Complementary Therapies
for Horse & Rider

Susan McBane & Caroline Davis

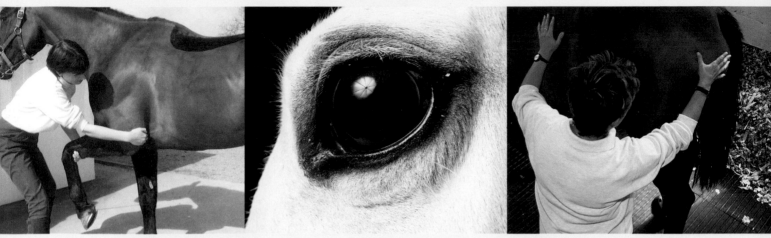

Complementary
Therapies
for Horse & Rider

David & Charles

ACKNOWLEDGEMENTS

The research demanded for this book has been tremendous, but most worthwhile, because we believe that the book covers more therapies than any other meant for horses and riders – maybe in an introductory way, but it does provide enough detail and information to encourage readers to look more deeply into the subject for themselves.

Because this book has been in preparation for a few years, before ever the Publishers approached the authors to write it, we have not always been able to keep track of the huge number of people we have conversed with, and have casually consulted. Countless organisations have been very helpful, umpteen individuals, patients, vets, doctors and therapists over the years have given opinions, facts and contacts, and so many observations made – and they have now all gone into the gigantic melting pot and come out as this book. Our gratitude to them is immeasurable.

A DAVID & CHARLES BOOK

First published in the UK in 2001

Susan McBane and Caroline Davis have asserted their rights to be identified as authors of this work in accordance with the Copyright, Designs and Patents Act, 1988.

A catalogue record for this book is available from the British Library.

ISBN 0 7153 1072 0

Printed in Italy by Milanostampa SpA
For David & Charles
Brunel House Newton Abbot Devon

PHOTO ACKNOWLEDGEMENTS

The publishers would like to thank the following for supplying photographs:

Academy of Systematic Kinesiology: p98
Adrenaline Sports Ltd: p39
Bob Atkins: pp 128(top), 130, 177
Edward Bach © pp 85(right), 86(both), 87(left), 88(top rt&btm)
Bee Health Ltd: p81
Frank Bell: p131
Caroline Bradley: pp 139, 140
Britstock–IFA: pp 7 (Hasenkopf), 9 (Zscharnack), 65(both) (Number Three Co.), 69(top) (Number Three Co.), 82(btm left) (Bernd Ducke), 62(top left) (Britstock–IFA), 89 (Option Photo), 153 (IPP), 154(all) (Number Three Co.), 157 (Option Photo), 169 (Esbin Anderson), 173 (Ostarhild), 174 (Gerald Schorm)
Jacqueline Cook: pp 22(top rt), 23(all)
Corbis: pp 159 (John Henley), 160 (Ronnie Kaufmann)
Emap Active Ltd/*Your Horse* magazine: p118
Equine Bowen (Beth Darrall): pp 52, 53
Forbes Copper: p66(both)
Ian Francis: p20
Greenshires Publishing/*Riding* magazine: pp 40 (Anthony Reynolds); 42 (Joanna Prestwich); 43, 92, 122, 124(both); 125(Jan Piper)
Hilton Herbs Ltd: p68(top&ctre), 70(left)
Kit Houghton: pp 6, 9(both), 11, 30, 32, 33, 34, 36, 37, 46–7, 58–9, 67, 70(rt), 72, 73, 74, 75, 76, 78–9, 83(both), 84(btm), 85(left), 97, 111, 112–13, 142(rt), 143(top left), 144(both), 147, 148(top rt), 149(top left)
Caroline Ingraham: p102
Artaine Jewell: pp120–1
Bob Langrish: p10
Magno-Pulse Ltd: p38
NHPA: pp 68(btm left) (Nigel J Dennis), 69(btm) (E.A. Janes)
John Walmsley Photo Library: p91
Photographs ©David & Charles on pp 8, 22(btm left), 24(both), 25(all), 28, 29, 44, 45, 49, 54, 57, 60, 61, 62(both), 84(top), 87(rt), 100, 101, 103, 104, 105(both), 106–7(all), 115(all), 117(both), 142(left&ctre), 143(btm left&top rt), 156 (Susan McBane); 12, 13, 50(all), 51(both), 55(both), 56(both), 63(both), 126, 128(btm), 165, 166 (Bob Langrish); 94–5, 114–115, 162, 163, 171, 176 (Kit Houghton)

Artworks by: pp 17, 116(both), 127, 145(all), 146(both), 148(all), 149(both) Maggie Raynor; pp 18, 141 Samantha Elmhurst
Artwork on p108 by Jean MacFarland courtesy of Ebury Press

Jacket photographs: (front cover, clockwise from top left) David & Charles/Bob Langrish, D&C/Susan McBane, D&C/Susan McBane, D&C/Bob Langrish, D&C/Susan McBane, D&C/Kit Houghton, NHPA/Nigel J. Dennis, Bee Health Ltd, NHPA/E.A. Janes (back cover) Kit Houghton

Contents & A-Z of Therapies

Introduction

Wheels have a habit of turning full circle: this seems to apply to medicine as much as to other areas of life, and where human medicine goes, veterinary medicine soon follows. Today, complementary therapies and remedies for all sorts of ailments are once again hugely in favour with horse owners, both for themselves, their families and for their horses and other animals, and all the signs are that this is no 'fashion passion'. Those under the age of about forty-five may feel that they have discovered something new in, say, herbalism, acupuncture, aromatherapy and so on – but older readers will probably remember when these types of treatment were as mainstream as any other.

PLEASE READ THIS BOOK!
The authors hope that readers will not simply use our book as a reference source, looking up a single therapy in which they are interested and ignoring the rest. The complementary therapy world is so vast and complex that although this approach may well give readers the immediate information they are looking for, it cannot even begin to tap into anything of the whole vast concept of complementary and holistic healing and living. Instead, we hope that the book also will be read from cover to cover as a book: in this way, we feel that something of the thread of continuity of holism and natural, complementary medicine and life-management for people and animals (in this case specifically horses and their owners) will become apparent, and a fuller understanding of, and feel for, the subject will be obtained.

AS WELL AS – NOT INSTEAD OF
Complementary therapies are often called 'alternative' therapies or medicines, as though they were an alternative, to be used instead of what we now regard as orthodox or conventional medicine. The authors of this book prefer the word 'complementary' because that is what most therapies are: complementary to, and usually able to be used with each other (although not always) and with orthodox human or veterinary medicine. Of course they can be used alone, if desired, and so can orthodox medicine; but excellent, often better results may be achieved by using a combination of healing techniques.

A holistic approach to horse health balances veterinary care with complementary therapies and leads to happier, healthier horses

A Bit of History

Until the middle of the twentieth century, even conventional medicine was based on natural remedies of animal, vegetable and mineral origin. Also, other 'fringe' therapies ran alongside the prevailing conventional sort. Every 'big house', monastery, school or even cottage had its herb garden which was used for both culinary and medicinal purposes. Housewives, nannies, grannies, cooks and housekeepers had their own armoury of remedies from all sources, and people were as likely to consult their pharmacist, local herbalist or other 'healer' (in some centuries regularly burned by The Establishment as witches – they were usually female 'wise women') for both themselves and their animals, as they were a conventionally qualified doctor or veterinary surgeon, when these came into being.

Then, around the middle of the last century, came the explosion in medical research, and artificially manufactured drugs and remedies, some of them extremely powerful and dramatic in action, swamped human and veterinary medicine, almost – though not entirely – to the exclusion of naturally sourced remedies. The latter came to be seen by most people as old-fashioned, not as 'strong', and as something to try if all else failed. Two generations have grown up in this environment, believing that modern, conventional medicine, human or veterinary, is the only 'real', effective sort.

Gradually it has been realised that not only did these powerful medications not always work, but they could also have extremely unpleasant side-effects, both long- and short-term, and people started looking for other ways of healing and health maintenance.

What we now call natural, complementary therapies are mostly far from new. Very many of them are hundreds and even thousands of years old and have been proved effective in practice over the millenia. Entire civilisations do not use a therapy for that long, or anything like that long, if it does not work. Despite this, modern, orthodox science generally looks askance at much complementary medicine because most therapies have not been proven effective by *its* parameters and criteria. Most medical research is undertaken or sponsored by commercial drug companies, and they normally will not do research if they cannot see worthwhile (financial) profits at the end of it.

No laboratory has ever isolated or described the mysterious life force, energy, Chi, Ki or prana which is at the heart of most Eastern medicine – but who in their right mind would say that therapies based on the balanced flow of this energy do not work, and have not been working for thousands of years, compared to the mere fifty or so of conventional, Western medicine? Just because there is no modern, Western, scientific proof that something works, it does not mean that it does not do so.

For generations, and probably for hundreds of years, people have known

The power of traditional Chinese medicine has been recognised for thousands of years

Shiatsu can help with horses who are head-shy or defensive of their ears. Here the practitioner is rubbing and rotating the base of the ear

HOLISM: THE BODY/ MIND/SPIRIT CONCEPT

The concept of holism was devised by Jan Christian Smuts (1870–1950) who presented it in a way that was understandable to modern Western scientists. Everywhere in nature, biological systems are interdependent and involve all the recognised sciences – chemistry, physics and also biology – each being involved with the other.

The main difference between holistic medicine and the conventional Western sort is that the former treats the whole being, hence (w)holism, taking into account the psychological and physical aspects, whereas the latter still concentrates almost entirely on the physical. It is being recognised more and more by practitioners of both human and veterinary conventional medicine that the mind certainly affects the body for better or worse, although the emphasis is still on the body. Other natural therapies may be used in support of holism or, indeed, of conventional medicine.

Holistic therapies and management principles are often highly individualistic, often because of their emphasis on 'wholeness'. It is not simply a case of 'one disease, one drug' but of finding the root cause of a disorder and treating that root cause with whatever is appropriate to the individual, taking into account the temperament, lifestyle and environment of the person or animal, as well as its physical aspects. Treat the patient, not the disease, is the usual rule.

that smoking causes ill health, but because there was, until very recently, no definite, acceptable, scientific proof that it did so, nothing concrete was done to discourage it. Vested interests continued to rake in the profits and taxes that it generated, whilst millions of smokers and non-smokers the world over continued to suffer and die from its effects. Now that acceptable (non-anecdotal) proof is available, attitudes have changed, but smoking did not suddenly become lethal just because science finally proved that it was – it always was.

A similar and tragic example is the drug thalidomide. It was said to have been scientifically tested and approved for use by the regulatory bodies involved in testing medicines – and everyone now knows the results.

There are other examples we could give; but finally, as this book goes to press, it has been announced that initial scientific trials in the West have shown what Ayurvedic herbalists may have long known, that the drug cannabis, from the Indian hemp plant *Cannabis sativa*, used both to make rope and

other hemp products and to produce the narcotic drug marijuana, does relieve the devastating symptoms of a multiple sclerosis-type disease in mice and probably in humans, too: further trials are starting in humans, and we may find that the illegal 'pot' of the 'Flower Power' 1960s becomes a valuable medicine in the twenty-first century. For those who lived through the sixties (and they say that if you remember them you weren't really there), the term 'Flower Power' had a significant dual meaning: flowers were the hippie symbol of peace everywhere, from wearing them to poking them down soldiers' rifle barrels – but plant power also acknowledged the recreational mind-altering properties of plants, of which hemp is only one.

There are very few panaceas in the world of healing. Both orthodox medicine and complementary therapies have their successes and their failures, and it would be good if we could all be a little more open-minded when considering what is available in the whole healing sphere.

DOES 'NATURAL' MEAN 'SAFE'?

Many complementary therapies are regarded as 'natural' and, therefore, completely safe and harmless, but this is not always the case, which is why professional advice should always be sought at least initially, although self-treatment may be possible subsequently, depending on the therapy. Apart from the fact that some of the most lethal poisons on earth come directly from natural sources, sensitivities can occur to some substances, and other substances and therapies may not mix well. To give only two examples, some forms of energy medicine (see Glossary) can cancel each other out, and some aromatherapy oils must not be used on people who have consumed alcohol or they could have 'nightmares to die for', as one therapist described it. As ever, professional advice is strongly advised.

HORSE MANAGEMENT, HEALTH AND FITNESS

It is not only when actually curing ailments that natural therapies are useful. Good health and physical fitness are mainly matters of good management, and holistic feeding is the major part of that. Holistically or organically produced feeds for horses are gradually becoming available, and holistic grassland management with its very wide range of grasses, herbs and other plants – one of the biggest steps forward (or rather back) for generations – is also now being promoted more and its importance

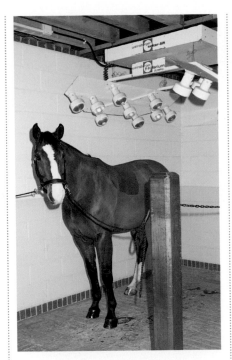

Technical advances in equipment, such as this solarium, have contributed to the number of treatment options available

being appreciated once again.

More attention is being paid to bedding materials which are not merely bland (almost dust- and spore-free), but treated with new, horse- and user-friendly products to help keep infection and toxins at bay. The full effects of saddling, bitting and shoeing horses are also now being studied and publicised, little by little, and the links between the all-round (whole) management of the horse are beginning to be more understood and appreciated, for example how a sore mouth can make a horse appear lame, how the wrong shoes or farriery method can create back problems, or how unsuitable food can cause disease and unsuitable housing behavioural problems. In everything, it all comes down to the holistic viewpoint of body, mind and spirit.

THE SPHERE OF HEALING

Healing can be regarded as an orange, with each segment representing a type of medicine or a therapy. There is orthodox medicine for both humans and animals, there is phytotherapy (general plant medicine), herbalism, homoeopathy, chiropractic, Traditional Chinese Medicine, Ayurvedic Medicine, physiotherapy, hypnotherapy, nutritional therapy, Reiki, faith healing and so on and so forth. Obviously those trained in one field usually think that their system is best, otherwise they would not have opted for it in the first place – but increasingly the more enquiring practitioners are thinking outside their own discipline and at least considering, sometimes studying informally and perhaps qualifying in, another quite different therapy.

The understanding of biomechanics and its affect on horse and rider, as promoted by teachers such as Mary Wanless, can help to maintain soundness and health

The 'Big Five' Therapies

There are five therapies which are informally referred to as the 'big five', and are generally regarded as being complete in themselves for specific, appropriate conditions, but which can still be used with other therapies when required. These are acupuncture, chiropractic, herbalism, homoeopathy and osteopathy – all of which, of course, are covered in this book. All these therapies are now widely, if not universally, accepted in both veterinary and human medicine as having a valuable place in health restoration and maintenance.

ACUPUNCTURE

Probably the biggest breakthrough for Eastern medicine into the Western healing system was that made by acupuncture a few decades ago. Very much a Chinese modality, acupuncture was initially regarded with everything from horror to ridicule. Now it is accepted as an effective, non-Western-orthodox form of healing and analgesia, and people do not laugh at it any more. It is available as an accepted treatment in most Western hospitals.

CHIROPRACTIC

Chiropractic specialises in the treatment of disorders and displacements of joints, particularly those between the vertebrae of the spine, and the subsequent effects on the nervous system and general health. It is a manipulative method used for humans and animals, and is based on the concept that the spine is the 'headquarters' of whole-body health. Chiropractors aim to redress misalignments through spinal manipulation or adjustment. Chiropractic is an effective and established therapy for humans and animals.

HERBALISM

Herbalism is a very ancient therapy. It is often referred to as 'Phytotherapy' but this actually means medicine from plants, but not necessarily those classed as 'herbs' – those which do not develop persistent, woody tissues above ground. It is probably the best known and possibly the most accepted complementary therapy.

Herbalism was almost the only, and certainly the main, kind of

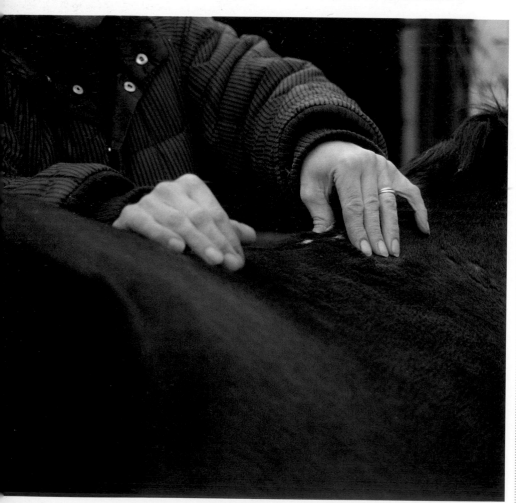

Chiropractic focuses on the healthy alignment of the spine. By manipulation practitioners can relieve not only stiffness and pain, but also more general health problems

medicine there was in the western world until around the middle of the twentieth century. Many orthodox medicines are still derived from plants, such as salicylic acid (aspirin) from the willow tree and digitalis from foxgloves which is made into medicines for heart disease. However, orthodox human and veterinary medicine still does not seem, on the whole, to have grasped the fact that the reason that phytotherapy is so effective and has so few side effects is because often the whole plant is used, with its balanced effect of several substances working synergistically together. This so often produces 'healing without harm' (if prescribed by a suitably knowledgeable practitioner), whereas when what orthodox scientists believe to be the active ingredient is isolated from its 'working partners' and then manufactured artificially in a laboratory, often into a very concentrated form – the standard practice in orthodox medicine – not only are the synergistic and regulating effects lost, but also what we term 'side-effects', often distressing ones, sometimes occur. If only conventional healers would work fully with complementary ones!

Possibly the oldest 'therapy' of all, herbalism can offer benefits without side-effects

HOMOEOPATHY

Homoeopathy, although based on ancient Greek principles, is one of the comparatively newer forms of healing, and it is one which conventional vets and doctors find very difficult to come to terms with. It is probably such an advanced science that we are surely only just beginning to scratch the surface of it. Conventional scientific medicine works on allopathic principles and just cannot seem to grasp the totally 'reversed logic' of homoeopathy: how can a remedy containing no molecules of the original healing agent possibly have any effect? A fair enough question. It takes a quite different way of looking at healing to be able even to start to come to terms with homoeopathy. We recommend as a starting point, the now classic book by Deepak Chopra, MD, *Quantum Healing.*

OSTEOPATHY

The philosophy of osteopathy is that the body, both human and animal, works as a whole, and that structure and function, often of seemingly unrelated parts, are interdependent. If the body is out of physical balance (misaligned or 'dislocated' in any way), its function must be impaired, and the osteopath aims to restore this physical balance so that it can work normally again. He works by adjusting the muscles and joints that are effectively perpetuating the misalignment, with a view to correcting it: these misalignments can cause extreme pain and loss of function to almost any area of the body due to pressure on, injury to, and loss of function of the nerves that serve it. Once balance is regained, function should be restored, unless nerve damage has been permanent, and often 'mysterious' diseases seem to disappear as the body is enabled to heal itself once more.

Osteopathy has now become a recognised and accepted treatment among the medical and veterinary professions.

The Role of the Veterinary Surgeon

This book is specifically for horses, their owners, handlers, riders and drivers. It will be available in many countries, and the laws in different countries regarding who may and may not, by law, diagnose and treat animals' diseases and injuries vary considerably. In some countries, no one other than a vet may treat an animal at all, even under referral from a vet; in others, like the UK, only a veterinary surgeon may diagnose and treat an animal, although the vet may refer the patient to another therapist who is not a vet; and in some countries there is a free-for-all situation where anyone can diagnose and treat diseases and injuries without a vet being in any way involved. It is completely impractical for the authors to state the law on this matter for every country in which the book may be sold.

We should like to make perfectly clear here that we are entirely in favour of involving a veterinary surgeon in any matter concerning the health and welfare of animals, whatever country readers live in. Veterinary surgeons/veterinarians have a long, meticulous training and qualification period, and their knowledge of animal anatomy and physiology must be second to none. Even in countries where veterinary attention is not demanded by law, the professional diagnosis and opinion of a vet is invaluable.

In some countries, training in certain therapies (such as physiotherapy in the UK) must be carried out first in human medicine, and then further training may be undertaken to allow the therapist to practise on animals, with or without veterinary referral according to the country. This, in our view, is illogical and restrictive and the law could, with advantage, be changed to allow student practitioners to train only in the animal field, with courses structured appropriately to take in veterinary-course levels of anatomy and physiology. Veterinary surgeons and veterinary nurses do not have to qualify to become doctors and nurses in human medicine before they embark on veterinary training, and other therapists should not have to do so either. In some countries, this situation could actually be seen as restrictive practice and against the law!

In practical terms, veterinary surgeons in the UK (of which we have most experience) are very much more open-minded than previously, and in general are quite

The well-being of your horse relies on the co-operation of a team. The invaluable support of your veterinary surgeon and farrier can be complemented by other therapists

ready to refer a client to a complementary therapist if they feel it could help a patient.

CONSULT A PROFESSIONAL

Whatever country you live in, and whatever therapy you wish to consider, whether or not a vet is involved according to your laws, rules and regulations, not to mention ethics, it is probably always best to consult therapists who are properly qualified by a controlling, registering body. This does not mean that unqualified personnel are not extremely competent in many cases; but it does mean that you *should* have more assurance of competence if the practitioner is qualified. There is also the matter of professional indemnity and/or third party liability insurance. Whether or not the practitioner is qualified 'on paper', do check that he or she has proper and adequate insurance, otherwise you could have little or no recompense in the event of a claim should things go wrong.

The subject of qualifications in complementary therapies is an extremely difficult one to address. In some therapies there are no formal qualifications; in others, one might consider the qualifications to be 'not worth the paper they are written on'; and in yet others again there are qualifications of an internationally recognised nature, either from a highly respected governing body or in the form of university degrees. Qualifications gained in some countries are not always recognised in others. Unfortunately the situation

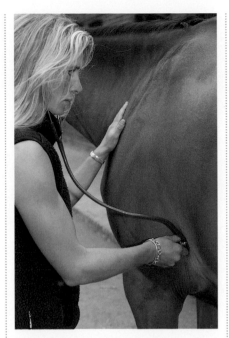

A veterinary surgeon has extensive training and understanding of animal health. It is therefore always advisable to consult such a qualified individual first

is somewhat confusing, and it is not likely to be much improved in the near future.

There are professional bodies registering practitioners in some therapies, and 'umbrella' organisations which register complementary practitioners of different persuasions from a professional practice point of view. Consulting one of these organisations when trying to find a practitioner should assure you of competence and professional standards of practice. Reference libraries are excellent sources of tracing such organisations.

There is a vast range of holistic and other therapies available, including the conventional. We can have the best of all worlds if we use them together wisely.

Warning

Neither the authors nor the publishers can be held responsible for the results of any statements made in this book in relation to any aspect of therapy, practice or healing disciplines. This book has been carefully researched over a number of years, but the information presented in it is the result of that research and often of information provided by the administrative bodies or practitioners of particular therapies: it cannot possibly all be from our own personal knowledge and we cannot guarantee its accuracy although we respect the sources from which it came. We have made all reasonable efforts to present helpful, accurate and relevant information but cannot stress too strongly that, in all matters relating to health and wellbeing it is always advisable to consult a relevant professional therapist and a doctor or veterinary surgeon, as may be most appropriate.

THERAPIES FOR

HORSE AND RIDER

Acupuncture

Acupuncture is at, and stems from, the heart of traditional Chinese culture, and is the science of puncturing the skin with needles at specified points (acupoints) in order to treat illness and to relieve physical and/or mental stress; it can also effect anaesthesia. It is used to treat a wide range of illnesses both mental and physical, its main aim being to treat the whole individual with a view to recovering the balance and harmony between the physical and emotional – and in the case of humans, spiritual – aspects which together govern life.

PHILOSOPHY

To fully understand acupuncture it is necessary to understand the concept of Chi (pronounced 'chee'), the vital life force or energy which the Chinese (and other cultures) believe flows through the body along channels or meridians beneath the skin, and which link all its systems and functions so that the body works as an integrated, harmonious whole. Chi keeps the blood and lymph on the move, warms the body and, crucially, fights disease and maintains health. It can be disturbed by emotional states, by poor nutrition, infection, injury, trauma, poisoning, hereditary factors and even by the weather and environment.

'Do these meridians exist anatomically?' is a fair question. Although they do not seem to have been described in any Western book on anatomy, human or veterinary, apparently an Eastern- and Western-educated doctor in China believes that he has discovered some of these meridians in the form of tissue-fine, membranous channels under human skin. A good way of thinking of meridians is to think of them as directions of flow. Like wind directions or water currents, no physical enclosing tube is needed, but anyone can tell they are there.

Acupuncture is regarded in China as only one part of the whole traditional medicine ethos, others being Chinese herbal medicine, exercise, massage and nutrition. It has various offshoots in other therapies, but all are based on stimulating certain points along the energy meridians (the locations of which all practitioners seem to agree on) with the aim of clearing the channels and allowing – indeed, stimulating – the body to heal itself. It aims to improve the overall wellbeing of the patient in this way rather than just treat isolated symptoms, although the condition or imbalance causing the symptoms of which the patient is complaining will also be treated.

HOW DOES IT WORK?

Acupuncture is believed by the Chinese to work by the stimulation of various sensitive points along the meridians by means of inserting fine copper or steel needles into them. This brings about a change in the energy balance and flow of the body

---

What is Acupuncture used for?

Studies have shown that acupuncture treatment can bring about:

- a rise in the bloodstream of the body's natural 'feel-good' chemicals, the opiate encephalins and endorphins, as well as serotonin and cortisol (this may occur both during and after an acupuncture treatment)
- a contented, relaxed state of mind and body
- an improved appetite
- raised energy levels
- an apparent stimulation of the actions of certain nerves, which not only promotes muscle function but also hormonal release, the combined effect of which has a very wide-ranging influence on the body and mind
- the alleviation of pain

ROUTES OF THE MERIDIANS

Large intestine meridian (continuous line) and lung meridian (dashed line)

Conception vessel (continuous line), kidney meridian (dashed line) and stomach meridian (dotted line)

Governing vessel (continuous line)

Gall bladder meridian (continuous line) and liver meridian (dashed line)

Bladder meridian (continuous line) and kidney meridian (dashed line)

Stomach meridian (continuous line) and spleen meridian (dashed line)

ROUTES OF THE MERIDIANS (continued)

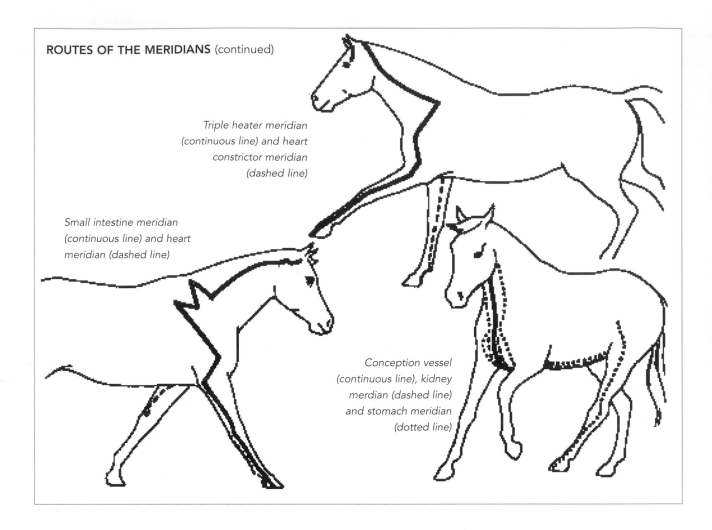

Triple heater meridian (continuous line) and heart constrictor meridian (dashed line)

Small intestine meridian (continuous line) and heart meridian (dashed line)

Conception vessel (continuous line), kidney merdian (dashed line) and stomach meridian (dotted line)

and helps to restore health. The use of a burning herb, moxa, in the tops of the needles (called moxibustion or moxabustion) is often used to make the process more effective in certain cases. Particular acupuncture points are stimulated to produce specific effects, and the knowledge of these points and their effects, singly or combined, requires extensive, dedicated training and practice.

The most recent development in acupuncture is to apply it by means of laser light. Light comes in widely varying wavelengths, and one in particular seems to be helpful in helping some nerves to regenerate after injury or illness. Obviously,

giving acupuncture by means of a beam of light which cannot be felt by the horse has great advantages.

Will my horse object? Few horses object to having an acupuncture treatment – indeed, an animal in pain will relax during treatment as its pain is alleviated, and some even doze during the process, a state known as 'daychi'. When the procedure is performed properly, the animals do not seem to be aware of the needles being inserted – only their owners appear to feel the pain! Human patients describe the sensation as either a tingling or a dull ache, with the occasional

person reporting pain as the needle goes in, though nothing like that of an injection. The needles may be left in place for just a few seconds, or for up to about twenty minutes; generally ten or twelve needles are used on any one horse, depending on how many are required to effect treatment. As long as the horse responds to the needles it will derive some benefit from them, some more than others depending on the ailment involved and its severity.

For those few horses who do object, acupressure can be used instead; the points can be stimulated by hand pressure, massage or tapping with a rounded probe, and electro-acupuncture or laser can be used.

How often and for how long? It is normally recommended that an average of at least five acupuncture treatments, at the rate of one or two treatments a week, should be given before any effect is likely to be seen. Some patients, though, need less and some more. Similarly, some may need further treatments periodically, and others may never need another for the rest of their lives.

A holistic ethos: In assessing a horse the acupuncturist would try to get a whole picture of it in order to determine the exact cause of the problem: if the cause itself is not treated – a badly fitting saddle, a painful tooth, bad feeding practice, a rough rider – the symptoms will reoccur; so whilst a horse is obviously suffering pain in a particular area, that area may not in fact be the root cause of the pain. The acupuncturist must therefore find out where that is and treat it first in order to alleviate the symptoms. For instance, it may be a problem in the neck, or perhaps lameness, causing the horse to carry itself incorrectly in an attempt to lessen the pain; in doing this it will be putting strain on other parts of its body, such as its back, which will then become uncomfortable and sore. Manipulation may be used in conjunction with acupuncture, as the two treatments complement each other well.

Acupuncture for the Rider

Although often regarded in the West simply as a means of pain relief, acupuncture is used to treat a wide range of illnesses both mental and physical and also spiritual, a concept difficult for many Westerners to understand. Everything revolves around believing that Chi is the main source of life and energy in a being. When a body dies, the being has lost only one of its aspects: its Chi continues to flow in another dimension or existence. Westerners who believe in some form or other of afterlife will find this easier to grasp than those who believe that when you die, that's it! Native Americans believe that we live on, in that our bodies disintegrate and become reabsorbed into the earth as the various constituent parts that we now understand as our body substances or chemicals – such as molecules making up carbohydrates, amino acids making up proteins, minerals, of course, and vitamins and other substances of which all organisms are made. These substances are used by other people and animals, taken by other organisms from the soil into which they have rotted down, and they 're-live' by becoming absorbed from food, either as plants which have grown in that soil, or animals (meat) which have first eaten them, into a new body. Whatever you believe, therefore, somehow we all live on and, according to Eastern peoples, our Chi continues to flow, if disparately.

The balance of the Chi is the balance of its opposite and equal, feminine and masculine, qualities – its Yin and Yang – and acupuncture aims to maintain an even balance between them, the 50:50 partnership of a well balanced marriage. It is when these qualities become unbalanced that disorders may result.

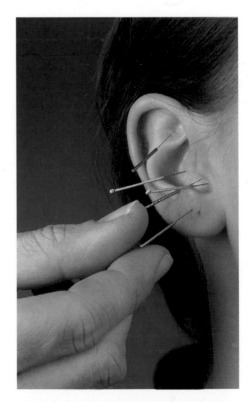

Acupuncture of the ear

ACUPUNCTURE IN PRACTICE

Ian Francis BVSc MRCVS

Having qualified as a veterinary surgeon at Liverpool University fifteen years ago, Ian Francis had no experience of using acupuncture to treat animals until several years ago whilst practising in Somerset. Says Ian, 'One of my colleagues was quite into acupuncture and was successfully using it to treat an Alsatian dog with a neurological condition. I think the thing that impressed me most at the time was the fact that my colleague didn't get his head bitten off when he inserted the needles!'

Ian's interest was such that he determined to become proficient in the art himself and proceeded to undergo training in order to do so. But was it difficult to learn? Does one have to possess a certain knack?

'I did find it difficult initially,' admits Ian, 'as there are so many acupoints on animals to become familiar with; you have to be particularly careful when inserting needles around the chest area as the fine copper and steel needles used are about two inches long and you wouldn't want one of these to end up in the chest cavity! There are places known as "booster points" as well, plus you have to be aware that previous treatment sites may be slightly sore so you need to work out carefully suitable new sites to put needles. It's essential that a person has a feel for practising acupuncture and how to tell if the animal is responding to treatment, otherwise he or she wouldn't be able to do the job effectively.'

Ian obviously has what it takes, as his client list these days confirms, with top performance horses in the worlds of racing and eventing benefiting from his 'magic touch'. He treats from his base on the Shropshire/Cheshire border,

and his success rate at alleviating and curing a problem with acupuncture is excellent. People usually contact him because they know he practises acupuncture and think it may be beneficial to their animals when other treatments have failed, or he is recommended to them by clients whose horses he has treated.

Says Ian, 'Sometimes you need to complement a natural therapy with another to get the desired effect, ie a cure. For example, I find that practising manipulation in conjunction with acupuncture seems to do the trick in some cases. However, you have to have a real feel for a particular therapy to be able to do it effectively. I dabbled with homoeopathy for a while, but found that it didn't work for me.'

So how can Ian tell that acupuncture is working on a horse, or any other animal for that matter? And does this therapy work on every animal treated with it? Explains Ian:

'Whilst some animals do not respond to this treatment, around 85 per cent benefit from it. The most rewarding aspect for me is seeing an animal in pain relax during treatment as its pain is alleviated; some even go to sleep, slipping into a state known as "daychi". Animals do not appear to feel the needles being inserted when this procedure is done correctly; in fact their owners look more worried at the prospect!

'As long as the horse responds to the needles it will derive some benefit from them, some more than others depending on the ailment involved and its severity. In one case, an equine patient of mine had a particularly severe back injury and it was generally thought that it could never be ridden again. Happily for the horse, and its owner, acupuncture has helped it recover to the point where it can lead a pain-free life and enjoy gentle hacks out again, although competition work is off the agenda.'

Ian generally uses between ten and twelve needles on each horse, 'depending on how many are required to effect treatment'. To minimise the risk of infection he always uses new needles, throwing them away after use.

There's more to this form of therapy than simply sticking needles into horses and hoping for the best. Ian works on the holistic principle of considering the whole horse physically and psychologically instead of merely treating what is considered the affected part of it. This is why he often uses manipulation in conjunction with acupuncture, having discovered that the two treatments complement each other. However, he warns:

'Where manipulation is concerned I strongly recommend that owners be extremely careful about who they employ to treat their horse. There are cowboys around who do more harm than good, so the safest way of finding a reputable practitioner is through a vet.'

So how does Ian ascertain whether or not an animal requires acupuncture? He explains:

'In assessing a horse I aim to get a whole picture of it so that I can determine the exact cause of the problem. If the cause itself is not treated, then it's obvious that symptoms will reoccur. I check the animal over from head to tail, inspect its teeth and rasp them if necessary, note what tack it is ridden in and how well it fits, and ask its owner how the horse is kept, what work it does, and how long the symptoms have been present and how they manifest themselves. If I think it necessary I'll ask the owner to ride the animal to see how it reacts and moves.

'Pinpointing exactly where the problem stems from in an equine back can be extremely difficult. To the uninitiated the obvious answer is to take X-rays in order to determine where the problem lies; however a horse's back area is awkward to X-ray accurately due to it being such a large mass, therefore isolating problem areas via this method is not a workable option. Besides, I find that many cases of back pain are due to a trapped nerve or injured muscle tissue, neither of which would show up on an X-ray.

'You must always bear in mind that whilst an animal is obviously suffering from pain in a particular area, that area may not in fact be the root cause of the pain so you have to find out where that is and cure it first in order to alleviate the symptoms. In some cases it may be a problem in the neck, or perhaps lameness, causing a horse to carry itself incorrectly in an attempt to lessen pain; because the animal won't be moving correctly it will put strain on other parts of its body, such as its back, which will then become uncomfortable or sore.'

Case History

Horse: Jasper, a Thoroughbred gelding in training at a point-to-point yard. A happy and talented horse who thoroughly enjoys his work.

PROBLEM: His jumping ability began to deteriorate and he suddenly began to 'buck for England'! His trainer asked vet and acupuncture specialist Ian Francis BVSc MRCVS to check Jasper over and he discovered, after a full assessment, that the horse was suffering tension in his back due to a muscle spasm, probably due to a trapped nerve.

TREATMENT: 'After the first acupuncture treatment' said Ian, 'Jasper looked and obviously felt much better and his improvement was even more apparent within a matter of days. Manipulation and remedial exercises helped to complete his cure. After two more sessions he stopped bucking altogether and he went from strength to strength performance-wise.'

RESULT: Jasper went on to novice steeplechase, and did very well at it, too, with no recurrence of a back problem.

Acupressure

Acupressure is a sister therapy to acupuncture (as is Shiatsu, to both of which readers are referred), and its basic principles are exactly the same, with the exception that needles are not used in acupressure and the skin is not punctured in any way: pressure (as opposed to a needle) is applied to specified points (acupoints) in order to cure illness, relieve symptoms or effect anaesthesia. It is, in orthodox parlance, a non-invasive therapy because the body is not entered or invaded.

A trained practitioner applies pressure to an acupoint which is effective for treating facial paralysis, jaw tension, toothache and eye problems

As a therapy, acupressure seems to have been used for well over 5,000 years. It is often more attractive to animals and owners alike because it is not in the least painful; however, it is a deceptively gentle therapy which can have a highly significant effect on the patient.

HOW IT WORKS

Acupressure works by the stimulation of various sensitive points along the meridians by means of pressure. This

Acupressure is applied mainly with finger or thumb pressure on specific points on the body, usually located on energy meridians but not always, depending on the school of thought of the practitioner

brings about a change in the energy balance and flow of the body and helps to restore health. The practitioner may use finger pressure, the heel of the hand, elbows, knees and even heels; in equine practice mainly the hands and sometimes the elbows are used. Rounded probes may be used, also laser and gentle electric stimulation. Particular points are stimulated to produce specific effects, and the knowledge of these requires extensive training and practise.

The acupuncture/acupressure points: These are located mainly along the various energy meridians of the body, and varying types of pressure can be used on them. Simple, consistent pressure can be used, or a pulsing or circular action until the trained, experienced practitioner senses or feels that 'enough is enough' for that point. The acupoints are places where the Chi, energy or life force flows close to the body's surface; these spots may be permanent or interim, the latter often

occurring during a state of disorder or energy imbalance, only to disappear once the patient is healed. This is only one reason why the practitioner has to do an assessment to feel what points have become available for treatment. The permanent points may be used at any time during either disease or health maintenance.

Acupoints can be described as transpositional or traditional, and, as in many forms of medicine, have long formed the basis of debate as to their locations and natures.

Traditional points are those which have been used for thousands of years and are not necessarily associated with a meridian.

Transpositional points are those taken from the human meridian system and anatomically transposed on to animals' bodies. This system is said to be less precise because of the great anatomical differences which exist between humans and animals,

What is Acupressure used for?

Acupressure works on the holistic principle of considering the whole horse physically and psychologically: its aim is to treat the individual with a view to recovering the balance and harmony between the horse's physical and emotional needs. As acupuncture and Shiatsu, it is used for:

■ the treatment and elimination of musculo-skeletal problems, including chronic and subtle lameness, back pain and stiffness

■ maintaining or restoring suppleness, health and wellbeing

■ maximising the horse's 'feel good' factor so as to optimise performance

■ in the event of injury, stimulating the circulation of blood and lymph, the nervous system and the release of hormones, including endorphins and cortisol, the body's own analgesics (pain-killers) in order to maximise the speed and quality of healing

■ resolving problems of behaviour and temperament, by identifying and reducing physical pain, and by soothing and relaxing the horse's mind

■ establishing a closer and more understanding relationship between horse and handler/rider

Treatment of the acupoint known as the 'Aspirin Point' is used to relieve arthritis of the hock and soft tissue injuries

Above: Acupressure points exist along the body's energy meridians. The one being activated here will relieve neck pain

Right: The points are not limited to a single effect on one part of the body, but may have multiple benefits. The point being pressured here can relieve pain in the neck, shoulder and lower back, it is also used for hock and stifle arthritis, and can relieve constipation and diarrhoea

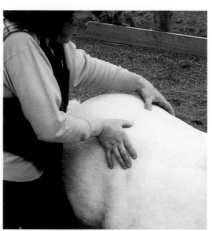

but transpositional practitioners seem to have as much success as those of the traditional school.

In any case, the exact locations of meridians and acupoints cannot always be precisely defined in each individual horse: a great deal is down to the sensitivity, experience and intuition of the practitioner. Unfortunately, this is one of the aspects of non-orthodox healing which some modern scientists use to put down complementary therapies.

SELF HELP

There are several books available on acupuncture and acupressure for horses. Intelligent perusal of these will familiarise readers with the basic principles of these therapies, and enable them to give their horses a basic, safe and effective acupressure treatment, provided all the guidelines are carefully followed. Instruction from a professional is strongly advised.

There are also simple techniques that riders can use on themselves which, again, are shown in basic books on acupressure. Bookshops have reference sources as to what is currently in print, and you can take your pick from the list.

Shiatsu

Shiatsu is a Japanese holistic system of healing and health maintenance. Working on the same principles as acupuncture and acupressure, the word 'Shiatsu' means 'finger' (shi-) 'pressure' (-atsu). There are no needles involved in Shiatsu: it is non-invasive, and practitioners work with their hands in a gentle, sympathetic way with muscles, tendons and ligements, and also with energy flow, to balance it within the person or the animal and so maintain the 'feel good' factor, or encourage, if necessary, a spontaneous, natural healing process. Shiatsu can also address problems of attitude, emotion and psychological distress or tension. It relaxes and energises both the receiver and the giver.

Gentle pressure is applied to the energy channels or meridians, usually firstly by 'palming' them. Here the right hand is resting on the horse as the 'mother' hand, keeping contact and sensing and transmitting energy, while the left hand (the working hand) palms a meridian

PHILOSOPHY

The main aim of Shiatsu and related therapies is to treat the whole individual with a view to recovering the balance and harmony between their physical and psychological needs. As in acupuncture, it is necessary to understand the concept of Ki or Qi (in Japanese) or Chi (Chinese), the name given to the vital life force or energy believed to flow through the body along channels or meridians beneath the skin – some shallow, some deeper – and which link all its systems and functions so that the body works as an integrated, harmonious whole when in health. Ki keeps the blood and lymph on the move, warms the body, and thereby fights disease and maintains health; but any one of several factors may unbalance it: a disturbed emotional

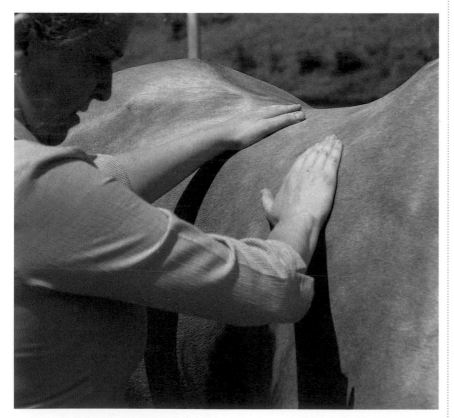

The shiatsu session begins with slow, all-over stroking with alternate hands to help the practitioner assess the state of the horse's body, its energy flow and any tensions. A hand is always on the horse to maintain contact, not being lifted off and moved until the other hand is touching the horse

What is Shiatsu used for?

- early recognition and treatment of problems before they escalate
- treatment and elimination of musculo-skeletal problems, including chronic and subtle lameness, stiffness and short or incorrect movement
- maintaining suppleness, health and wellbeing and restoring poor health and condition
- reducing susceptibility to injury
- maximising physical potential
- activating the immune system
- stimulating circulation of blood and lymph, the nervous system and the release of hormones, including endorphins and cortisol, the body's own analgesics (painkillers)
- behavioural and temperamental problems
- a closer and more understanding horse/handler relationship

Gentle stretches, always with the horse's co-operation, stretch and work soft tissues and various meridians in the leg depending on the type of stretch

Gently pinch and work the horse's cheeks and muzzle area to reduce head-shyness and 'mouthiness'. Most horses really enjoy this sensation

With the web of your hand gently but firmly press into the crease between lip and gum, top and bottom, where there are several acupressure points, to relieve tension and mouthiness. On the whole horses usually like this and do not need even a gently restraining hand on the front of the face

state, poor nutrition, infection, injury, trauma, pain and discomfort, poisoning, hereditary factors, a poor environment, stress, and even the weather.

Clearly horses may be affected by any of these, and stress in particular is nearly always the cause of stable vices such as weaving, crib-biting, wind-sucking and so on.

HOW DOES IT WORK?

Shiatsu works through the stimulation, by means of direct pressure or specific movements, of various sensitive points along the channels or meridians along which energy flows. This brings about a change in the energy balance and flow of the body, and helps to restore health. Specific points on the body, called tsubos in Shiatsu, are stimulated to produce specific effects.

Practical application: In Shiatsu, fingertip pressure is used, also pressure from the edges of the hands, the elbows, pads of the thumbs and the forearms, according to the judgement of the practitioner. More emphasis is placed on using pressure along the whole or part of a meridian rather than just on acupoints or *tsubos*, where the meridian is accessible, of course. In addition, the careful stretches and rotations used in Shiatsu can also work the meridians. As well as encouraging the flow of energy, Shiatsu pressures also stimulate the action of certain nerves, which not only promotes muscle function, but hormonal release too, and this can have a very advantageous effect on the body and on the equilibrium of the mind.

For example: Pressure applied to a horse's bladder meridian – which runs from the face, over the poll, the neck and back, over the hindquarters and down the hind legs to the hooves – can relieve neck and back pain, hind leg soreness and stiffness, bladder disorders, a clamped, stiff tail, and general fatigue; and in helping to relieve these, the therapy inevitably helps to resolve any psychological stress or tension, and relax the horse in mind as well as body. The bladder meridian is a key meridian used generally to encourage the excretion of toxins and other unwanted substances from the body, and so aids general health.

Studies have shown a rise in the bloodstream of the body's natural 'feel-good' chemicals and pain-killers – the opiate encephalins and endorphins as well as the hormones serotonin and cortisol – after an acupuncture treatment; so this is believed to be at least one result of a shiatsu session.

Complementary manipulative therapies: Many practitioners will use an energy therapy in conjunction with a manipulative therapy, and specific stretching exercises and rotations are part of Shiatsu.

SELF HELP

There are currently two books available on shiatsu for horses but the authors strongly recommend that any owner contemplating treating their own horse should have initial instruction from a professional practitioner. For contacts for training courses in Shiatsu from beginner level onwards (see page 186).

C A S E   H I S T O R Y

Horse: Part-Thoroughbred grey gelding called Haze, owned by an agricultural college for teaching equestrian students. Used at moderate level for flatwork and jumping.

INITIAL ASSESSMENT: Haze had no specific veterinary diagnosis and was officially sound and in work. It was not possible to speak to any of his riders. The Shiatsu practitioner assessed him during a walk-up in hand and saw that his head and neck movement was slight, his back, ribcage and tail hardly swung from side to side and his loins seemed to have excessive muscular development with little movement of hips and pelvis. He barely tracked up in walk. He seemed calm but anxious outdoors.

SESSION PRACTICE: Once stabled, Haze became more restless and would not eat or drink. The practitioner, during her initial hands-on assessment, found areas of lack of energy or Kyo (weakness, 'emptiness') in the fore part of the back but considerable Jitsu (energy build-up and blockage, tension) in the loins and hindquarters.

■ She began with all-over firm, continuous stroking to calm him and gently percussed the Jitsu areas. Haze walked away every few minutes and seemed distracted but, to avoid further tension, the practitioner declined to restrain him. She applied pressure with finger-pads and from the heel of her hands on Haze's bladder meridian (see notes on function, above). She worked on the entire bladder meridian twice on each side after which Haze was relaxed, mouthing and concentrating on his body.

■ More gentle percussion was given plus hind leg stretches, forwards and backwards, and also gentle side-to-side rocking of the crest of the neck using the hands, arms and bodyweight, all aimed at loosening muscles and joints. Haze also received tail-pulls which benefit the whole spine.

RESULT: Haze was walked out again and a significant improvement was noted. His head and neck moved more normally and his back, ribcage and tail were swinging noticeably. The loins were less tense and the horse over-tracked by one hoof-length.

Jin Shin Jyutsu

The purpose of Jin Shin Jyutsu is to release the tensions that cause various physical symptoms. It is deeply healing, penetrating right to the core of a physical problem, and greatly reduces the time the body takes to heal from injury and illness. It is a valuable complement to conventional healing methods, inducing relaxation and reducing the effects of stress.

PHILOSOPHY

The art of Jin Shin Jyutsu is derived from man's innate, original wisdom and knowledge of how to heal himself. It was first recorded in the Kojiki, the Japanese Record of Ancient Things, written over 5,000 years ago, and has been passed down by word of mouth from generation to generation.

HOW DOES IT WORK?

The body contains energy pathways that feed life into all its cells; when one or more of those pathways becomes blocked, the damming effect can lead to discomfort or pain. In the same way as acupuncture and acupressure, Jin Shin Jyutsu re-harmonises and balances these energy flows. Unlike acupuncture and acupressure, however, there are no needles and no pressure applied: Jin Shin Jyutsu is the most gentle of techniques, using only the lightest touch of the hands.

Even so, despite its gentleness, Jin Shin Jyutsu is a profoundly deep treatment, claiming to go through the skin right to the marrow of the bones where blood cells are formed. It is said to be fully effective through clothing, bandages and even plaster casts and braces. Human recipients of Jin Shin Jyutsu remain fully clothed while receiving treatment, and horses keep their rugs on.

A preventative therapy: Jin Shin Jyutsu is being used increasingly throughout the world, to balance and harmonise the bodies of both people and the horses in their care, to *prevent* injury and illness before these occur, especially those in high pressure environments, where optimum performance is needed. A harmonised body is a strong body, and far less likely to succumb to illness and injury than a disharmonised body. In this context it has particular relevance to horses in competition, helping them to cope with its attendant problems, such as the pressures of travel, a regimented diet, long periods of being stabled, and the stress of competition itself.

A constructive therapy: Jin Shin Jyutsu is widely used in the United States of America, South America, on the continent of Europe, in Australasia and throughout the Far East to promote optimum health, fitness and wellbeing in both horse and rider.

What is Jin Shin Jyutsu used for?

- to release the tensions that cause various physical symptoms
- to induce relaxation and reduce the effects of stress
- to balance body, mind and spirit
- to balance and harmonise the body to *prevent* injury and illness
- to promote optimum health, fitness and wellbeing in both horse and rider

Reflexology

Another ancient therapy used thousands of years ago by the Chinese and Egyptians, reflexology is a physical means of balancing, stabilising and co-ordinating the entire body/mind entity, although the emphasis seems to be placed mainly on physical disorders.

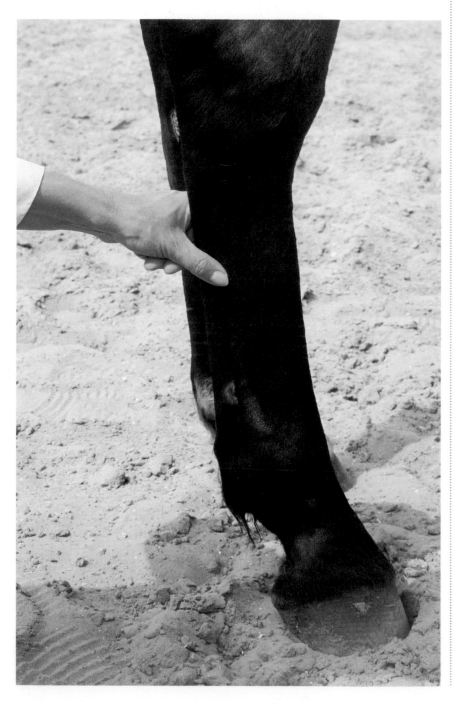

PHILOSOPHY

In the person: Practitioners believe that ten channels run through the body, from the fingertips to the head to the toes. These channels give access to all body parts and organs via points of input that occur at various places on the body: the soles of the feet are especially rich in these 'access points'. By firmly yet gently pressing or massaging the correct, carefully charted points on the feet, every part of the body can be reached and treated by regulating the flow of life force or energy within the ten associated areas of the body.

In the horse: The horse's 'foot' in fact starts at his hock, which is the equivalent joint to the human ankle, and the lower hind leg. The horse's coronet and his heels are amply supplied with points which can be massaged and pressed, so long as the practitioner knows how to transpose the points correctly from the human foot.

HOW DOES IT WORK?

The trained, experienced and sensitive practitioner can discover a good deal about the health of a person or a horse by gentle exploration of, and pressure on, appropriate points and channels on the feet/leg. For example, it is claimed that by following the appropriate channel along the correct part of the human foot or horse's leg, each vertebra in the spine can be 'felt' or 'sensed', and that pressure on the correct part of the foot/leg can encourage realignment of any which are out of place.

Will it tickle? Relaxation is essential for the flow of the energy, and after any initial apprehension both human and equine patients soon settle down and relax. A properly trained reflexologist will apply the right sort of pressure to relax the patient without it in any way tickling. Neither will the practitioner painfully manipulate the feet or pull the horse's leg about.

Does it work? Like other therapies, it seems to be very effective for most patients: this may be immediately, or a few hours or days later, and sometimes they need only one treatment, sometimes more. It is not unknown for a patient, be it person or horse, to feel a little unwell for about twenty-four hours after an initial treatment. This is a good sign that the body's energy, which flows on a twenty-four-hour cycle, is rebalancing and doing its work.

SELF HELP

This is a very specialised therapy, and not one that you can practise yourself without instruction. Nevertheless, it is as well worth looking into as any other complementary therapy. However, finding a practitioner who will work on a horse may not be easy (see Useful Addresses in this book for an initial contact point).

As the horse's foot begins at the hock, which equates with the human ankle, it becomes clear that the zones and points used in reflexology can be transferred to equine use by a skilled practitioner with equine knowledge

What is Reflexology used for?

■ to relax the patient, thereby enabling a maximum flow of energy to optimise health and fitness

■ to treat any physical disorders by regulating the flow of life force or energy

■ to resolve skeletal problems – and specifically the back – through gentle pressure on the appropriate access points on the rider's foot or the horse's leg

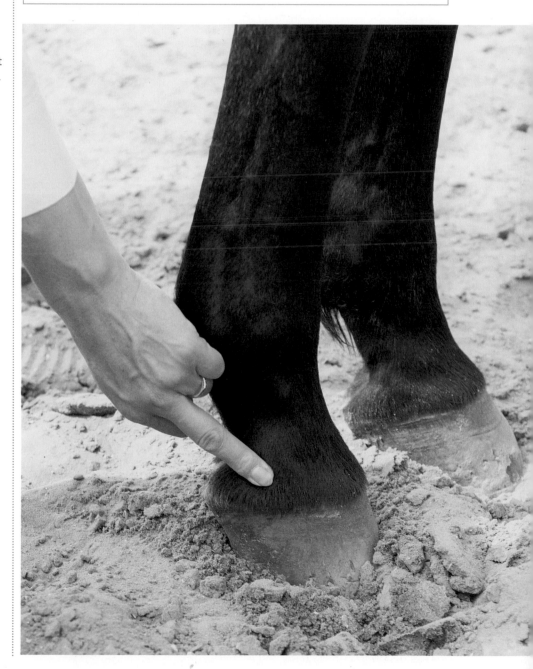

Physiotherapy

The word 'physiotherapy' is an umbrella term covering a wide range of therapies used on humans and animals. These therapies are used in the treatment of disease, injury or deformity, and involve massage, manipulation, specialised machines, exercise, and/or the application of heat or cold. Physiotherapists do not prescribe or provide drugs for their clients or patients: that is part of the doctor's or vet's role, when appropriate, although in many cases of injury, anti-inflammatory orthodox drugs may be used as well as, increasingly, homoeopathic and herbal medicines, plus magnetic wraps, boots, rugs and pads.

PHILOSOPHY

Thirty years ago, the new genre of healers called physiotherapists were still regarded by most members of the human medical profession as quacks, and it was unheard of to apply physiotherapy to an animal. How different things are today!

Physiotherapy is fully recognised by, and available via most countries' state health services for humans, and it is a regular part of the fitness and soundness regimes of most competition horses, both for maintenance and rehabilitation, sometimes under veterinary referral and sometimes not, depending on which country you live in.

There are various schools of thought, and various modalities or healing techniques covered by physiotherapy, which is now an extensive subject in its own right: many books have been written exclusively on this valuable discipline, and we can give only an overview of it here.

HOW DOES IT WORK?

Diagnosis and assessment: Although diagnosis of an equine disorder may, by law, have to be carried out by a veterinary surgeon (depending on your national laws), physiotherapists must assess the horse for their own professional satisfaction, and will first study any veterinary diagnosis and report available; only then will they look at the way a horse stands and holds himself, and how he moves at liberty, in hand and, if appropriate, under saddle and in harness. Physiotherapists are very aware that it is natural and normal for the horse's body to compensate for pain or difficulty by moving in non-natural ways in order to relieve the discomfort.

The therapist will probably ask the owner/rider/trainer about the horse's normal or previous way of going, and also his schooling and training programme with specific reference to the exact exercises and type of work the horse is asked to do. He/she will then work out a programme of treatment aimed at healing, recovery and rehabilitation.

Physiotherapist working on rider at the World Endurance Championships

MASSAGE, STRETCHING AND MANIPULATION

All of these therapies form part of physiotherapy and may be carried out by a physiotherapist, if appropriate. All have been dealt with elsewhere in this book under the individual headings as above.

MACHINES

Electrically operated machines are often used in physiotherapy for various purposes. Some work on the principles of electro-magnetic field therapy, which works on the cells of the body and creates a magnetic field to enhance healing. The idea is that the cells' own magnetic fields are disrupted by injury and over-stress, and the field applied by the machines helps the cells' own magnetic fields to return to normal, so enabling them to heal themselves more effectively. Machines which are attached to the horse, as opposed to being hand-held, usually have pads of varying sizes which are taped to, or stick to the horse and are connected to the machine by wires down which the current passes. A selection of machines, not all electro-magnetic, are described below.

Massage machines: Massage that is knowledgeably carried out is nearly always beneficial and hardly ever harmful. Small, hand-held machines are available which work by means of vibration: both horses and people seem to enjoy the sensation which may be experienced at varying depths in the soft tissue of the body. Normally a mild, shallow setting is

> ## What is Physiotherapy used for?
>
> The various methods involved in physiotherapy are used to achieve the following:
>
> - to relieve pain and enhance healing
> - some encourage muscular effort, which helps to disperse cellular fluid, promote lymphatic drainage or flow, improve blood circulation, and prevent the deterioration which results from loss of use
> - some help to increase the blood supply in deep tissues, and so are good for injuries which could not otherwise be reached
> - to stimulate cellular activity which produces heat, which promotes healing
> - to speed up the healing of injuries; laser, for instance, is particularly beneficial in the treatment of bruising, muscle injuries and wounds, and also tendon and ligament injuries, and injuries to joint capsules
> - to help reduce the formation of adhesions (scar tissue)

used until the patient becomes used to it. The machine is pressed to the body, and the pressure plus the vibration assists in the dispersal of excess fluid and in the process of venous return (the passage of blood in the veins back towards the heart) and the flow of lymph in the body.

Niagara machines: These are available for owners to use at home without direct supervision, although expert advice is issued as to their use. If the horse is quiet enough, the machine may eventually be strapped to his body and left in position, though obviously it is vital that the horse is first accustomed to the machine and its effects.

H-wave: This is normally very well tolerated by horses, and seems to have a soothing effect on them. It can relieve pain if used at high

frequencies, and is believed to work by preventing the sensory nerves from transmitting pain signals to the central nervous system and, possibly, by stimulating the production of encephalins and endorphins. The lower frequencies produce muscle contractions, an active process which massage, mainly a passive process, cannot produce. Muscular effort brings the advantages of cellular fluid dispersal, lymphatic drainage or flow, and an improvement in blood circulation.

Ionicare and Electrovet: Often considered together, these both work on the same basic principle that if the electrical activity of the charged particles or ions in the cells is disturbed, loss of function results. Therefore both aim to restore the ionic balance more quickly than would occur naturally. The Ionicare machine produces an electrical current which passes through the tissues and beneficially influences the activity of ions; the Electrovet can have a similar effect, but also stimulates muscle activity to prevent the deterioration which results from loss of use.

Short-wave diathermy: This provides soothing and healing deep heat to tissues by means of passing a high-frequency, alternating current through them. The tissues resist the current, and this creates heat which, in turn, increases tissue activity and blood supply. The denser the tissues, the more heat is created. The therapy increases the blood supply in deep tissues and so is good for injuries which could not otherwise be reached.

Ultrasound: This therapy has many uses, always working at the cellular level. It is used in treatment to raise the temperature of deep tissues, but also for diagnosis, scanning and measurement. It emits sound waves which act as an energy source to stimulate cellular activity, and can cause mechanical vibration of cells which produces heat; it also has a non-heating function which basically gives the cells what has been described as a 'micro-massage'. It is a wide-ranging tool – and it is also the most specialised and potentially the most dangerous item of equipment currently in general physiotherapeutic and veterinary use. Sound waves can actually break bones, and these machines are certainly not for unknowledgeable owners to hire and buy.

The treatment head contains a crystal which vibrates when subjected to an electrical charge. As air is a poor conductor of sound, a gel is applied to the area to be treated to enhance the passage of the sound waves. Ultrasound can be applied under water to good effect, water being a good conductor of sound.

Ultrasound should only be used by experienced specialists.

Laser: The word 'laser' came about from a description of the technique, namely 'Light Amplification by Stimulated Emission of Radiation'. High-powered lasers were first used in the late 1960s to perform laser surgery; the lasers used in physiotherapy are not of this type, but of the low-powered variety that speed up the healing of wounds and other injuries. There are various types of laser, both machines and therapies, which appear to heal different types of injury.

The therapy is non-invasive (there being no actual penetration of body tissues); it is well tolerated by horses as there is no sensation felt from the beam of light waves emitted; and in most cases there is a noticeable speeding up of healing. As well as being useful for bruising, muscle injuries and wounds, laser is also beneficial for tendon and ligament injuries, and injuries to joint capsules, according to which light wavelength setting is used. Laser techniques can also be used to stimulate acupuncture points.

Again, only experienced, qualified personnel should apply laser therapy.

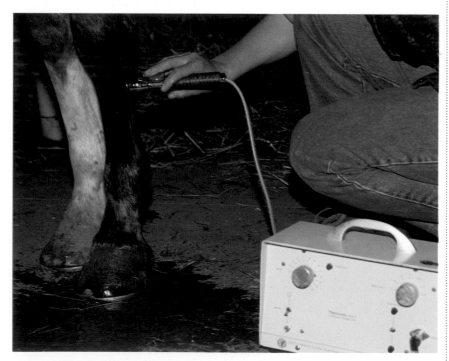

Ultrasound is certainly not a therapy for use by untrained personnel. It can be very dangerous in the wrong hands as the equipment can cause severe injury when used incorrectly

TENS: Transcutaneous Electrical Nerve Stimulators: These machines are now very popular as pain relievers. Electrodes are applied to the skin, and a pulsed signal (sixty pulses per second) is generated which blocks the transmission of pain signals along the sensory nerves from an injured part. If a lower number of pulses per second is used, this causes a 'muscle ripple' which, as with more or less any active muscle activity, increases the blood flow to an area, eases muscle spasm, and helps in the dispersal of fluid and swelling. This combined action will, without affecting nerves, help to reduce pain.

Electrical muscle stimulators: There are various of these machines now in use. The original Faradic machine has been largely superseded, although some practitioners still use them, mainly for greater stimulation of larger muscle structures.

Electrical muscle stimulators can relieve pain, and stimulate the flow of blood and lymph, so removing fluid swelling and reducing muscle spasm; this in turn will increase mobility and help to reduce the formation of adhesions (scar tissue), and encourage wound repair, again minimising the growth of adhesions.

HOT AND COLD THERAPIES

These have long been used by owners and trainers for sprains, bruises and torn muscles.

Cold therapy: This is used to reduce inflammation: although this is the

Faradism as a therapy is not as widely used as it was in former years, but still has a place in the healing repertoire of many physiotherapists particularly when treating larger muscle masses

body's natural reaction to injury, it involves heat, swelling and pain, and can actually result in fluid becoming congested in an injured part, thus 'jamming up' the area, restricting circulation and so *hampering* healing. Cold applications will cool down the area, mildly reduce pain, and reduce swelling – though this is in part due to the gentle pressure of the actual application, whether it is the force of water, bandaging on of a pack, or the fact of standing in water. This enables the fluid in the area to flow better, thus enhancing healing.

Heat therapy: Strangely enough, the application of heat also seems to reduce pain: it directly increases the circulation by causing the superficial blood vessels to dilate (vasodilation), thus enabling them to hold more heat-carrying blood. This enhances muscle elasticity, cell function, and general 'tissue tone' – and so assists healing, it is felt. Heat therapy is mainly used when an injury is forty-eight hours old or more, by which time natural inflammation will hopefully have settled down.

There are various methods of applying heat and cold, by machines and also by packs, wraps, poultices and lamps, for example.

HYDROTHERAPY

Swimming: This has been used increasingly for about the past twenty-five years
- to help get horses fit without over-stressing their limbs
- to keep the cardio-respiratory system at specific fitness levels during, say, limb injuries
- to develop good muscle tone
- as an enjoyable treat.

Warning

It is essential when swimming horses that the personnel involved are not only experienced but highly perceptive of the signals coming from the horse. It is very easy to miss the signs of real distress, and taking a horse to this point merely for the purpose of getting him fit is inexcusable

The importance of monitoring: Horses very quickly become exhausted when swimming, and their time in the pool must be very slowly built up, *and their pulse monitored by means of a heart-rate monitor.* It must be remembered that a swimming horse – usually led round or along the pool by means of two assistants holding lunge-lines clipped to the headcollar – is totally helpless, and may be unable to indicate his distress if he becomes overtired through inexpert handling and observation, if those controlling the session are over-enthusiastic, or do not understand equine physiology and psychology.

However, because horses do not find swimming a particularly natural activity – although even young foals know how to swim instinctively – great care must be taken when introducing them to swimming, and it is normally safest to do this with experienced, *concerned* personnel in a specially built equine swimming pool. Some riders do swim their horses in rivers or the sea, and although it can be very enjoyable, there must be a good deal of risk attached to this practice.

When swimming, horses use their bodies in exactly the opposite shape or outline to that required when riding so this should be counteracted by other work.

Pool design: Pools can be either straight or round, straight ones being the most favoured type as the horse is not stressed by constantly having to swim on a bend. The round type is often used, however, for fitness swimming, because the horse can be kept in the water for a set length of time. This removes the problem with leading him up and down a straight pool, where he must come out of the water and turn around after each length.

Aftercare: When the horse leaves the pool, any signs such as shaking, shivering, staggering, stiffness, inco-ordination, very rapid breathing, bleeding from one or both nostrils or, of course, excessive heart/pulse rates are not normal, and are sure signs that the horse has been swum to the point of distress or exhaustion and/or is extremely cold.

Pools are not normally heated, and although horses do not feel dry cold as acutely as humans, they are certainly susceptible to the combined effects of cold and wet, as when almost totally immersed in cold water in a swimming pool. In particular, fit horses rarely have any spare fat layer under the skin, so they have no insulation and can become bitterly cold very quickly, even to the point of hypothermia, despite the heat-generating effort of swimming.

Guarding against abuse: Of course, the heart and lungs must be stressed to achieve fitness, but owners should make themselves well aware of their own horse's normal parameters and recovery rates so that they can guard against this type of abuse. If a horse is brought out of the pool for a rest or change of direction and shows reluctance to re-enter it, on no account must he be forcibly persuaded to do so. If he does not want to re-enter of his own accord within a very short time of being re-presented, perhaps with calm, verbal encouragement, there is obviously a very good reason.

Water walks: If you are fortunate enough to live within reasonable reach of the sea, you will probably already have paddled or waded your horse, if only for fun. The cold water has the dual benefits on feet and legs of keeping them cold, and of massaging them, this from the force of the water moving against them; also, walking through water necessitates stronger muscle use, either to lift the legs if in fairly shallow water, or to push against it if deeper. It is likely that walking almost a mile nearly knee-deep in the sea is equivalent to a two-mile canter on the gallops – or the beach. However, in the experience of Susan McBane, the water depth must be carefully monitored otherwise the horse ends up with quite the wrong muscle development: thus, just less than knee-deep is good exercise and aids muscle development – but if the water is only slightly deeper than that, the horse has to lift the feet and legs too high and this produces a strenuous, artificial gait which is not beneficial and could produce a permanent shortening of the stride which can occur when horses have to spend too much time and effort lifting the legs to clear the water. Taking the horse in further, however, to almost elbow depth, produces a lower action with the horse pushing against the water, which is good and produces good muscle development.

On no account must the horse be rushed or allowed to go at all fast, as he can easily lose his balance and fall. Nor is it a good plan to stand still in the sea admiring the scenery, as the horse will sink in the soft sand and then be unable to get his feet out quickly enough – with the same result. The voice of experience!

Other water walks: If you have access to a river or lake with a known safe bottom and no undercurrents, you can swim or wade in that, with care, of course; but otherwise specially built water walks can be used, normally found at hydrotherapy, rehabilitation or pool establishments.

On the whole, walking or wading in water is, like so many things in life, excellent in moderation – say, two or three twenty-minute spells per week – and when it is combined with other exercise to ensure even muscle development.

Equine jacuzzis: These are useful in that the horse can stand in a moderate depth of water whilst underwater jets play on his legs, the force of the water exerting a massaging effect on the legs whilst the cold cools down any heat.

TREADMILLS

These have made the study of equine exercise physiology very much easier in recent decades, and horses can be quickly trained to work on them at any gait, from a walk to a fast gallop. Again, knowledgeable, concerned personnel are required, to ensure that the horse is not over-worked and exhausted, or taken faster then he can go.

How useful are they? Not as useful as was first believed: it has been found from biomechanical studies that because the surface moves underneath the horse, work on the

Warning

There is no doubt that treadmills are very useful for other studies involving the cardiac, respiratory and locomotory systems, and they have enabled much ultimately useful research and diagnosis to be done. However, horses certainly can be pushed beyond their capacity during this work; sometimes this is simply to find out just what the heart and lungs are capable of, but as with any aspect of working athletic horses, ethics must come into our use of them, whatever our qualifications or intentions.

If a horse that has previously been worked on a treadmill shows reluctance to go on it again, or appears worried, tense or frightened whilst being installed on it, despite obediently stepping up onto it, he has obviously had a distressing experience previously. Ethically we cannot ask the horse to go through that type of work again, for whatever purpose. If at any time any horse, experienced or not, is becoming distressed during the work, indicated either by means of monitoring equipment or the horse's appearance and/or behaviour, the work should be stopped.

treadmill is not as effective from a fitness point of view as work on the ground, because the muscles that the horse uses to keep his balance and move against the moving surface are different from those he uses to push himself along over static ground – although the movement does make him take evenly spaced steps which he may not do otherwise. This makes treadmills useful for rehabilitating horses with gait abnormalities however they are caused.

Guarding against abuse: Most treadmills can be slanted slightly upwards to increase the physical effort necessary, but it should be remembered that, in this mode, the horse is effectively working uphill on a non-giving surface and this has the same effect as working a horse with long toes and low heels, stressing the tendons and ligaments at the backs of the lower legs and in the feet, and perhaps transferring significant pressure to the sesamoid and navicular bones. On good, natural ground or on a prepared surface, the toe will have the chance to sink into the ground somewhat at its breakover point, enough to relieve the angle: not so on a treadmill. It is possible that hock strain may also occur if the angle is too steep or the pace too fast. It is now felt that level treadmills are probably best.

HORSE WALKERS

Used in moderation, these machines have proved invaluable in many busy yards, for the following reasons:

- for loosening horses up, and cooling them down
- to give horses a break from long periods of being stabled
- for maintaining fitness in resting horses (two 30min walks a day,

Working a horse on a treadmill without genuine concern for its wellbeing can result in severe distress and even injury. Heart-rate monitors (not worn by this horse) should be regarded, in the opinion of the authors, as essential

including trot where appropriate)

■ from a therapy viewpoint, they help to exercise horses recovering from injuries to prevent the formation of adhesions

■ they also help horses being re-educated in their gaits to get used to their new way of going without carrying weight, and with no close control such as being led in hand. If the horse's head is restricted this always alters his gait, yet it is surprising how many handlers seem to be incapable of allowing a led horse a free head even when a physiotherapist has explained why this is essential. There are no such difficulties on a walker.

Horse walker design: Probably the best type is that in which the horses walk free in individual pens (not tied),

Work in moderation on a horse walker can be beneficial both mentally and physically. The most common and best design today seems to be the type that provides an individual section for each horse. Horses soon learn how to work in the horse walker and appear to enjoy sessions, in moderation

with plenty of room at their sides, and with about a horse's length in front of, and behind them, to allow for slight slowing down or speeding up. Horses take to these very well indeed, and several can be walked and watched by one person, saving a lot of time and labour. The horses listen to the person controlling the machine and soon learn to trot on, walk, stop, turn and start again on the other rein. They actually seem to enjoy their sessions, provided they are not too long – up to 30min at any one time is sufficient.

In the unlikely event of a horse playing up or bumping against the pen divisions, the machine will stop.

SELF HELP

Although physiotherapy is a specialist subject, there are several aspects of it that owners can use themselves, probably after initial advice and instruction from a physiotherapist. There is a general, daily, all-over rub-down type of massage which the horse will surely enjoy; pre- and post-ride stretches; safe home-massage machines; hacks down to the river for a paddle; and in-hand and groundwork (see Groundwork, p114).

There are also several books and booklets available on physiotherapy techniques which will give readers good background knowledge.

Magnetic Therapy

The use of magnets as a tool for healing is an effective, ancient remedy that has so far defied scientific attempts to prove how it works to the satisfaction of most orthodox scientists, doctors, vets and health care professionals. Yet just because we don't understand how something works doesn't mean that it can't work and cases show that magnotherapy really can help.

HOW IS IT USED?

Any condition or situation that would probably be improved or alleviated by encouraging blood flow benefits from using magnets. For a fracture, for example, a magnet would be of benefit to improve blood flow to the affected area in order to repair the damaged bone; and magnets may well help any horse that has a tendency to be stiff. Magnets on their own will not necessarily cure ailments: it is generally when combined with other treatments that they can be extremely beneficial.

PHILOSOPHY

Some professionals accept that it does work, and have their own theories as to how it may do so:

Theory one: that magnetism improves the efficiency of the blood. This does not mean that it speeds up blood circulation or increases blood pressure: it is believed by some to improve the haemoglobin-carrying capacity of the erythrocytes or red blood cells. Haemoglobin is the red protein pigment which carries oxygen and also

Magno-Pulse® pastern boots in place. Boots such as these can be used to relieve fetlock and foot problems, alleviating stiffness and pain

iron in the blood: it could be that iron, a metal, is affected by the magnetism (which is attracted to certain metals) so that the blood's ability to carry life-giving oxygen, and also nutrients, to the tissues is enhanced, as is the removal of toxins, so promoting healthy tissues, healing and pain relief.

Theory two: that the natural magnetic field of the creatures on this planet is disturbed by all the man-created electro-magnetism that now charges the atmosphere, interfering with their natural functioning. Wearing magnets, or undergoing electro-magnetic treatment, helps to rebalance our natural magnetism, promoting health and healing.

Theory three: that our bodies are composed of countless atoms which all have a positive or negative electrical charge, each atom being a microscopic magnet. Opposites attract: positive charges and negative charges are attracted to, and are held to each other in unimaginably complex ways in our bodies, and in effect, hold tissues together – and because electricity is energy, they are also responsible for driving all the biological processes of both ourselves and our horses. It is reasonable to suppose that placing a magnet (which has a charge) on tissue which itself is charged could effect some change in the tissue's structure and/or function – and if it can create change, it must also have the potential to heal injured tissue.

HOW DOES IT WORK?

There are two types of magnetic therapy in use: static field therapy; and pulsed magnetic field therapy, where the effect of the magnetism is said to be increased by electricity. The electric power is provided by mains electricity or via a battery supplying electric coils, built into a belt or a bracelet for humans, and boots or a rug for horses. The electrically enhanced version is said to speed up the passage of oxygen and nutrients, and of toxins, through the cell membranes, and to be more effective than the static version.

Those wearing magnets in whatever form feel absolutely no physical sensation whatsoever: there is no tingling, certainly no electric shocks if the products are correctly made and used, no 'pulling' feeling, and nothing to worry even the most sensitive horse or fussy human. And most of those who try magnetic therapy swear that it works.

What type of therapy? It is often hard for a lay person to know just what type of therapy to use, but experienced personnel at any company selling the products needed – such as boots or rugs – should be able to advise.

Not a cure-all: Therapists will often use magnotherapy products – for example boots or rugs – in conjunction with other therapies. They are anxious that people should not construe them as a 'cure-all', because a human patient or a horse may have an underlying problem that needs to be resolved before applying magnets. Thus a horse with a structural problem – back injury or tendon strain, for instance – causing soreness and stiffness needs this addressed first with veterinary consultation, after which magnets may well help to speed the healing.

Particular benefits: In certain instances magnotherapy products may be used for their own merit:
- in a rug on a horse that gets tense and tight muscularly when travelling

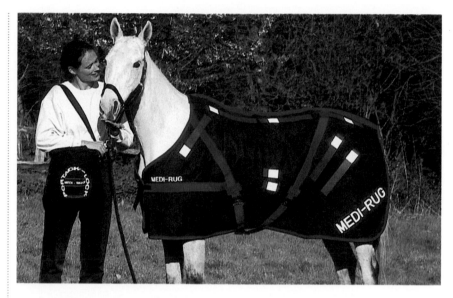

- on a daily basis for horses with a diagnosed musculo-skeletal problem
- in a rug pre- and post-exercise for increasing blood flow (warming the muscles prior to work, helping the removal of metabolic wastes, such as lactic acid, after work)

Medi-Rug™. These appear to be beneficial for whole body treatment

PREVENTATIVE QUALITIES
During travel: It is said that wearing a magnetic rug helps horses to withstand the stresses on their

---

What is Magnetism used for?

Static field therapy is commonly used for:
- friction and bruising injuries
- swelling and/or heat in an area
- new splints
- fatigue and stiffness
- most soft tissue and bone diseases, such as sore backs, strains and sprains, osteoarthritis, windgalls, ringbone, stiffness, pedal osteitis and navicular disease

Pulsed magnetic field therapy is used for:
- recent tendon and ligament injuries
- osteoarthritis
- new splints, sore shins and fractures
- stiffness and tiredness from over-work
- physical shocks sustained in falls or blows
- general stiffness caused by old age or lack of exercise

Magnets are also said to have a relaxing, calming effect on hyperactive children and horses: this may be because of their stated pain- and discomfort-relieving properties, or there may be some other effect.

When should magnetic therapy not be used?

It is advised not to use magnetic therapy on:

- pregnant mares
- haematomas
- infected wounds and abscesses
- serious acute injuries
- any person or horse taking cortisone
- any area which contains a metal plate, screws or pins, such as a broken limb or replacement hip
- inflamed areas

Some topical injury treatments such as liniments, iodine-based preparations and some leg washes can also cause blistering of the skin if exposed to magnetism.

muscles and other tissues caused by travelling and their need to constantly brace and rebalance themselves, particularly during a long journey, as it helps the body expel the toxins created by this constant muscle use. As far too many horses are travelled to competitions, meets and so on and are expected to work before they have recovered, this could certainly be a good preventative measure. Always bear in mind that, generally, it is advised that a horse should be allowed one hour's recovery time for each hour spent travelling, before being expected to undertake strenuous work, and recovery is quicker if the horse is led about a good deal rather than being left in

'What's good enough for the horses is good enough for me!' Using a pulsed electromagnet therapy system which he uses on his horses, showjumper Tim Stockdale was 'back competing in half the expected recovery time' after his knee was shattered by a kick from a young horse

Focus on the Rider

One of the authors of this book suffered from repetitive strain in an ankle, and riding exacerbated the condition. She was introduced to magnetic therapy by her doctor, who advised her to get some 'little stick-on patches with magnets in the middle' from her chemist; after wearing these for a couple of weeks her symptoms were considerably relieved, and this was without any reduction or change in her riding routine.

the horsebox or put into a stable to just stand still.

For older or hard-working horses: Magnetic rugs with static magnets sewn into pockets in the rugs do seem to help older or hard-working horses who may suffer from general stiffness – they appear to pull out looser after standing in, say, overnight, and this makes it easier for them to warm up if they have to work.

SELF HELP

The use of magnetic therapy, usually the pulsed variety, is now quite common in physiotherapy, applied by machines operated by trained personnel. A word of caution, however: some companies, mainly interested in selling machines, have been known to provide these with little back-up knowledge or advice, and have claimed that magnetism will treat 'almost anything'. Nevertheless, it is strongly advised that expert advice is sought from a vet, doctor, or care professional experienced in its use such as a nurse, physiotherapist or exercise physiologist, for example, before using any type of magnetic therapy, static or pulsed, in any situation; then you will be sure that the right product is being used for the right condition.

Correctly used, the therapy is perfectly safe and effective. Because of its pain-relieving effects, though, it should not be assumed that an injury, for example, has actually healed, and veterinary advice should always be sought on this matter.

MAGNOTHERAPY IN PRACTICE
Chris Caden-Parker BSc, MSc, M.F.Phys, AIPTI

Equine sports therapist Chris Caden-Parker runs a therapy and rehabilitation yard known as 'Equine Sport Therapy' in Kent, in association with former European three-day event champion Lucy Thompson. She has a combined BSc Honours degree in Zoology and Botany, an MSc in equine science, and she qualified as a human sports therapist before training in America in equine sport and physical therapy and massage. Chris has completed a qualification in Traditional Chinese Medicine and acupuncture, taking her final exams during the summer of 2000. As well as her primary aim of helping veterinary-referred horses and ponies back on the road to soundness, particularly top-level equine athletes, Chris is a part-time college lecturer and has been the official equine sports therapist for the Irish three-day event team since 1997.

Chris uses many types of therapy in her treatment regimes, including magnotherapy, and says: 'I would tend to use magnotherapy, for example boots or rugs containing magnets, in conjunction with other therapies. It's important for people to realise that they cannot be construed as a "cure-all"; equine patients may have an underlying problem that needs to be resolved before applying magnets or any other modality. I use them where appropriate as part of a specific treatment, depending on the individual's need.

'The only time I would use a magnotherapy product for its own merit and the particular benefits it can offer would be, for example, the use of rugs on a horse who gets tense and tight muscularly when travelling, or on a daily basis for horses with a diagnosed musculoskeletal problem. Magnetic rugs are very good pre- and post-exercise for increasing blood flow and so warming the muscles prior to work, and later facilitating the removal of metabolic wastes such as lactic acid.

'Most of the clinical work involving the use of magnotherapy has been done in the previously Iron Curtain countries. Drugs in these nations are extremely expensive, if they can be obtained at all, and magnets provide a cheap form of medicine. There is excellent scientific evidence available that magnotherapy does work.

'In my experience, any condition or situation that would probably be improved or alleviated by encouraging blood flow benefits from using magnets. I believe magnets may well help any horse that has a tendency to be stiff. Working the muscles in conjunction with other forms of therapy must also be a part of the healing process.'

So are magnets 100 per cent safe to use? Says Chris:

'A horse with a structural problem causing soreness and stiffness needs this addressed first with veterinary consultation, after which magnets may well help to speed the healing. The potential danger with 'off-the-shelf' products is that people may buy and use them instead of calling out a vet to ascertain the exact problem. Take a lame horse for example: what is causing the lameness might actually be extremely serious, even life-threatening, so you need to know exactly what you are dealing with before deciding on a course of treatment. That's my only concern with them. Like any form of medicine, when used correctly, magnets can provide immense benefits; however they won't do any good, and at worst will cause actual harm, when used incorrectly. Magnets are superb for some things, but for others they are not going to make any difference if they are used.

'In my opinion it is far safer to call out a vet to diagnose a problem in the first place; and in actual fact, reputable complementary therapists won't treat a horse without a vet's permission or referral.'

What sort of ailments can magnets help heal? Says Chris:

'Any ailment that can be helped by improved blood circulation. For a fracture, for example, a magnet would be of benefit to increase blood flow to the affected area in order to repair the damaged bone. However I am not inclined to say that magnets on their own will cure ailments, only that combined with other therapies they can be extremely beneficial.'

CASE HISTORIES

1 *Horse: Dutch-bred stallion Cassander, advanced dressage performance horse owned by David Pincus BHSI.*

PROBLEM: Long-standing lameness in Cassander's left fore foot, with the vet unable to determine what was causing it. Says David: 'Conventional treatment, including corrective shoeing and medication, was tried and did achieve a slight improvement, but we couldn't seem to find a satisfactory long-term remedy.'

Cassander and David Pincus (Picture: Joanna Prestwich)

TREATMENT: David spotted an advert in his daily newspaper for a Medicur electro-magnetic pain-relief device which had been developed specifically for people suffering from chronic long-tern ailments such as rheumatism and osteoporosis. David thought it worth trying on Cassander and bought one. Says David: 'I used it three times a day on Cassander's foot, and within two weeks his lameness had disappeared.'

RESULT: Cassander went on to have an extremely successful competitive season, winning and being placed at advanced level on a number of occasions. Following that successful 'experiment', David says he has no hesitation in using magnotherapy when he considers it could be helpful:

'My international Grand Prix horse Son of Charm suffered a back injury after a fall and I thought he would lose the use of his tail. After four weeks of regular magnotherapy treatment I noticed a marked improvement, and now both his back and tail have been restored to perfect health.

'In addition, I have found magnotherapy to be effective on severe foot bruising – an injury which, in my experience, takes a considerable time to heal. Yet the horse that I treated with magnotherapy was back in work within three days. It was the shortest recovery time I have ever witnessed with this type of injury.'

CASE HISTORIES

2 *Horse: Snoopy, an eighteen-year-old, 16.3hh ex-event horse owned by Marvyn Anderson.*

PROBLEM: Explains Marvyn: 'I have owned Snoopy since he was three. He was a great all-rounder, but suffered two lamenesses in his life that the vet could find no cause for, despite X-rays.

'Two summers ago, when he was sound, I turned him away for three weeks whilst I moved to start a new job with horses. When I brought him back in to work after his short lay-off he didn't feel quite level, and he didn't look 100 per cent sound in the field.'

TREATMENT: 'I had him checked over by my vet but nothing could be found that was causing the lameness, again despite X-rays and nerve blocks. I turned him away again to rest for a month, hoping that this would help. Then someone lent me a pair of Bioflow magnetic horse boots to try, which I did – after all, I'd nothing to lose.'

RESULT: 'Within a month Snoopy was completely sound. I also noticed that a leg which sometimes swells up due to an old tendon sheath injury was completely cold and tight. Snoopy went back into full work without any problems – and is continuing to stay sound, which I feel is due to the magnotherapy treatment. It has given me back an active, sound horse.'

Marvy Anderson and Snoopy (Courtesy: Greenshires Publishing)

Chiropractic

Chiropractic is an independent therapy specialising in the treatment of disorders and displacements of joints, particularly those between the vertebrae of the spine, and the subsequent effects on the nervous system and general health. It is a manipulative method used for humans and animals, and is based on the concept that the spine is the 'headquarters' of whole-body health.

Misalignments of the spine however caused, either through injury or bad posture, result in pressure on the nerves which pass out between the vertebrae. (The spinal column is itself, of course, one giant nerve.) This pressure can lead to back problems, reduced motion, pain and stress-related illness – there are few things as stressful as being in constant pain.

Above and right: Chiropractors use short, sharp blows to adjust what are believed to be skeletal misalignments, probably caused by muscle spasm, which creates pain through nerve pressure.

Manipulation

Manipulation is a term used to describe any therapy in which parts of the horse are moved by the practitioner during treatment; obvious ones are osteopathy, chiropractic, shiatsu and massage, or possibly by application of machines (as in physiotherapy) which stimulate muscle movement electrically. Some might include therapies such as acupuncture and acupressure on the grounds that although they do not manipulate the horse's body in the accepted sense, they do manipulate his energy flow.

PHILOSOPHY

Chiropractors aim to redress misalignments through spinal manipulation or adjustment. With human patients this does not cause much problem, because doctors and others know that our spines and those of smaller animals can become misaligned. But with horses the matter is less clear cut, and certainly almost every vet believes that a horse's spine cannot become misaligned. However, muscle tension, and particularly muscle spasm, can undoubtedly cause 'pulls' on the spine through the soft tissues surrounding and attached to it, and therefore on nerves in the area. So although a horse's back vertebrae and inter-vertebral discs may not be 'out' (presumably meaning 'out of place' or 'out of line'), he can most certainly suffer from painful back problems, as most of us know.

Chiropractic versus osteopathy: Often confused with osteopathy, chiropractors believe that the natural and correct working of the nerves is more important than the circulation of the blood, which is a central belief of most osteopaths – and it is hard for a lay person to know which comes first, the chicken or the egg. The blood supply controls the health of all tissues, but without nervous control the circulation is adversely affected.

McTimoney chiropractic: For horses, the most common method is that devised in the 1950s by John McTimoney, who adapted chiropractic techniques developed for humans, for animal use. The word comes from the Greek and means 'done by hand'.

HOW DOES IT WORK?

Assessment: As with so many therapies, it is essential to establish first of all the cause of the horse's injury or discomfort. The practitioner will therefore study the horse's history, together with any available veterinary diagnosis, and will feel down the spine and pelvis and other areas of the body. In some countries a veterinary diagnosis is required by law, but even where it is not, and practitioners are able to offer a diagnosis themselves, it is a good plan to have the co-operation of the horse's vet.

Outside influences: A good practitioner will also check the horse's feet, shoes, tack and way of going, and may also ask to see him ridden by his normal rider, or lunged. Bad riding and badly fitted and adjusted tack are often found to be a direct or indirect cause of injury or of poor action or accidents: in trying to avoid the pain the horse will attempt to move in a different way; this is known as compensatory action, and it puts all sorts of unnatural stresses on his body – and this in itself causes injury, because the body is being forced to work in a way in which it was never intended to move.

An uncomfortable or painful saddle; a heavy-sitting, unbalanced rider; a rider with heavy, harsh hands; and 'gadgets' or training aids which are wrongly used, wrongly fitted or inappropriate for the horse – all these contribute to significant discomfort, avoidance behaviour and even pain in the horse.

Technique: The chiropractic technique is gently manipulative, and aims to correct misalignments by realigning and balancing the horse's musculo-skeletal system. The practitioner will direct a series of short, sharp taps (not harsh, strong blows) onto the spinous processes of the vertebrae in the back. This is done, not with a view to 'putting the back back in', but to help move muscle and other soft tissue, and to release muscle spasm. This in turn releases trapped nerves, or those under pressure, which in combination are holding the

What conditions can Chiropractic treat?

Any condition such as those discussed in this chapter. Pain always alters a horse's way of going and usually his attitude to life, and certainly his attitude to work. Chiropractic may therefore be useful in reversing any of the following changes, depending on the root cause:

- in attitude, such as irritability, listlessness, lack of interest in, or reluctance to work
- in action, such as dragging the hind feet in particular, but sometimes the front ones, too
- in his work, particularly when jumping – for instance refusing, running out or rushing, twisting or kicking back during the jump, and running off on landing; refusing to flex or 'round' during schooling work; difficulty in performing bends and circles; lack of balance
- in soundness, such as asymmetry either when standing or in action; lameness, especially after a fall or slip-up when other causes are not evident; any sort of 'unlevelness' (ie lameness)
- in behaviour, such as resisting, bucking, rearing, napping, bolting
- in fitness, such as unreasonable stiffness on one rein, back pain, difficulty in performing hillwork up or down, and a general lack of zest in action

structures in an unnatural and painful state.

A holistic system: Although it is mainly the spine which is worked upon, the practitioner will assess the horse's entire body; for example, limb and foot problems can cause back pain, and vice versa. This is a holistic system that eliminates the root cause of a problem, and it is often found that two or three treatments plus rest and remedial exercise are enough to restore the horse to health.

Some owners will arrange for a chiropractic check-up for their horse every year, or before the start of a fitness programme, as a way to pre-empt strains and/or injury.

SELF HELP

Chiropractic is an effective and established therapy for humans and animals. Humans can obtain chiropractic either by looking in their local directories and having private treatment, or by asking their doctor for a referral.

For equine treatment, see the Useful Addresses list on p186. Do not attempt this therapy yourself as more harm than good can come of it in the wrong hands.

Chiropractic is a popular therapy amongst owners for their horses. It is a gentle and apparently very effective treatment, which forms a part of many competition horses' fitness regimes

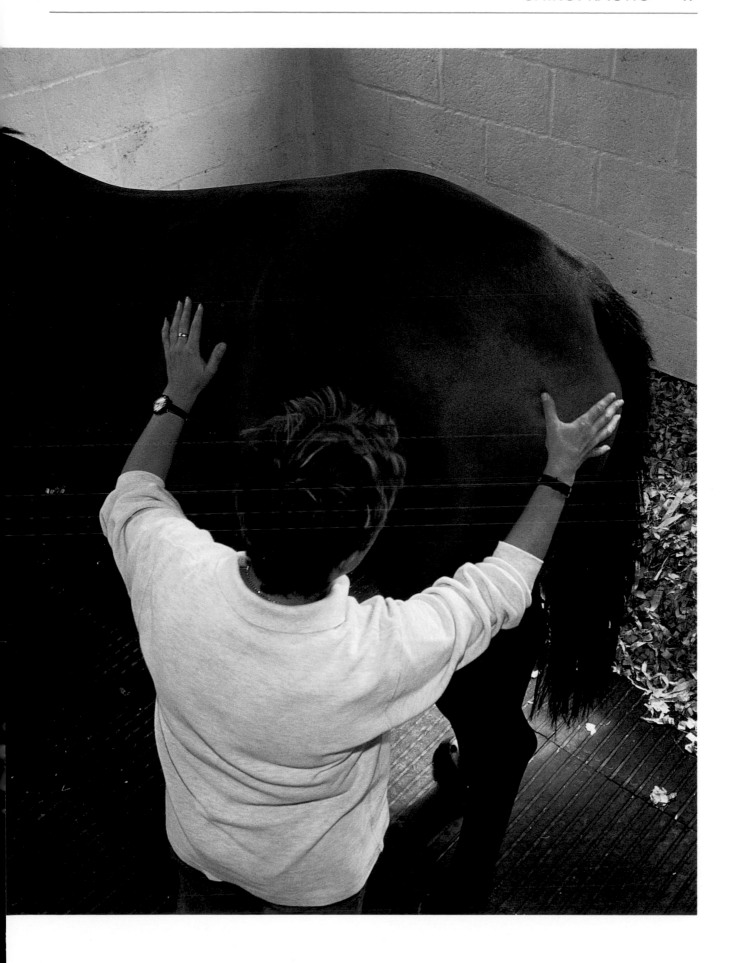

Osteopathy

Osteopathy is a highly effective treatment for humans and animals; even animals which have been regarded as permanently incapacitated have been restored to full fitness by means of osteopathy. It is a healing art and science which aims to resolve painful conditions caused by misalignments of the skeleton – and not only the spine; it works by adjusting the muscles and joints that are effectively perpetuating the misalignment, with a view to correcting it.

These misalignments can cause extreme pain and loss of function to almost any area of the body due to pressure on, injury to, and loss of function of the nerves which serve it. Internal organs may also come under stress due to tension on the musculo-skeletal system, with far-reaching effects.

PHILOSOPHY

Modern osteopathy was developed by Dr Andrew Still in the late nineteenth century, although manipulative therapies were widely used in medicine in ancient civilisations, especially ancient Greece. The philosophy of osteopathy is that the body, both human and animal, works as a whole, and that structure and function, often of seemingly unrelated parts, are interdependent. If the body is out of physical balance (misaligned or 'dis-located' in any way), its function must be impaired, and the osteopath aims to restore this physical balance so that it can work

normally again. Once balance is regained, function should be restored, unless nerve damage has been permanent, and often 'mysterious' diseases seem to disappear as the body is enabled to heal itself once more. Problems of temperament and behaviour, both in hand and under saddle, are also often the result of physical pain or discomfort, of course, and are often righted after osteopathic treatment.

Osteopathy is now a recognised and accepted treatment among the medical and veterinary professions. Along with chiropractic and some

other physical or manipulative therapies, practitioners may treat animals under the direct supervision and/or referral of a vet. Different laws apply in different countries, but in general osteopathy is now a well recognised and respected therapy.

HOW DOES IT WORK?
INJURY AND THE ROLE OF THE OSTEOPATH

First of all it is important to understand the sort of physical damage that the osteopath is called upon to resolve. It may be caused by unco-ordinated or inappropriate muscle movements, or as a result of perhaps a blow, a fall, or repeated strain. Back problems are very common in horses and may be caused by many things, including incorrect saddle fitting, bad riding, poor farriery, in short, any thing that causes the horse to hold himself in a manner that is defensive and unnatural.

When injury does occur, whether this is suddenly or gradually, the physical consequences may be far-reaching. The muscles associated with the damage may go into spasm,

What is Osteopathy used for?

Osteopathy aims to treat ailments by adjusting muscles and joints with a view to correcting misalignments of the skeleton. It will therefore help to resolve:

- back problems
- stiffness and loss of mobility in the joints
- sciatic pain
- muscle tension/spasm/fibrous knots caused by skeletal misalignment

and form a hard, fibrous knot: this is the body's natural protective mechanism, used to prevent further movement and so further injury of a part. As a result of this, joints may become locked at the limit of their range of movement or even dislocated, and obviously great loss of function of the part can result; in time the tissues can become more fibrous, the flow of blood and lymph through them will be considerably reduced, and this will ultimately cause muscle atrophy or 'shrinkage' (because of the lack of nutrients and oxygen) and poor tissue health. This restricted range of movement will in turn adversely affect other parts of the locomotory system.

The osteopath's role is to identify the physical damage responsible for the specific condition, and to attempt to resolve it through manipulation.

TECHNIQUE

Osteopathy makes use of manipulation, often in the form of slow, deliberate and wide-ranging massage movements and joint manipulations, depending on the school of thought (there are various forms of osteopathy). Treatment is usually slow and gentle, and is guided by the horse's response to the movements carried out. There is no 'bone cracking' or 'joint crunching': causing pain by over-stressing the body is always counter-productive, and generally the osteopath aims to move tissues to enable them to realign – and it takes great skill and training to know just how far to manipulate the body, and in exactly what way, for best effect.

ASSESSMENT AND DIAGNOSIS

In some countries, only veterinary surgeons are allowed by law to diagnose illnesses and injuries. In these cases, the osteopath will discuss the case and diagnosis with the vet, make his own assessment as to treatment, and work with the vet's permission.

The horse will be examined

The osteopath will observe the patient moving and examine him or her closely before deciding on treatment. Here, the practitioner is checking the level of the horse's hips and his muscular development of the hindquarters

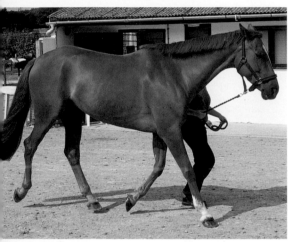

standing still, and the osteopath will look and feel for any areas of soreness and pain. The quality of muscle tone, ranging from 'knots' to atrophy, will be noted, and the horse will then be walked and trotted in hand on a straight line and in a circle, turned short, and made to step backwards. The osteopath will be looking for any abnormal functioning in the spine, head and neck, and limbs, and will note pelvic symmetry or balance. Sometimes he or she may ask to see the horse ridden, as bad riding or an uncomfortable or even painful saddle may be causing the problem (either or both of which may have been suspected initially). Very often problems in one area of the spine stem from injury or damage to, or pain in, a quite different part of it. Horses also suffer fetlock injuries much more than is generally realised.

Diagnosis and assessment of injuries can now be greatly assisted by the use of thermography (described in this book under that heading).

SEDATION AND ANAESTHESIA AS AIDS TO TREATMENT

Animals in pain are often highly resistant to those trying to help them, and osteopathic treatment is sometimes performed under sedation, or even general anaesthesia today.

After the initial assessment, a horse can be sedated to enable the osteopath to manipulate or palpate (examine by feel) joints and deeper muscle areas, an examination which may not be possible otherwise due to the resistance or even violent objection of the horse. If sedation does not help to relax the horse, a general anaesthetic may be administered so that the osteopath can carry out further manipulation. Some practitioners feel that this greatly assists in identifying the problem areas exactly, as the head, neck, tail and limbs can be used to their full extent in a way not

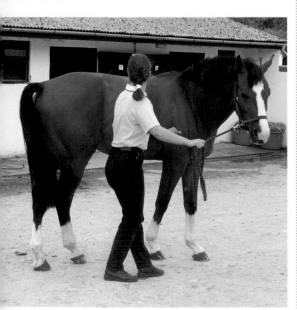

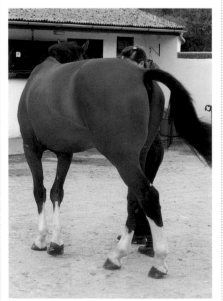

possible under sedation. Sometimes, more can be achieved in one treatment under anaesthesia than in several with or without sedation.

The skills of the osteopath and vet are needed to decide whether or not manipulation in the fully conscious, standing horse will be appropriate for his treatment, whether sedation would help, or whether general anaesthesia will be more helpful.

SELF HELP

Locating an osteopath should not be difficult if you need to be treated yourself; in most countries people can generally obtain whatever treatment they wish to explore if they are able to pay for it. If they want free treatment under their country's state health service, they will normally need a referral from their doctor. In any case, it is a good plan to see the doctor first to get an opinion as to whether or not osteopathy would

Focus on the Rider

Riders with physical problems often alter their posture when sitting on a horse, either because they simply cannot put themselves into a good position due to skeletal misalignment, or because pain causes them to adopt a defensive position: this causes stiffness, and prevents them moving correctly with the horse. Very often problems in one part of the body actually stem from injury to another part; for instance, whiplash injuries sustained in a car accident often cause lower back pain, and headaches can stem from misalignment of the lower spine and pelvis, which is unbalancing the cervical or neck vertebrae. Riders also frequently suffer from shoulder and knee injuries, generally sustained in a fall.

be appropriate for the condition concerned.

TREATMENT FOR HORSES

Horse owners who wonder if osteopathy could help their horses should consult Useful Addresses, starting on page 186, for a contact with the administrative body and, in some countries, discuss the matter with their veterinary surgeon to obtain a referral.

Left and below: The osteopath will probably request to see the horse walked and trotted in hand, moving in tight circles in both directions and backing up. He or she may also ask to see the horse ridden, if appropriate. These are important aspects of assessment

Bowen Technique
Muscle Release Therapy

The Bowen technique is an extremely gentle, non-intrusive, hands-on way of releasing misaligned muscles in humans and animals. It was pioneered by Thomas Ambrose Bowen, born in 1916 in Geelong, Australia. His deep interest in sport, massage and bodywork caused him to observe sports participants and trainers, and he gradually developed his own technique of remedial bodywork.

The effectiveness of the Bowen technique has caused it to be adopted by osteopaths, chiropractors, physiotherapists and sports therapists and masseurs.

Its use is spreading amongst animals, and at the time of writing, training courses in Equine Bowen Therapy are being set up under veterinary supervision and approval in the UK and other countries.

HOW DOES IT WORK?

Horses seem to respond particularly well to the Bowen technique. Their active lives mean that they are often subject to stress and strain, and by balancing and realigning the body's systems, the skilled practitioner may alleviate their discomfort. Initially he or she will assess the horse's muscular, skeletal and nervous states, and obviously will consider any veterinary opinion and diagnosis available. It is claimed the technique activates the body's own healing abilities, releasing muscle spasms and realigning skeletal imbalances as well as increasing the lymph and blood supply to the affected areas, to enhance the healing of damaged tissues.

TECHNIQUE

A Bowen practitioner in human or equine therapy will use his or her hands on specific parts of the body such as muscles, other soft tissue, and at proprioceptor neuro-muscular trigger points, using rolling-type movements with a view to disturbing the muscles and soft

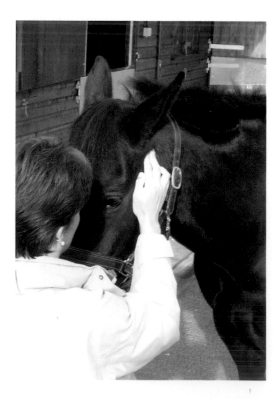

What is Bowen used for?

Equine conditions which may be relieved, depending on the root cause, include:
- loss of performance
- resistance in work
- irritability
- uneven muscle development, or muscle wastage
- uneven shoe wear and dragging of the hind feet
- undue stiffness on one rein
- intermittent or unresolved lameness
- incorrect gaits
- back problems
- filled legs

The joint between the lower jaw and skull is crucial to flexion to the bit. Lack of flexibility plus injured tissues around it can make it very difficult for the horse to work willingly and freely

Focus on the Rider

Conditions in people that Bowen will generally relieve, are back, neck and knee problems, sports injuries, frozen shoulder, tennis elbow and respiratory conditions. Lymphatic drainage is encouraged by the technique, which strengthens the immune system and improves general body health. Conditions such as chronic fatigue, respiratory allergies, headaches, tension, indigestion, kidney problems, sciatica, arthritis, whiplash injuries, injuries sustained in falls, infant colic and many others have been relieved by this technique.

A treatment takes about forty-five minutes, and can mostly be performed through light clothing. It appears that just two or three treatments at weekly intervals are often sufficient to bring long-term relief from even chronic, painful conditions, although further treatments may be sometimes needed. The improvement in body movement and control, and therefore in riding technique and comfort – and the horse's performance – can be most noticeable.

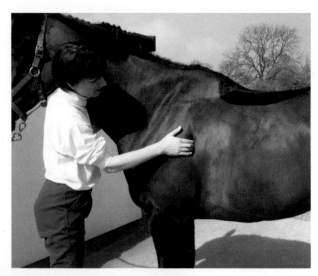

The Bowen technique consists partly of gentle rolling movements of tissues, which horses appear to find relaxing, and which aim to balance and realign soft tissue structures

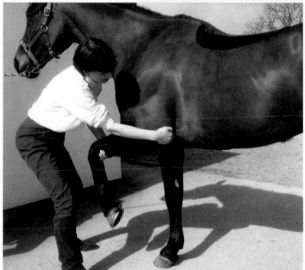

Because the Bowen technique is very gentle, people often do not feel that it can be doing any good. However, in practice the technique appears to be most effective and, as its use expands, more and more people appear to be appreciating its benefits

tissues and also moving the body's energy. This aims to encourage the body to realign itself, to ease muscle spasms and tensions on other tissues, and restore correct, natural and pain-free movement. The techniques are very gentle and there is no actual massage, adjustment of hard tissue or force of any kind.

How many treatments? Two treatments a week apart are usually recommended, and post-treatment instructions given by the practitioner should be followed carefully to ensure maximum benefit.

SELF HELP

Bowen Technique is a therapy requiring a good deal of training and the addresses of administrative organisations are given in Useful Addresses (p186). Consulting a professional therapist may produce a few techniques riders may be able to use themselves. At the time of writing, Bowen is not a widely used therapy and the authors know of no book which explains it.

Massage

Massage might be defined as a deliberate manipulation of muscle, sinew and joints in order to increase the range of motion, the elasticity, and also the circulation within the tissues, thereby enabling muscles to work at their optimum efficiency.

Over recent decades, the demand in the competition horse world for experienced equine massage therapists has greatly increased. Once thought of as pointless and slightly amusing – even if those who expressed derision had experienced beneficial massage themselves – it is now considered a valuable therapy both to keep competition horses supple, loose, even and relaxed, and to help to heal muscle injuries and ease stiffness occasioned by their work.

This light chopping movement done with the edge of the hand is used by some therapists, on both humans and horses, towards the heart to encourage circulation and generally loosen up, free and help align muscle fibres

INJURY AND ITS CONSEQUENCES

First of all it is important to understand the type of condition or injury the massage therapist will be called upon to alleviate. Muscle damage is probably the most common, and any sort of tension that will impair the good functioning of the body.

Muscle injuries in horses may be caused by:

■ *bruising*, when the tissues receive a blow such as during a fall, a kick, or unsympathetic use of spurs (which can also actually cut or tear the skin and flesh); a badly fitting saddle or poor riding causing pressure injuries to the back or girth area; or banging the legs on fences

■ *general cuts and tears* caused by injuries during travelling, in the field, falls on the road and so on

■ *tearing of the muscle fibres*, usually caused by lack of co-ordination of opposing groups of muscles, so one group, or just one muscle, comes under unreasonable stress and the fibres are put under more tension than they can take. Supreme effort on the part of the horse can also cause this

Inflammation is another situation where careful massage may be of benefit. In all cases of damaged tissue, fluid will be released from inside tissue cells as their walls are broken, and blood will accumulate in the damaged area due to broken blood vessels. The fluid congests the area preventing normal circulation and healing, and may separate muscle fibres (cells) further, causing pain and weakness. This natural inflammatory process, as we know, brings pain, heat, swelling and loss of use.

Before healing can take place effectively, this congested fluid has to be removed: anti-inflammatory drugs can be used, and gentle massage will also help to disperse the fluid – this can be hand massage, or by means of machines. Some simple, vibratory machines are safe for lay owners to use, but physiotherapists will have access to others (See Physiotherapy). However, before buying any machine to use yourself on your horse, first discuss its merits with your vet and/or a physiotherapist or equine sports massage therapist, or someone similar (see Self Help, below).

HOW IT WORKS
HANDS-ON MASSAGE
Specialist massage therapists, probably working under the supervision of, or as a team with, the veterinary surgeon, can do a great deal to help prevent adhesions forming in healing tissue: adhesions are new tissues which may attach healing parts to each other in such a way that, when work resumes, further tearing of tissue may occur, and so further injury. Muscle spasm, too, is a common affliction both during work and post-injury in horses: this is because muscles and soft tissue contract around a site of injury in order to protect it, but in doing so

often cause painful tension on bones and joints; so once the injury is mended, it is necessary to relax the contracted area and restore a range of motion to it by 'stretching' the muscles in order to get the area working again as it should do. Helping the tissues to realign themselves will help the body heal itself.

It has been acknowledged that the skin is a site of many acupuncture/acupressure points, and that firm stroking, careful pressures, kneading, pulling and pushing of the skin and underlying tissues not only feels good (ask anyone who has ever had a professional massage) but stimulates those points. This helps to keep the body's energy flowing; it promotes the secretion of hormones, including the now famous encephalins and endorphins which make the body feel good and have a significant pain-relieving effect; it stimulates and 'invigorates' nerve endings; and it assists not only with an improved blood circulation, but that of lymph, too – which, unlike blood, is entirely dependent on body movement to keep it flowing and is essential to the effective functioning of the immune system.

MAIN HAND TECHNIQUES
Massage can be hard work for the masseur, but a good deal of the effort can be reduced if the body weight is used as much as possible to apply pressure, rather than always using the muscles of the back, shoulders and arms in a pushing movement. There are three main techniques for hand massage:

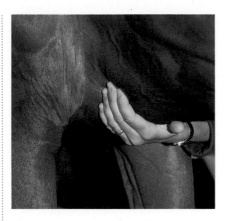

Petrissage

PETRISSAGE (KNEADING)
The hands are placed flat over the relevant area, pressing down, and then the underlying tissues are grasped gently and lifted up slightly by pressing the tips of the fingers around them towards the palms of the hands. The action is repeated several times in one spot before being followed by effleurage.

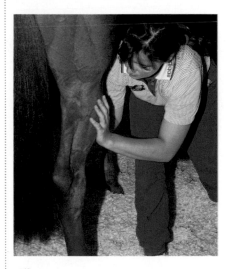

Effleurage

EFFLEURAGE
The hands are moulded around the shape of the muscle tissue to be massaged, and the masseur applies downward and inward pressure, leaning on the hands and letting

them travel in the direction of the muscle fibres and of venous return (generally the forehand is massaged backwards towards the heart and the hindquarters forwards, again towards the heart, with all four legs being massaged upwards). The hands maintain light contact with the skin at the end of the stroke as the masseur brings them back to begin another stroke: maintaining contact with the horse like this has a psychological 'connection' effect. Bony areas are treated lightly, and muscular ones with more force; a general area may be massaged for about ten minutes before moving on.

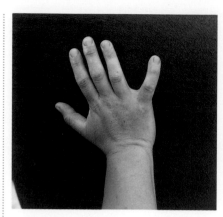

FRICTION

This is used for very localised pain due to muscle 'knots', adhesions, scar tissue, chronic hardened swelling, tendon and ligament injury and similar problems. Although it sounds slightly uncomfortable it has a most relieving feel to it if done with great sensitivity. Although the

Friction applied with (left) the heel of the hand and (right) wtih index finger and supporting pressure from the middle finger

areas to be treated may be uncomfortable or painful, the careful pressure applied by friction massage does not cause further distressing pain (no massage should do that) but is a sort of welcome, therapeutic, mild pain that is difficult to describe unless you have felt it.

The heels of the hands can be used, especially on areas large enough, but mostly fingertip pressure is used, usually the end of the index finger with supporting pressure being applied on its nail by the pad of the middle finger, although some therapists find it easier to do it the other way round. The skin is pressed carefully down and is moved, usually in a small, circular action, or side to side across the direction of the tissue fibres, in such a way that the tissues below it are moved with the skin. The skin is not moved over the tissues.

Massage therapists who have a great deal of experience, 'feel' and intuition often develop their own

---

What conditions will Massage alleviate?

There are many uses for massage: it
- helps improve muscle tone, and frees movement
- promotes the circulation of blood and lymph in horses on box rest
- prevents muscle wastage
- gets a horse back to work and fitness more quickly than if he had just been left standing
- helps in the repair of damaged tissue, and prevents adhesions forming in healing tissue
- relieves stiffness after a journey
- before strenuous work or competition it goes a long way towards loosening up a horse, and it gets his blood flowing through his muscles in preparation for his warm-up work
- after work, it helps to disperse the toxic waste products that are the result of the muscles creating and using energy for fuel
- alleviates stiffness as the horse cools down and recovers
- keeps horses in good working tone during ordinary working days, freeing muscle spasms and 'knots' which restrict movement and cause resistance in the horse
- promotes the secretion of hormones that make the body feel good

touch techniques along with a therapeutic rapport with their patients, human or animal, and can add greatly to their comfort, relaxation and functioning, all of which helps to improve attitude.

SELF HELP

A word of caution: It is very tempting to think that you cannot hurt your horse with a gentle massage, but in practice you can, and you can also exacerbate any injury he may have, and of which you may not even be aware. There are several good books on massage techniques for horse owners, and it is strongly advised that you read and study one of these and/or pay for a practical lesson from a professional massage therapist who will show you safe techniques to use on your own horse. He or she may also warn you of techniques you may have seen or read about, but which are safer avoided without specialist training.

Strengthening exercises: You will find that, to start with, massage is a considerable strain on your hands and arms, and some strengthening exercises to help this would probably be in order, although the massage itself will strengthen them. Squeezing a semi-soft ball will strengthen your hands and fingers, and doing 'press-aways' will strengthen your arms, shoulders and, to some extent, your back: stand with your feet a metre or so away from the base of a wall and place your hands flat on its surface at about shoulder or chin height, with

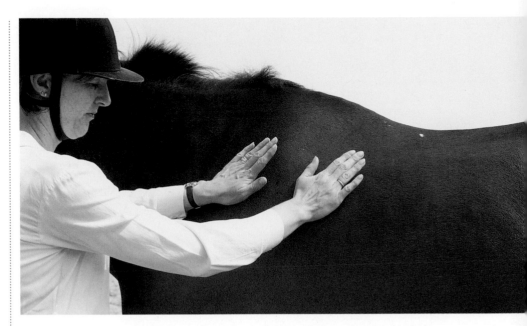

Specialised pressure and movement of muscles and other soft tissues are used to help prevent adhesions forming, release muscle spasms and to generally tone the muscles and free their movement, the aim being to promote healing by encouraging a normal, healthy blood flow. Here, effleurage is being used

your feet slightly apart and your back straight; then let yourself go forwards towards the wall (not moving your feet), then push yourself back to arm's length, repeating this carefully without in any way forcing yourself, only as many times as you feel comfortable with. It is not clever or 'tough' to make your arms ache!

Do-it-yourself machines: beware! Some vibratory machines are said to be safe for owners to use themselves on their horse, but before buying one, first check with your vet and/or therapist that it is really what you want: unfortunately some are sold with little or no instruction as to how to use them, or have only the most basic of instruction leaflets, or are even sold for quite inappropriate purposes. Other suppliers are

perfectly reputable; however, do seek professional advice before purchase, from an independent source.

Focus on the Rider

The rider as well as the horse can undoubtedly benefit greatly from regular massage – and so would grooms or carers, with all the heavy work they do. Riders and grooms can suffer all kinds of injury: in falls; by lifting heavy loads, especially if this is done incorrectly by letting the back instead of the thighs take the strain; by being pulled or pushed about by horses; by carrying heavy buckets of water; by bending down to pick up droppings or to pick out the horse's feet – and so on.

MASSAGE IN PRACTICE

Chris Caden-Parker BSc, MSc, M.F.Phys, AIPTI

As well as practising magnotherapy and other complementary therapies at her equine rehabilitation yard in the south of England, equine sports therapist Chris Caden-Parker uses sports massage techniques to help her patients along the road to recovery, as well as helping sound horses to work at their peak performance. Chris defines massage as 'a purposeful manipulation of muscle, sinew and joints in order to increase range of motion, elasticity and circulation within the tissues. At the end of the day I use it to enable muscles to work at their optimum.'

In the course of her work she employs basic (effleurage) massage and friction (deep) massage; however, the latter is only used to remove post-injury adhesions.

Chris applies massage mostly to horses afflicted with muscle spasm, and explains why it is so beneficial to helping this particular ailment: 'Muscle spasm can be a result of a range of causes, the most usual being post injury. This is because muscles and soft tissue contract around the injury site to protect it; so once the injury is mended, it is necessary to relax the contracted area and restore a range of motion to it by "stretching" the muscles in order to get the area working again as it should do.

'Another instance of when massage is appropriate is at a three-day event. When horses come off the cross-country course I use massage on them to help remove lactic acid from their muscles, by improving blood flow through the tissues which carries away waste products, so that they are less likely to be stiff and sore the following day.'

Not everyone is fortunate enough to have Chris, or any other expert in equine massage, on their doorstep to help keep their horse in tip-top condition, but there are a few safe and simple massage techniques that benefit equines who are a bit stiff or sore which anyone can administer. Chris explains:

'Horses are very in touch with their bodies and amateur masseurs can do little harm provided they listen to their horses' responses. When you work a horse, you should be looking and keep checking for signs all the time as to whether it is content with what you are doing or not. It's extremely obvious whether you are doing the animal any good when working on it because if you are massaging properly, the horse should be relaxing and enjoying your touch. If the horse is tense and obviously not enjoying the procedure, then you are not massaging properly and may in fact be doing more harm than good.

'When you train to be an equine masseur you must train on humans first. A person can turn around and tell you if what you are doing hurts, whereas an animal cannot. If a horse starts to become uneasy, moving away from your touch, then this should tell you one of two things: either your touch is too hard, or there is something more serious wrong which hurts when you touch that area.'

How can a horse owner find a person competent enough to carry out correct massage on their animal? Advises Chris: 'With any complementary therapist, find out if that person has insurance, including public liability, because to get insurance cover a person has to have some sort of qualification that the insurance body concerned recognises. In addition, it's also a good idea to satisfy yourself that the therapist is a member of a relevant governing body or society.

'Anyone can call themselves a therapist, but you can't contact an insurance company and say you'd like liability cover simply by saying "I'm a therapist", as the company will ask where you have trained and what evidence you have that you are competent enough to carry out the therapy concerned.

A sensitive and perceptive approach must be adopted when practising massage techniques. Chris Caden-Parker explains that the horse 'must be relaxed and enjoying your touch', any uneasiness or attempt to move away is a sign that the trained practitioner will pick up on, and consequently modify the treatment appropriately

Stretching

Stretching has become a practice which, with some expert instruction and personal study, owners can easily carry out themselves with their horses as a beneficial part of their daily routine. Human athletes have long experienced the benefits of stretching, and now many horses are enjoying them.

WHAT ARE THE BENEFITS?

- **For the horse in work:** They can be very helpful when warming up a horse before work, as they gently pull the muscles into relaxation, ironing out any tiny kinks or unwanted contractions, loosening up the muscle fibres and allowing good circulation to provide oxygen and nutrients and remove toxins. As the tissues are

prepared for work, there is less chance of injury. Stretches also free the action, encouraging a longer stride, lift and scope.

In cooling down a horse after work, stretching again maintains looseness in the tissues, promoting good circulation and reducing the tendency of the muscle to protectively 'clam up', and so discouraging stiffness and cramp which can occur due to

tightness in response to hard work. The natural reaction of muscle to even minor injury is to tighten up into spasm to prevent further movement which might cause further injury. This is counterproductive, and can be counteracted by careful stretching to maintain alignment and good circulation. Horses who have just

one stiff or cramped area should nevertheless receive whole-body stretching to help maintain symmetry and discourage compensatory movement.

- **Remedial stretching:** Regular, correctly carried out stretches promote even alignment of muscles and balanced muscle development in opposing muscle groups. Horses that are very slightly 'crooked' can often be

---

What is Stretching used for?

As we have seen in this section, stretching can be useful in the alleviation of many conditions, and beneficial in a host of situations; here is a synopsis:

- in helping to warm a horse up before work
- in cooling him down after work: it maintains looseness in the tissues and so discourages stiffness and cramp
- promotes even alignment of muscles and balanced muscle development
- promotes co-operation in the horse, encouraging him to relax and also to trust the handler
- increases flexibility, thus improving agility and willingness to work
- maintains the physical wellbeing of resting horses
- to loosen up/reinstate tissues before/after they have been stressed, eg before/after travelling, farriery

---

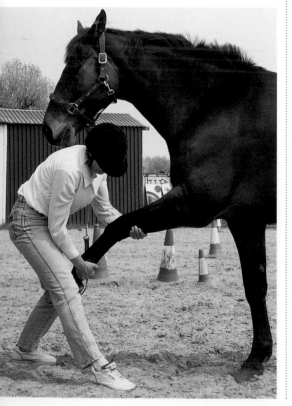

Left: A well-performed, comfortable and safe foreleg/shoulder stretch. The horse is unperturbed and co-operative and the handler in a safe stance and position and supporting the leg below knee and fetlock

corrected by careful and appropriate stretching techniques.

Out-of-work horses can have their physical wellbeing and flexibility maintained by regular stretching, say two or three times a week, to prevent tissues 'shortening' due to lack of exercise, and to keep them in an amenable state for healthy circulation.

Horses on box rest should have stretches performed for a little while every day to maintain elasticity (as long as this doesn't interfere with their recuperation); they also enjoy the activity and the attention during a very boring existence.

■ **Preventative therapy**: It is also worth considering a little massage and stretching before and after farriery (to loosen up and 'put back' muscle tissues), and before and after travelling, which can place considerable stress on the muscles and other soft tissues.

■ **Psychological benefits**: Regular stretching promotes co-operation in the horse and active participation in what his handler or owner is trying to do for him. It encourages him to relax and 'give' himself into the stretches and so to trust his handler, horses being particularly defensive of their heads and feet.

Stretching increases a horse's flexibility in all aspects of his life, including under saddle, making all movement more comfortable for him. This improves his agility and willingness to comply with his rider's aids.

Safety Tips for the Handler

There are right and wrong ways of performing stretches on horses, and wrong ways are sometimes promoted by people who should know better. The safety of both horse and handler are paramount.

From the horse's point of view, he must in no way be forced in these procedures, and you must on no account let a fight or even an argument develop. The horse should be patiently encouraged, and you should be happy with a little progress at a time in a process which he may find quite strange. For a newcomer to stretches, it may be enough during his first session to simply lift the feet and bring them slightly forwards and back, maybe slightly in and out to the sides, and to hold the limb for a few seconds; then praise the horse as you put the foot down again. Do not just let go and drop it or let *him* put it down when he feels like it: gentle control and permission from you encourage co-operation from him.

A most important factor is that the horse must always feel comfortable and safe, and that he can trust you, otherwise he will not relax, your efforts will be in vain, and it will be all the more difficult at the next session.

From the handler's point of view, always wear strong boots to protect your feet in case you are trodden on, but without metal toecaps, as these can be pressed down onto your toes by a half-ton horse, and they will not spring back but will trap your toes and make a painful injury worse. Hard leather toecaps are safer, or one of the designs of protective synthetic workboots. Always stand in a well balanced way so that you can let go and not fall should the horse move suddenly; do not stand directly in front of, or behind the horse.

It is advisable to wear a jockey skull cap.

Take care of your back: keep it straight, and let your legs and knees take the weight. Support weight with your elbow on your thigh, when appropriate, to save your back.

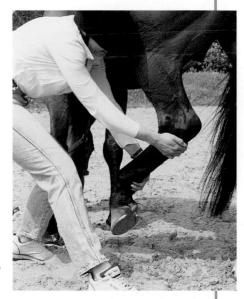

The handler's body is 'open' to the horse (her closest leg is back and her outer one forward). The wide base provided by her feet provide stability to her stance. Her inner hip could be a little closer to the horse. The horse's leg is being supported at the middle (hock) and end (fetlock) to give him a feeling of security

Left: In a backwards foreleg/shoulder stretch, the horse may not at first want to let his forearm be taken backwards: this movement tends to cause more resistance than the forward stretch. Keep up a gentle pressure on his knee with your inside hand and wait for him to offer to stretch. If all you get is what is shown here without resistance, praise him and leave further movement until another time

Below: In doing tail pulls, the dock should continue the line of the croup/quarters: do not raise the tail and pull. Hold the dock itself, not just the hairs of the tail, and lean back, rather than pulling with your arms. The horse should, ideally, lean forwards against your tension, stretching himself along his spine: for this reason, release the tension very slowly so that you do not 'drop' the horse

HOW DOES IT WORK?

Developing a routine: If you do the stretches in the same order each time, the horse will eventually work through them with you like a routine (as when owners pick up their feet in the same order each time for picking out). Generally, a good plan is to stretch the neck and back first, as this will loosen up those muscle groups and help the horse to feel loose and comfortable, and better able to keep his balance during the other stretches. Then stretch the forehand and fore legs on both sides, and finally the quarters and hind legs on both sides.

Warming up: Warm up a stabled horse's muscles first by walking and trotting in hand on both reins for about ten minutes to prepare the tissues by movement and to get the blood and lymph flowing. With any horse, a basic preliminary massage (see Massage, p54) will further warm up and loosen the muscles in preparation for stretching. Trying to stretch cold, stiff muscles without sensible preparation can result in discomfort or pain for the horse, and can even cause tissues to tear.

TECHNIQUES FOR LIMB STRETCHES

Stand a comfortable distance away from the horse so that he has room to move and you do not risk being trodden on, but close enough for you to hold the limb supportively and stretch it safely.

Carry the limb out to its fullest comfortable extent, and develop the feel for whether or not the horse is holding and pulling back (which most do at some time). Give a little if he pulls back. Do not pull against him, as he will probably become worried and pull back more; also, force from you can actually further tighten muscles. Talk to him encouragingly, and when he relaxes and lets you take the limb further, give a tiny pull slightly beyond the extent he has offered you to actually stretch the tissues. You can hold this for two or three seconds if the horse is willing and used to it, then return the leg to its normal position, still supporting it, and put the foot down. Praise the horse.

There is no need to, nor is there any advantage in, holding the stretch for many seconds as is sometimes recommended, as no further benefit is achieved by holding it for more than two or three seconds. Inexperienced horses will also start to panic if they think they cannot 'have their leg back'.

If a horse refuses a stretch, do not insist, but try again later in the session. Even if you do not manage it this time, he will probably agree next time.

WHEN SHOULD STRETCHING NOT BE PERFORMED?

Certain injuries will be exacerbated by stretching, and owners or therapists should always check with the vet handling the case as to whether or not particular moves are appropriate.

■ **Horses with a badly sprained or broken limb** will not be able to respond to stretches of their other limbs because these will be bearing the weight of the body in compensation for the injured one, and a horse may lose his balance if a person without the knowledge or experience tries to get him to stretch. Horses in this situation could benefit from techniques such as careful massage, Bowen, Shiatsu, Jin Shin Jyutsu, depending on the opinion of the vet or therapist.

■ **Horses suffering from osteoarthritis/ degenerative joint disease** must also be treated with great care because of their inability to use their bodies to their full extent. Professional advice must always be taken in such cases.

HOW CAN I LEARN MORE?

It would be well worthwhile paying a physiotherapist or equine sports physiologist or therapist to come and give you a lesson in basic massage and stretching techniques. Also, excellent books and videos are available on the care of the equine athlete which detail stretching techniques for horse and rider. Shiatsu stretches are also effective.

Focus on the Rider

The main problems riders have, in my experience, is stiffness in the hips and shoulders.

Stiffness in the hips can be improved with the following exercises. The rider stands erect, facing the back of a firm dining (upright) chair, holding on to the top of it. He or she then swings each leg up to the side, no more than half a dozen times to start with. Eventually over weeks, or even months, the rider should be able to lift the leg sideways as close to waist height as possible. The leg can, similarly, be swung forwards and backwards as far as is reasonably comfortable, again to help loosen and supple the hip joints. Other useful stretches are pictured below.

It is essential not to overdo this type of exercise. Only stretch as far as is comfortable and then a little further. If you feel no pull at all you are not actually stretching the relevant tissues but if you overdo it and feel a strong pull or even pain you can cause yourself injury.

Hunched shoulders can be improved by the rider standing erect and gently stretching both arms straight up and then carefully swinging them down and back, as if swimming backstroke with both arms at once. Good posture is vital for a correct riding seat. The shoulder should be held in a gentle but unmistakable tension downwards and backwards.

There are several videos currently advertised which promote various schools of thought on bodywork techniques. Almost any workout video will include stretches for people and advertisements in equestrian magazines will probably be the best source of suitable tapes for riders.

Cranio-Sacral Therapy

This very gentle, hands-on physical therapy is based on remedying distortions in the structure and function of the cranio-sacral regions – the skull and sacrum – and the soft tissues surrounding and linking them.

PHILOSOPHY

Developed by osteopath and surgeon Dr John Upledger, the therapy, like others, aims, by means of very gentle touches, to help the body help itself to readjust any misaligned tissues or bones: gentle hand pressure on the relevant areas helps the body realign the elastic soft tissues so they can pull back to their original, natural position, thereby relieving tension, distortion, discomfort and pain.

Like other gentle, physical therapies, it is greatly intuitive and requires a practitioner who is in tune with his or her patient, sincerely caring and intending to heal, and able to feel the smallest movements of the body.

HOW DOES IT WORK?

The practitioner appears to do no more than touch or hold gently certain parts of the body; these can be seen to twitch or move sometimes under his or her hands, even though they are not actually being manipulated or even poked or prodded. As a practitioner told one of the authors: 'I simply point out to the muscles where they should be, and allow several seconds for them to right themselves.'

Those who have experienced a treatment, or witnessed an animal being treated, say that nothing seems to happen, particularly in the latter case – although animals often respond by communicating their feelings to the practitioner by becoming drowsy, relaxed, by yawning and mouthing – or conversely, by showing irritation if the practitioner is working on the wrong area.

How often is treatment needed?
This seems to vary with the practitioner, but sometimes only one treatment is required, with a follow-up a few weeks or months later. The results seem to be lasting, regular treatment not being required unless the causative circumstances recur.

SELF HELP

Finding a practitioner: At present there are not many cranio-sacral therapists around, particularly ones who can, and will, treat horses;

Focus on the Rider

In humans, the symptoms that may be treated by this therapy are equally varied: subtle or more marked aches and pains, indigestion, headaches and loss of body flexibility – and a host of others. Human patients claim to feel very small, involuntary movements of the body, a release of tension and pain, if not immediately, and a greater freedom and mobility.

What is Cranio-Sacral Therapy used for?

Any condition can be treated which has injured or disturbed the body structure and is causing discomfort, pain, restricted movement and distress. In horses, the usual symptoms may be present of:

- poor performance
- resistance
- lameness and/or back pain
- bad behaviour in the form of bucking, rearing and napping
- also refusing, rushing and/or running out at jumps
- difficulty in doing hillwork
- general lack of flexibility and willingness, or sheer inability to work as required

however, they may be found through your doctor or local directories, through advertisements or word of mouth, or through complementary therapy organisations (see Useful Addresses, p186). Horses can be treated, though possibly through veterinary referral if your national laws demand this.

Do it yourself: Some of the simpler techniques of this therapy can be taught to owners so they can help their own animals, and courses for this purpose may be seen advertised or publicised in equestrian magazines. Its benefits are a more comfortable horse, satisfaction for the owner and a closer bond between the two. The therapy is so gentle that it is said to be impossible to harm your horse even if you do it wrong. The body naturally 'wants' to be in the correct alignment, and the tissues will not follow your guidance if you are directing them wrongly.

Crystal and Gem Therapy

How can what amounts to a crystal of precious or semi-precious material possibly induce healing in the human or animal body or mind?

The therapists' answer to this perfectly legitimate question is that, through energy waves, each type of crystal can heal many ailments both physical and mental – and some people receiving crystal and gem therapy do claim to experience relief from distressing or painful conditions if they carry a suitable crystal or wear jewellery containing the right sort of gem. This may or may not be your birthstone!

HOW DOES IT WORK?

Gem stones and crystals can be carried in a pocket, sewn into an appropriate place on a horse's rug (where it will not cause bruising if the horse lies down), placed in a dog's bed, or under your own pillow. They should be 'cleansed' weekly by leaving them in cold water overnight.

WHAT IS IT USED FOR?

Rose quartz is said to have a calming effect and to help heal the heart; amethyst is said to promote brain function and to be helpful during study and creative pursuits; and pink rhodonite may help to stabilise erratic emotions.

Rose quartz

Some gems are claimed to have adverse effects, and it seems to be important, in this therapy, to consult a comprehensive book on the subject or an expert therapist.

WHAT ABOUT HORSES?

If you wish to use crystal therapy on your horse, the stones can be attached to halters, rugs, or inside bandages but you must ensure that they are not placed so that they can cause bruising to the horse.

Electro-crystal Therapy

Said to enhance and increase the electrical charges given off by gem stones by using a computer and high frequency electro-magnetic waves.

How does it work? The consultant will discuss and assess the patient's disorders, and then use crystals and computers to find out where there is an imbalance in the body's energy, subsequently using crystals and other healing techniques to deal with the problems.

What is it used for? Like so many complementary therapies, this one aims to restore the body's energy to its natural flow, so helping it to heal itself.

Amethyst quartz

Copper Therapy

Copper worn next to the skin is said to have a pain-relieving and strengthening effect on body structures affected by rheumatism and osteoarthritis.

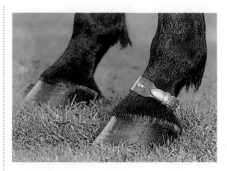

Make sure that a pastern strap does not rub the skin, to avoid this it may be worth swapping it from one leg to the other on a daily basis

When copper-lined pastern straps and dog collars became fairly widely available during the 1960s, many people sniggered and asked what possible use they could be. But the father of one of the authors had been wearing a copper bracelet for the self-treatment of osteoarthritis for years, and even though his family and friends thought he was a crank, he swore that when he took it off his hands soon started aching.

Perhaps they were wrong to scoff, because in ancient civilisations, copper was used therapeutically for what appears to have been osteoarthritis, and it is mentioned in mediaeval medical and farriery texts (up to and including the nineteenth century, farriers worked as healers as well as shoeing smiths).

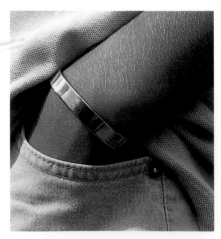

When wearing a rigid item like a copper bracelet there is a risk that it may catch in tack or other equipment

COPPER AND HORSES

It is always possible, when treating humans, that patients will claim an improvement because they want there to be one. This, of course, cannot apply to animals, and the significant improvements in some animals after wearing copper pastern straps, collars or neck chains cannot be the effect of a vivid imagination.

Firms supplying copper products have on file many case histories – but it has to be said that it does not work for every person or animal. Some claim that the copper has to be kept very clean to work; others say that after a few years it has to be replaced (although as a natural element this seems unlikely); and others claim that putting it next to an animal's coat will 'block' the skin's absorption of whatever remedial substances are there to be taken in.

HOW DOES IT WORK?

Unfortunately, no one is sure of the answer to that question. But sufferers know just how painful and debilitating rheumatism and osteoarthritis can be, as do the owners of animals afflicted by them: anything which may help will be tried, and remedies which do not work will not be recommended in the way that copper therapy is so widely.

An experiment: Copper is a nutrient needed in very small amounts. Some research work in Australia during the 1970s seemed to indicate that copper can be absorbed through the skin – in the course of this work it certainly appeared to relieve the symptoms of some human patients suffering from rheumatism/arthritis-type conditions: in the same experiment, imitation-copper bracelets were provided to a control group of patients, and they were the only ones to complain that there had been no improvement.

Copper in drugs: Copper preparations have also been included in anti-inflammatories prescribed for the relief of the symptoms of these diseases, and seem to enhance their effects.

SELF HELP

Provided a pastern strap or neck chain is fitted correctly and does not rub or irritate the horse, and cannot get caught up in any way, there can certainly be no harm in trying this therapy, in which so many people have such profound confidence.

Herbalism

Herbal medicine works in two ways: either, by providing the body with substances that will stimulate its immune system to counteract the disease from which it is suffering, or, it uses substances found in plants to clear the body's energy channels and allow energy to flow freely again, clearing toxins, pathogens and other general debris.

The principle of clearing energy channels is common to most complementary therapies, and is achieved in their various different ways either through 'taking the medicine', or by means of physical stimulation practised by therapies such as acupuncture, acupressure, chiropractic, shiatsu, massage and so on. Conventional drugs often act as a back-up to the body's own efforts, providing extra substances and effects, rather than stimulating the body to heal itself.

PHILOSOPHY

Herbal medicine is the oldest form of medicine in the world. Long before recorded history began humans and animals would almost certainly have been using vegetation of various types as nutritional medicine, and many animals, at least, still have the nutritional intuition that helps them to medicate themselves in this way. In the late 1990s, for instance, researchers found that feral American mustangs were clearing their own parasite burdens (monitored via their faeces) by seeking, selecting and eating specific plants. Ancient texts, inscribed on clay tablets, have been discovered giving details of medical treatments comprising plant materials for the ailments of humans and animals. For thousands of years civilisations have used herbalism as

Nettles are generally used as a diuretic and circulatory stimulant and blood tonic. They are also rich in vitamin C, chlorophyll, sodium, iron and protein, and can be used in preparations or, if cut and allowed to wilt, may be fed whole to horses

What can Herbal Remedies be used for?

Herbalism can be effective in the treatment of most problems that owners might encounter in their horse, both physical and of temperament. Here are just a few of the conditions it might help:

- poor condition
- anaemia
- gut damage due to parasites
- soft tissue strength and integrity, such as ligament damage and muscle atrophy
- bone damage due to osteoarthritis and rheumatism
- to calm a highly strung, difficult temperament
- stress
- indigestion
- insomnia

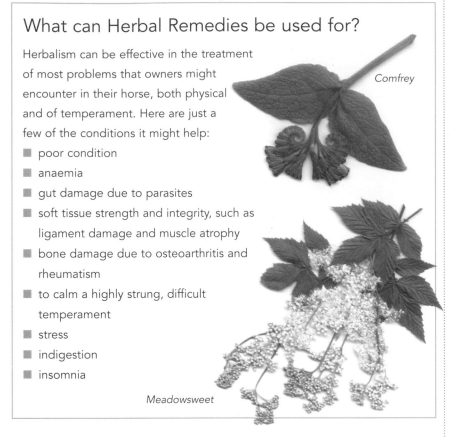

Comfrey

Meadowsweet

HOW DO HERBAL REMEDIES WORK?

Herbalism works by stimulating the body's immune system and by helping to clear its energy channels, and there is generally a herbal remedy that can be used in the treatment of most conditions likely to be encountered by horse owners. For example, comfrey may be used in the treatment of osteoarthritis and soft tissue damage, and also as a demulcent to help heal gut damage caused by worms, and to aid nutrient absorption. Cider vinegar is often recommended for rheumatism and osteoarthritis, and herbs such as celery seed, kelp, nettles and burdock can help alleviate stiffness and maintain health in older horses.

Herbal treatment can also be given to animals on long-term phenylbutazone therapy to help counteract the effect on the liver

Devil's claw is a commonly used natural anti-inflammatory, effective for both soft tissue damage and bone conditions

respected profession. It is only our recent reliance on synthetic drugs that has diminished its importance.

their chief form of medicine and for health maintenance. The art and inexact science of herbalism (plant therapy specifically centred on herbs) and phytotherapy (general plant medicine) has long been a highly refined process and a

Side effects

Orthodox human and veterinary medicines have always used substances derived from plants but with a tendency to isolate and concentrate the active ingredients by omitting the other, balancing ingredients which are present in the whole plant. This has resulted in patients sometimes suffering unpleasant side effects.

Side effects can appear when herbal remedies are prescribed by unknowledgeable users, usually because the plants are harvested at the wrong time of year (or even of the day), are used in the wrong amounts, or prepared in the wrong way. Herbalism is not an amateur home remedy to be used casually by the uninitiated. Generations ago, healers had extensive knowledge of plant remedies and administered to their communities: nowadays there are far fewer of these people, and it is safer to consult a qualified medical herbalist in conjunction with one's veterinary surgeon. Some companies selling herbal products have qualified herbalists on staff.

and intestines; the demulcent (and conditioning) herb fenugreek can help protect the intestines from its effects, which can include diarrhoea.

Chamomile, valerian and passiflora are used to help calm down a highly strung, nervous temperament.

SELF HELP

Identity crisis: Herbal remedies cannot, under UK law, be sold as medicines. The National Institute of Medical Herbalists qualifies medical herbalists to treat human beings, and they can also treat animals on referral from and/or in conjunction with a veterinary surgeon; but whilst several vets are qualifying as veterinary homoeopaths, few are as yet qualifying as veterinary herbalists. Because herbal remedies are often taken by mouth, and because they consist of plants, they can be regarded as foods, and so this is how they are sold. The British

Above: Burdock is widely used to treat blood disorders, skin conditions resulting from toxicity, to enhance liver and kidney function and as a digestive stimulant. Burdock root can be made into a poultice to speed the healing of wounds and ulcers

Below: Chamomile grows readily in the wild in the UK and is used as a calming herb

Focus on the Rider

Herbalism is quite widely used by many people and herbal remedies are available over the counter at larger pharmacies. However, as herbs generally tend to work fairly slowly and need to be taken consistently, according to instructions, it is normally more effective to consult a herbalist or at least a retail source with a qualified person on hand to advise. There are certainly herbal remedies which, longer term, may help with nervousness or a highly-strung nature, which are the main psychological problems suffered by riders. There are also herbal remedies which may help heal injuries such as strains, bruises, broken bones and so on.

Dandelion is well known as a diuretic (stimulating the production of urine). The root can also be used as a coffee substitute or to replace onions

Equestrian Trade Association is currently forming a Feed Sub-Committee to try to bring in a code of practice for manufacturers of feeds and supplements so customers can be assured that there are safe manufacturing procedures, quality assurance, traceability and correct labelling, so that no medical claims are made for products.

Where to look: Those horse owners who want to know which particular plants can be used for which disorders should consult one of the many good books available on herbal remedies to know what to look for on a product label. Many labels will say, in necessarily non-committal terms, that such-and-such a plant has traditionally been used to treat such-and-such a condition, or similar wording: this gives the customer accurate guidance without actually stating that the product is a medicine active against that condition.

Tea-tree oil (Ti-tree oil)

Tea-tree oil can be regarded as a herbal remedy as it is distilled from the leaves of the tea tree, *melaleuca alternifolia*, but it is also an essential oil used in aromatherapy. Whatever category we wish to put it into, tea-tree oil, like aloe vera and propolis, is now almost regarded as a separate remedy in its own right because it has such a wide range of applications.

What is it used for? Diluted in a base oil, it is claimed to be a mild anaesthetic useful for soothing inflamed wounds and skin disorders; to be antiseptic, having anti-bacterial properties; and to be antifungal. It also seems to be an effective, natural insect and skin-parasite repellent, with both stimulating and soothing effects when used in massage.

How does it work? Commercially available products for horses containing tea-tree oil are many, comprising mane, tail and coat sprays, insect repellents, shampoo, cleansing wipes, creams and lotions for skin disorders and even as a crib-biting deterrent.

Like any essential oil, in its undiluted form it is a powerful chemical which must never be applied direct to skin. However, in this form it can nevertheless be used as an effective, old-fashioned type of inhalant in respiratory infections or allergies: simply add a few drops of the essential oil on top of some hay in a sack or bucket and add very hot water to it, then carefully let the horse inhale the steam.

Focus on its use for humans: For many years tea-tree oil has been prized as a skin conditioner in human health and beauty circles, and has been made into conditioning creams and lotions, antiseptic preparations for home and hospital use, cosmetic skin care, and as a gentle but effective skin healer and disease-preventative agent. It can be used as an inhalant to help expel mucus in respiratory infections, and is even used in poultices and compresses.

It is available as a massage oil, although clients can have this made up for them by an aromatherapist for use on people and animals; it is useful in soothing bruising, and irritated and infected skin, and it may even help relieve the inflammation connected with sprained ligaments and tendons and damaged muscle tissues.

Where can I buy it? Look out for it in good equestrian stores, or have products made up by an aromatherapist or herbalist.

C A S E   H I S T O R Y

Horse: 23-year-old Thoroughbred mare, Duchess, a former flat racer, show-jumper and broodmare.

PROBLEM: On purchase in the autumn: poor condition, anaemia, sharp teeth, gut damage due to parasite burden, chronic ligament damage in hind fetlocks plus early symptoms of osteoarthritis but not lame and enjoyed work. Severe muscle atrophy below and behind withers due to badly fitting saddle. Unable to reach her left side with her muzzle. Highly-strung, sometimes wilful but not a nervous temperament. When in season, Duchess could be excessively difficult and, at times, almost dangerous to handle.

TREATMENT: The (orthodox) veterinary surgeon, who had known the mare for five years, felt she would 'probably last this winter'. He corrected her teeth and parasite burden and supplied a concentrated supplement to correct the anaemia. On a carefully devised diet, her bodyweight gradually improved throughout the early winter. An osteopath, on referral, corrected the left side and spinal stiffness which also improved the hind leg action.

The owner tried herbal supplements from a reputable commercial company but the mare refused to eat them. The owner, therefore, requested a referral to a medical herbalist to help with the temperament problems, the gut damage, the soft-tissue strength and integrity and the bone damage due to osteoarthritis.

The herbalist supplied a herbal tincture (liquid) containing comfrey (for osteoarthritis and soft-tissue damage but also as a demulcent to help heal the gut damage and aid nutrient absorption) and chamomile (for the temperament), prescribing its addition to the mare's feeds at the rate of ten drops three times a day. Duchess accepted this.

She would not take the recommended cider vinegar (for rheumatism and osteoarthritis) but did take an additional herbal supplement for 'old age problems' containing celery seed, kelp, nettles and burdock.

A major step forward came when Duchess was assessed by a radionics practitioner, on referral from a homoeopathic veterinary surgeon. A few mane hairs were sent (see Radionics, p90) and Duchess was found to have a severe hormonal imbalance which caused the problems when she was in season. After only one treatment her behaviour during oestrus became very affectionate and relaxed, which was unheard of for her!

Her problem never recurred, and the owner built on this improvement by giving Duchess a herbal preparation produced by Hilton Herbs (see Useful Addresses, p186), called Regulate.

She was subsequently vaccinated and wormed homoeopathically and, constantly receiving her herbal products, enjoyed two-and-a-half further years of a contented life as a hack with a much more relaxed temperament and no noticeable progression of the osteoarthritis or ligament problems until the age of 26 when her hindquarters and hind legs began to lose strength. The vet prescribed phenylbutazone which she had in addition to her herbal therapy. The demulcent (and conditioning) herb fenugreek was then added to her feeds (which she did eat) to help protect her intestines from the effects of the phenylbutazone (which can result in diarrhoea). Herbal treatment can also be given to animals on long-term phenylbutazone therapy to help counteract liver damage.

RESULT: The owner and Duchess' orthodox vet both felt that the complementary therapies used greatly enhanced and extended her life to the age of 26, which was totally unexpected at the time of purchase.

Aloe Vera

Aloe vera is taken from a plant, a succulent member of the lily family, which grows in hot regions: it is included in this book as an individual therapy because it has such a wide range of therapeutic uses, and because it is becoming an increasingly popular remedy with very many applications for humans and animals.

Aloe vera plant

It is another ancient remedy used by the Greeks, Persians, Romans, Chinese, Egyptians and several other civilisations, and one which is enjoying a new lease of life today. Although many of the claims made for it can be described as anecdotal, some come from medical professionals in practice, and some clinical trials have been carried out sporadically which have confirmed many of the claims made for aloe.

THE ALOE PLANT

Aloe vera, as it is popularly known, is a member of the *Aloeceae* family which contains about 450 species. Native to Africa, the Arabian peninsular and nearby islands, it will grow in any suitable area where the temperature remains above freezing, and in greenhouses. Types range from almost stemless plants to tree-like giants, and they have clusters of succulent, spiny-toothed, spiky, thick, grey-green leaves which have a soft green gel inside. There is a tough, outer skin, then a layer of yellow sap which contains a bitter alkaloid called aloin, and then a chamber containing the green gel.

HOW IS IT PREPARED FOR USE?

Aloins are extracted from the yellow layer under the outer skin but the inner gel is often dried and prepared as a powder in capsules as a food supplement. The gel is also made into lotions, ointments, drinks, skin creams and liquids for varied uses. More recently, whole-leaf extracts are proving, according to some doctors and healthcare professionals, to be the most effective way to harness the remedial powers of aloe.

REMEDIAL USES

Aloin is a powerful laxative, and was once the old farriers' favoured purgative and conditioner for horses when made into aloes balls. Bitter aloes – a bitter, brown liquid readily available in any chemist's shop up to about thirty years ago – was a popular remedy amongst nannies and mothers to stop children sucking their thumbs and biting their nails (although it stained them brown), and it could be used in stables to stop horses chewing rugs, wood and so on.

These, however, are only the start of a long list of the remedial uses, internal and external, of aloe for both people and animals. It is also used in health maintenance and preventative medicine. Herbalists certainly use it, and commercially available products such as skin conditioners and food supplements can be bought in health food shops and some chemists; and horse products are usually obtainable by mail order, details of which can generally be seen in horse magazines.

Again, few clinical studies have been done as yet, but as interest in and use of complementary therapies regenerates rapidly worldwide, more work will doubtless be done on aloe.

What conditions is Aloe Vera used for?

Gleaned from various sources, the following compilation details, at random, conditions of both humans and animals which are claimed to have been helped or 'cured' by the use of a suitable aloe preparation:

- the immune system
- blood disorders
- exercise intolerance
- wounds
- sprains
- osteoarthritis
- bruising
- digestive disorders
- burns from any cause (and it appears to protect against radiation burns, including sunburn)
- skin diseases
- irritable bowel syndrome
- some cancers
- ME
- allergic conditions
- gum disease
- and some AIDS patients have reported an improvement in their condition after its use

Other diseases it appears to have helped are:
- vaginal tract infections
- diabetes
- respiratory tract infections
- tuberculosis

HOW DOES IT WORK?

Therapeutic properties: Experts seem to feel that aloe's main therapeutic property is due to its containing a class of long-chain sugars called glycosaminoglycans (GAGs), found in the basic substance of connective tissue and important in, among other things and for example, joint lubrication and tissue strength and elasticity.

GAGs have other functions too, among which are the ability to prevent toxic waste products re-entering the bloodstream from the hind gut. One molecule, acemannan, protects cells against the invasion of harmful pathogens ('germs'), stimulates the immune system by encouraging a type of cell called macrophages to engulf and deactivate pathogens, and produces substances which help the body to fight disease, such as interferon and interleukin. Because of this property, aloe could well be invaluable in treating a wide range of disorders which ultimately stem, it is believed by many, from a poor immune system, and disorders which are resistant to modern Western human and veterinary medicine.

Aloe also contains various essential nutrients such as vitamins B1, 2, 3 and 6, C and E, calcium, iron, magnesium and zinc, seven of the eight essential amino acids and some essential fatty acids, valuable enzymes and other substances. It is also claimed to stimulate uterine contractions, to be analgesic, strongly laxative, detoxifying, anti-inflammatory, anti-viral, anti-

Aloe vera gel and pills

bacterial, 'cleansing', and to have a steroid-like effect without the side-effects of steroids.

SELF HELP

Where can I buy aloe vera products? Many commercial ranges of human and animal products are available from ordinary retail outlets such as pet shops, chemists and healthfood stores. There are several mail order sources listed in Useful Addresses (p186). More specialised products can be obtained after consultation with holistic veterinary surgeons and medical herbalists.

Beware self-treatment: Although the normal commercially available ranges of products should be able to be used with confidence if administered in accordance with the directions on the packs, self-treatment can always pose risks if users abuse those directions. The wisest course is always to consult a suitably experienced and qualified professional such as a doctor, a veterinary surgeon, a nutritionist or a medical herbalist.

Nutritional Therapy

The subject of nutritional therapy is one which causes a good deal of debate in the horse world among owners, vets, nutritionists, scientists in general and anyone interested in the all-round care, management, wellbeing and health of horses.

It is obvious that horses (and humans) have to eat in order to live. If we do not eat we lose weight, our systems do not obtain the nutrients and energy they need, and eventually our body temperature drops and we die. Therefore just ordinary food can be said to have a physiological effect on the body. However, various professional bodies are claiming that anything which does have a proven physiological effect on the body is technically a medicine, and that its availability and use must therefore be strictly controlled.

PHILOSOPHY

'We are what we eat' is an old phrase revitalised in the 1960s. Wise eating is much more widespread than it was decades ago, and people are increasingly concerned about what they themselves eat and what their horses and other animals eat. We are learning that certain food additives create allergic reactions and other disorders in humans and animals, and as a consequence there is a strong demand for 'pure, clean' food that is free from artificial fertilisers, pesticide and weedkiller residues, genetic manipulation, synthetic vitamins and minerals, and noxious substances which may get into our foods from soil contamination (such as lead, cadmium and radiation).

HOW IT WORKS: HOLISTIC FEEDING

Even if we cannot always obtain entirely organic, holistic feeds and grazing for our horses, there are certain steps we can take to minimise disorders and other problems caused by their eating a not-entirely-suitable diet.

GRASSLAND MANAGEMENT

As far as our own land is concerned, we should ensure that the grazing comprises generally low-nutrient grasses of widely varied species to ensure as wide a nutrient spread as possible. We can avoid the use of artificial fertilisers, pesticides and weedkillers as much as possible, and use organic treatments – though even then, only when necessary. We can use inter-species grazing, cattle and sheep being particularly good for horse pastures, and we can conscientiously carry out all land-improvement techniques such as drainage, harrowing, rolling and so on, and reintroduce hedges and ditches.

Avoid fertiliser: Some reasons for treating land more naturally are that much lowland grazing in the UK and Ireland, and in some parts of central Europe, produces grass which is too lush for horses, especially ponies, cobs and heavy horses, and breeds and types of those extractions including warmbloods. It can also be too low in the fibre a horse needs, and these faults are aggravated if the land is fertilised at all, even with organic fertilisers in some cases. This is because if the land is fertilised, the grass becomes high in soluble nitrogen compounds (nitrates and nitrites) which can cause metabolic and digestive disorders in horses; it also becomes low in some important

In mixed grazing the companion species eat and kill each other's internal parasite larvae and prefer different grasses and parts of grasses, so helping to ensure balanced grazing

minerals, but too high in potassium. This produces a nutritionally unbalanced sward which, of course, translates to a significantly unbalanced diet for horses, with all the problems that can bring. Expert advice is always recommended.

The benefits of inter-species grazing: Many horse paddocks are never grazed by other animals because the owners mistakenly believe other animals 'steal the horses' grass'. Nothing could be further from the truth, however, because cattle, sheep and horses like different grasses and plants, and different parts of the plants; they are complementary grazing partners, as in nature. Land over-grazed by only one species gradually becomes deficient in the plants that that species prefers because they never have a chance to be pollinated and to go to seed; so they die out, and less palatable, less useful plants take over,

thereby reducing the value of your land. The end result is fewer grass and plant species, a less varied diet and a poorer supply of essential nutrients.

Modern grassland management: a downward spiral: This type of misused land also favours the growth of species not favourable to horses' digestive systems and needs, such as too much clover, buttercups and poisonous plants. This process has resulted in one of the most significant changes to adversely affect the health of today's domesticated horses: namely, because of modern farming techniques and poor or non-existent grassland management on equestrian establishments, the estimated numbers of plant and grass species in pastures in general has been reduced to less than a quarter of those present before World War II. Because the hay and haylage commonly fed to horses nowadays are both made from this

Pasture management is not as onerous as many think, and is a fairly simple way of ensuring an excellent supply of nutritious balanced food

grassland, the nutritional quality, variety and balance of these forage crops, too, has been significantly compromised.

Today, grassland is cultivated mainly for quantity, not quality in the form of nutritional value and balance. Much cultivated grassland is now a green desert, a deformed monoculture produced by the application of artificial, quick-release fertilisers which produce quick-growing grasses at the expense of many valuable slow-growing ones – and, of course, herbs. The result can be a sward of unbalanced grazing selection and nutrient content, where the 'good' grasses are often not competitive enough to keep genuine weeds at bay; this then necessitates chemical weed control, and so landowners may be drawn into an inexorable downward spiral unless they take positive steps to improve matters.

The benefit of wildflower meadows: Many of us think wistfully or nostalgically – the older ones amongst us – of what an old English meadow used to be like – and what it could be like again, with the will and effort to make it so. It is not just a case of its looking pretty: it would contain a vast array of grasses, herbs and other plants which would provide an equally vast range of nutrients, many brought up from lower soils and rocks by deep-rooted plants. The old 'Dr Green' remedy very often truly worked in restoring horses and other animals to health, not only because of the tremendous psychological benefit to them of being out grazing (a benefit which worked wonders on their bodies as well as their minds) but also because of the broad spectrum of nutrients which were naturally available in such pasture: carbohydrates from both sugars, celluloses and hemi-celluloses, limited fats and oils, vitamins and major and trace minerals.

Before grazing it, a hay crop would possibly be taken, and the full range of nutrients in the grass would be present – hence the value of such 'good, old-fashioned', first-cut meadow hay. It also smelled like nothing you ever smell today – and so did the hay-hold, when full of sweet, loose hay.

Re-establishing a holistic method of grassland management: Farming practices and land management techniques in those days – such as carefully planned mowing, fertilising with manures, rolling, harrowing, tilling, re-seeding, rotavating when necessary and so on – were an art and a science in themselves, as was understanding what grass and plant species were best for which animals. Fortunately this knowledge is not lost, because a very few farmers have always farmed this way, and still do, and this type of management is slowly creeping back into use in some areas. Certain agricultural organisations are also able and willing to advise on old, more natural and holistic methods of grassland management – although it must be said that some 'land managers' are becoming even more environmentally unfriendly in their methods, sometimes due to lack of sensitivity, but also because of constrictions placed on them by successive government policies, mainly financial.

Horse owners with their own smaller establishments, however, are well placed to bring back one of the most beneficial aspects of the past, and useful contacts for those wanting relevant advice is given later in this book.

Grassland is probably the most valuable psychological and nutritional resource available to us, and to waste it is foolish in the extreme – and expensive, because bought-in food is much more costly than well cared-for grazing.

Putting it right: To give your grassland a holistic make-over is not as big a job as you might imagine. You do not have to plough up and totally reseed and have your fields out of use for a year or more. You may be able to over-sow beneficial species and herbs (or create a herb strip on the driest part of the field) and fertilise, when necessary, with your own very well rotted (over a year old) horse manure (bearing in mind

---

Nutraceuticals

Nutraceuticals are products which have been described as not quite drugs but more than foods. They are feed supplements which have sufficient quantities of nutrients, and combinations of nutrients, in them to effect a definite physiological change in the body consuming them. The most common nutraceuticals are those intended for joint maintenance and repair in athletic horses.

Controversial effects: On a worldwide basis, some nutraceuticals have been banned in competition purely because they do have a significant effect which some regard as unfair, yet others claim that they contain only nutrients, not drugs. Other authorities have declared that if they result in the horse consuming 'more than normal levels' of the nutrients, the products are regarded as drugs or medicines.

There is no doubt that some products do have a definite beneficial effect, and these are now a standard part of the diet of many sports and performance horses. In many cases, there has been no other change whatsoever in a horse's routine or diet, just the addition of the nutraceutical, and the improvement in the horse's condition (whatever it was) has been very noticeable. Scientific work on the various brands for the various purposes, however, has been sporadic and not always conclusive.

Keep up to date: It is well worthwhile keeping up to date via your vet, nutritionist and the equestrian press on the latest findings about these products. If you compete, your administrative body will let you know whether certain products are prohibited or not. Whether or not you compete, experience – the sort that orthodox scientists call unreliable anecdotal evidence! – is showing noticeable benefits from their inclusion as remedies in a horse's diet; although the same can also be said of other supplements, particularly herbal ones. This is quite a grey area, and one well worth learning about.

that it may not be organic if you use conventional worming drugs which may be retained in the muck) or with cattle slurry very judiciously applied (again, it will not be organic unless it comes from a certified organic farm, and may contain hormones and other substances). Avoid chicken and pig muck as they do not produce the sort of 'non-lush' grazing needed by horses. Muck from barn-wintered sheep may be acceptable depending on the products fed to them.

FORAGE FEEDS

Hay, haylage, semi-wilted forage and straw are valuable fibre/roughage feeds for your horse, but unless they are cut from old-fashioned meadows their nutrient content may be deficient and unbalanced by the standards of holistic feeding. There may well also be chemical residues from any products used on the growing crop, unless these are from approved organic/holistic sources.

Hay and haylage: Today, specially sown seeds hay, and meadow hay cut from old pastures are available; however, more and more farmers are producing haylage as it is less risky to harvest; it is also popular amongst horse owners because it is not prone

Supplements

The argument as to whether or not feed supplements of vitamins and minerals can be classed as actual medicines continues, and their future availability is far from assured; even more so is that of herbal supplements, because herbs have been used for thousands of years, for humans and animals, as a source of medicine to help in the treatment of disease and injury. They most certainly do have the ability to bring about a physiological change. However, they are also very obviously foods, many of them deep-rooted and able to reach and bring to their leaves or roots minerals and other nutrients which grasses cannot access, thereby benefiting both grazing and foraging animals. In natural conditions horses will graze herbs to choice where they can, and herbs were, and still are, certainly part of the normal diet of wild and feral equidae.

either to dust, unless allowed to become too dry, or to mould. The white yeasts which some haylages exhibit are not normally harmful; also, there is usually too much air in haylage bales for the bacteria responsible for botulism to proliferate and cause trouble, because these are anaerobic bacteria.

Whatever you buy, a reputable supplier should have a full nutritional analysis ready for you. If not, send a small sample to a laboratory for analysis, maybe via your vet's surgery, so that you and your advisers know what you are dealing with and can adjust the rest of your horse's diet accordingly.

Some countries have ready

supplies of legume hay – clover, lucerne/alfalfa and specialist hays with vetches and high-nutrient grasses in them. These will be higher in protein because of the protein content of the plants from which they are made. They also have a tendency to become bitty and dusty, and alfalfa tends to be rather strong in taste which a few horses find off-putting.

Semi-wilted forage: This is grass which is cut and sealed into plastic sacks before it has dried. It is a popular feed today for horse owners who want to avoid dust, want guaranteed levels of nutrients because most good makes come in various grades, and don't

want to bother soaking hay. Most horses love these products.

Feeding straws, mainly oat and barley, are excellent for ponies, cobs, 'heavies' and good doers because of their lower nutrient content. And if your other forage sources are rather 'rich', the straws can be mixed with them to lower the total nutrient content. However, the likelihood that straws have been treated with chemical sprays is probably even higher than it is with hays and haylages, as they will have been grown to produce grain for the human food market, and every effort will have been made to keep diseases and pests at bay.

Short-chopped forages: A variety of these is now readily available for horses, and resemble old-fashioned chop (sometimes incorrectly called chaff, which is actually the outside husk of grain). However, they are normally more nutritious – although again, different grades are available. The type which is significantly treated with molasses should be avoided as this can cause digestive and metabolic problems in some horses, as well as behavioural problems where the total diet is high in energy, molasses being sugar. Alfalfa is an integral ingredient in most of these excellent products,

which may also contain straw and a wide variety of grasses.

CONCENTRATES

Happily the trend now is to feed horses fewer cereals, as these are not a natural feed for horses in anything but very low quantities, and to giving more nutritious fibre feeds. Sugar beet is a valuable high energy, high fibre root for horses, as well as certain beans and high-nutrient forages. These are often found in pellet/cube form in coarse mixes/sweet feeds.

HERBAL PRODUCTS

Probably one of the most effective ways in which modern horse owners can add any nutrients that might be missing from their horses' diets is by using a broad-spectrum herbal product from a reputable company with holistic sourcing and manufacturing policies.

STATEMENT OF FEED VALUE

Some countries make it mandatory for the ingredients to be listed on supplements and feeds, and some demand that the actual formula is revealed – highly unpopular with manufacturers, of course! However, this is vital information for the customer (you) and the consumer (your horse). A nutrient analysis, at

Caution

Feeds formulated for one species of animal must not be fed to a different species without taking advice, as some ingredients which are beneficial for one may be extremely harmful to another.

It is always advisable to take truly expert, qualified advice before formulating or changing your horse's diet: certainly never assume that because a product is 'natural' it is safe, because some of the world's most potent poisons come from humble plant sources.

Finally, do not go over the top in your desire to be organic and holistic. Suitable products are thin on the ground in some countries, and your horse has to eat something!

least, is essential so that you can tell whether or not the feed contains adequate and balanced amounts of nutrients. If you experience any problems with any company, or have any queries about their products, do seek independent advice from a nutritionist and/or vet interested in nutrition.

Propolis

Propolis is a product of bees, and has been used for thousands of years in health maintenance, and in the treatment of disorders in humans and animals. It consists mainly of a resin which the worker bees take from the buds of certain plants and trees, mainly poplars, plus beeswax, essential oils and pollen; they mix these ingredients together with their saliva to cement together portions of honeycomb, to fill up crevices, and to line and seal their nests and hives to protect them from the outside environment. The bees also coat the inside surface of the hive with propolis, and so create what has been described as the most sterile environment known to nature.

HISTORY OF PROPOLIS

The word 'propolis' comes from the Greek and means 'before' or 'in front of' (pro) 'the city' (polis): it is loosely translated as 'defender of the city' (the bee-hive). The Greeks themselves used propolis for treating wounds as well as supposedly incurable diseases. Hippocrates, described as the father of modern medicine, prescribed it to heal internal and external ulcers and sores, and the ancient Egyptians used it as an effective healer for very many diseases and injuries. The Romans, too, used it because it 'extracts stings and all substances embedded in the flesh, reduces swelling, softens indurations [hardened tissues], soothes pain of sinews and heals sores when it appears hopeless for them to mend'.

In the Middle Ages and onwards, propolis was used widely as a proven healer for diseases and injuries, as an anti-inflammatory used both internally and externally, and as an early form of 'oral vaccination' because of its preventative qualities. It was accepted as a valued healing substance right up until the end of the nineteenth century in Europe when it gradually fell from favour, only in the last twenty or thirty years being internationally investigated, researched and used therapeutically for its healing potential. There is ample scientific evidence now as to its efficacy.

A proven healing agent: Propolis acts as a combined antibiotic, antifungal and antiviral substance, and it also has anaesthetic properties. Today, when bacteria are becoming widely resistant to synthetic antibiotics, and since we do not yet have even a synthetic antiviral which will work without destroying healthy tissue as well, these properties are particularly valuable to us and our animals.

Scientists have found that no single ingredient is predominantly

What is Propolis used for?

As well as its vital mechanical qualities, propolis contains a wide variety of other substances; these include organic and amino acids, vitamins, minerals, and natural bioflavonoids which, as anti-oxidants, are strongly believed to:

- delay ageing
- strengthen tissues
- strengthen the immune system by improving the ability of white blood cells to function at their optimum level
- 'mop up' various toxic substances in the body resulting from everyday metabolism

Propolis also seems to act as a combined antibiotic, antifungal and antiviral substance, and it also appears to have anaesthetic properties.

active in propolis – they all work in harmony as a powerful organic, natural product. As such, propolis is an invaluable aid to preventative medicine and an effective, long-term healing agent which some doctors believe is ultimately more effective than most synthetic ones.

Propolis for animals: Ancient and more modern records have shown that propolis and other bee products such as honey and royal jelly have been used traditionally, and most effectively, for animal treatment for thousands of years. Propolis does not seem to have received so much attention from the modern veterinary profession in general as from the human medical profession, but any of the increasing number of holistically-minded vets should be willing to help owners investigate its potential and prescribe it appropriately.

PROPOLIS FOR HUMANS

Many forward-thinking doctors in general practice and in hospitals (where antibiotic-resistant pathogenic organisms are rife, and may be responsible for many deaths) are using propolis in the treatment of injuries and potentially fatal diseases. We understand that recent studies and trials of propolis at the UK's National Heart and Lung Institute have shown it to be effective against a comprehensive range of disease-producing microbes including MRSA (multiple-resistant staphylococcus aureous – the 'Hospital Staph' as healthcare professionals have nicknamed it), which is resistant to most orthodox antibiotics and is now a dangerous hazard in hospitals worldwide.

SELF-HELP

There are several suppliers of propolis products – supplement capsules, tinctures, creams, and so on – in the UK: please see Useful Addresses (p186).

Propolis, which is also available in capsules and tablets

Homoeopathy

Unlike conventional medicine, homoeopathy does not simply prescribe one remedy for one ailment. The whole personality, lifestyle and environment of the patient are considered. Observation of the horse's behaviour, its relationships with other horses, how it reacts to given circumstances, to its environment and its entire circumstances are crucial to understanding its personality and, therefore, to knowing what remedy will best suit it. For this reason, two horses suffering from an identical disease may well not be prescribed the same remedy or remedies, and this is what makes homoeopathy so hard for horse owners to understand.

Homoeopathic remedies are taken from animal, vegetable and mineral sources and prepared in many different ways

PHILOSOPHY

Modern homoeopathy was formulated by a German doctor, Samuel Hahnemann, in the eighteenth century, on the principle that 'like cures like'. In earlier times, the ancient Greeks (specifically Hippocrates in the fifth century BC) and also mediaeval alchemists were familiar with the principles of homoeopathy, which are that the symptoms caused by an overdose of a substance in a healthy being are the symptoms that can be cured by a small dose of that substance in a being that is sick. Homoeopaths regard symptoms as expressions of disharmony in the patient, which is why the whole horse (or other animal or person) is treated. It is the aim to restore harmony, balance and energy flow to stimulate the body to rebalance and cure itself.

HOW DOES HOMOEOPATHY WORK?

PREPARATION OF REMEDIES

Homoepathic remedies are derived from animal, vegetable and mineral sources. They are prepared by an accepted pharmaceutical process called potentisation which releases the therapeutic properties of the various substances used. The substances are diluted time and time again and vigorously shaken in a solution of water and alcohol, and the number of times this takes place (ranging from three or four, to many thousands of times) produces a wide range of potencies of the remedy.

Arnica is popular in competition horse yards to help counteract bruising and general soft tissue soreness

Those who do not believe homoeopathy can be effective understandably base their belief on the fact that, often, not a single molecule of the therapeutic substances can be found in the final remedy. At the time of writing, however, news is coming through from the United States that scientific tests have, indeed, found traces of remedial substances in homoeopathic remedies.

Healing intuition plays a big part in the practice by a therapist of his or her specific therapy, and there are many therapies which are completely inexplicable to conventional medicine, human and veterinary. Homoeopathic remedies may contain no more than what has been described by American doctor Deepak Chopra as 'a memory of healing' – yet its levels of success make it undeniably effective.

ADMINISTERING REMEDIES

Homoeopathic remedies have to be treated with care and used conscientiously in strict accordance with the instructions of the practitioner. They may be provided as powders, pills, tiny pilules or as liquid tinctures and water dilutions. Horses normally best accept their remedies in powder form fed on a piece of apple or carrot. Putting the remedies in the animal's feed is not a very effective way to give them in view of the danger of their being missed, blown away, not swallowed or 'lost' among a host of other material. They can also be diluted in

Calendula (marigold) is used for treating open wounds and slow-healing ulcers. It is an extremely reliable healing agent and can also be used for wounds around the eye and with hypericum can help to treat open wounds involving nerve damage

BIOCHEMIC TISSUE SALTS

A form of homoeopathy, this therapy involves giving mineral salts to horses thought to be suffering from certain mineral deficiencies; there are twelve main minerals or tissue salts used. It is felt that they may be better absorbed in this form, being taken in by the tissues in the mouth, than as a supplement in the feed when they have to pass through the very acid environment of the horse's gut, which may compromise their efficacy.

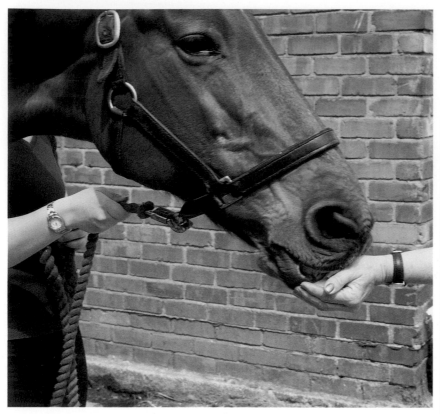

Homoeopathic tablets are best tipped into the bottle cap and on to a piece of apple or carrot, pressed in lightly with the bottom of the bottle, and fed to the horse. Do not let them touch your fingers as this will depotentize the remedy

More can mean less

Selecting the right potency or 'strength' of a remedy is important. Some practitioners find that higher potencies are more effective in treating acute conditions (sudden in onset) whereas the lower potencies are better for chronic (longer-lasting) conditions. Certainly many find that the lower the potency or 'weaker' the remedy, the more effective it can be, another confusing principle for the animal's owner to get to grips with!

a little sterile water and carefully squirted under the horse's tongue and lips from a small syringe.

They must not be touched by any living person or animal other than the intended patient for fear of depotentizing them, and must be kept away from strong-smelling substances and bright lights.

SELF HELP

Homoeopathic remedies are available for horse owners to buy and use over the counter or by mail, but it is always better to take initial advice from a qualified practitioner as to what remedies should be kept on hand for this type of use, and how and when to use them. In practice, a consultation with a homoeopathist (a vet or other qualified practitioner working on referral) may take up to about two hours, as the practitioner thoroughly quizzes the owner and observes the horse to get a full 'symptom picture' of him or her. A remedy which, according to its known properties, matches the patient's symptom picture is then selected. The patient will be sensitive only to the most 'similar' or 'like' remedy.

Rhus toxicodendron is used for injuries affecting skin, muscles, mucous membranes and fibrous tissues involving blisters and pain. It is commonly used to relieve stiffness caused by overwork. A useful remedy for muscle and joint disorders which tend to improve on exercise

C A S E H I S T O R Y

Pony: Six-year-old mare, Minnie, family all-rounder used for riding and driving.

PROBLEM: Minnie lived out with others but suffered from recurrent spasmodic colic which none of the others had. This involves spasm of the muscle of part of the wall of the large intestine. The spasms would last for a few minutes, cease, then recur roughly half an hour or so later.

The grazing was changed to less fibrous keep and stabling introduced at night in winter but the colic recurred, although less often. It appeared to be large amounts of grass which triggered the colic. None of the ponies on the field ever had laminitis.

INITIAL ASSESSMENT: The (orthodox) vet suggested that, despite regular worming, the pony could have aneurisms ('ballooned' arteries) due to worm damage of the arteries, or that previous damage had caused a restricted blood supply to the gut, resulting in slow passage of food through the intestines and, hence, colic. He suggested specialist diagnostic tests, but the owner wished to try homoeopathy first.

HOMOEOPATHIC ASSESSMENT: Minnie was referred to a homoeopathic vet who stressed that homoeopathic remedies were mainly used in colic as an emergency, first aid measure. As Minnie was kept at home and there was always someone on hand, it was agreed to keep a supply of homoeopathic remedies to administer both whilst waiting for the vet to arrive and subsequently.

TREATMENT: Aconitum napellus 6c was to be given every hour for four hours in the early stages. This remedy is for panic, shock and fear.

- Colocynthis 30c was to be given every 10 minutes until relief was apparent. This remedy is to relieve spasm of the smooth or involuntary muscle of the intestinal wall.

- Nux vomica 6c was to be given every two hours for four doses. This remedy is used for colic caused by over-eating rich food.

Other remedies were given for slightly differing symptoms but were not needed. The above remedies resulted in controlling and relieving the colic during two bouts over a six-week period. Bach Flower Remedies (Rescue™ Remedy and Rock Rose) were also given to ease the panic and fear caused by the pain.

The remedies appeared to control the colic well and the homoeopathic and orthodox vets worked together to give Minnie 's owners a management regime which included a probiotic in the diet, no more than 12 hours grazing in any 24 and ideally not all at once, good quality, low-energy feed during stabling and careful dental care and de-worming. The homoeopathic remedy Teucrium marum 6c (used in redworm infestation) was prescribed to be given every two weeks as a permanent precaution.

RESULT: On the new regime, Minnie has had no colic for 12 months.

Flower Remedies

Probably the most famous flower remedies worldwide are the Bach Flower Remedies; however, there are, in fact, other brands of flower remedy which work on very similar principles. Whilst the Bach range concentrates on healing a patient's emotional state and so aiding physical healing, other brands claim to help heal physical conditions directly.

Clematis is a useful remedy for inattentiveness during work by both horse and rider

PHILOSOPHY

Flower remedies are very closely related to homoeopathy. Dr Edward Bach, a conventionally trained and qualified doctor, was the physician who developed this therapy. He believed that it was essential to treat the whole person – body, mind and spirit – if healing were to be effective, and that in order to prevent the disease reaching its final, noticeable stage, it was necessary to trace its development back to the very beginning to learn how and why it began. He believed, like homoeopaths with whom he had worked closely, in treating the person, not the disease or symptoms, and felt that personality traits were ultimately responsible for bringing on physical diseases. Disease was, he felt, 'the consolidation of a mental attitude'. If these traits and attitudes could be treated, he reasoned, the diseases could be prevented or stopped in their very early stages.

HOW DOES IT WORK?

After years of realising that treating a diseased body was not enough, Dr Bach developed a system of using the healing powers or 'signatures' of flowers. He believed that the flowers of our countryside held the key to treating excesses of personality traits and mental attitudes – although at a time when herbalism was going out of fashion in favour of the new, fast-developing synthetic drugs and antibiotics, and when homoeopathy had not been widely accepted, he knew he was facing ridicule, maybe even professional ruin, by following his intuition.

Cherry plum can be useful to calm aggression and for horses with little self-control

Preparing a remedy: Dr Bach found that by leaving flowerheads in a clear glass bowl in pure water and in strong sunlight, the healing signature of the flower was taken up by the water, which then became, as he termed it, 'potentised' or empowered to heal. The liquid was then filtered, and an appropriate amount of alcohol was added as a preservative.

dropper in the lid. However, this is obviously quite impractical for treating a large animal such as a horse, so for these it is suggested that owners buy a bottle of the stock concentrate (if using Rescue Remedy™) and add about ten drops of it per 4.5 litres (1 gal) of water in the drinking bucket each time the water is changed, which it should be at least two or three times a day.

Five drops of any appropriate single remedies may also be added. For horses, the remedies can also be given at the rate of four drops of Rescue Remedy™ or two of single remedies on a lump of sugar, carrot or apple at least four times a day.

As with most remedies, flower remedies are not intended as a substitute for proper veterinary attention, advice and diagnosis, but

Flowerheads are left in pure water in a clear glass bowl in strong sunlight when the 'healing signature' passes from the flowerhead into the water which is then mixed in equal parts with brandy

WHICH REMEDY TO USE?

Flower remedies always treat the presenting or surface emotion. As the layers of emotion are stripped away the mix changes to reflect the new emotions that have been brought to light. This means that over time even quite complex and deep seated issues can be treated, just by selecting the most obvious remedies at each stage.

FLOWER REMEDIES FOR HORSES

Practitioners usually supply remedies in dilute form in small bottles with a

Carefully squeeze drops of the remedy from the dropper just inside the horse's lips. Alternatively, about ten drops of the remedy can be added to each fresh bucket of water. It is not so much the strength of the remedy that matters as the frequency of taking it: this way, the horse gets some remedy each time he drinks

as a complement to any other treatment given. Their success with animals, and especially horses it seems, has earned them a place in the first-aid cupboard of any yard.

Bach Rescue Remedy™: Due to its wide-ranging nature, this remedy is particularly suitable for treating animals, which seem to respond very favourably to it, whatever their specific problem.

SELF HELP

It is impossible to list here all the remedies, but most brands of flower remedy, and certainly the Bach Flower Remedies, have detailed books, booklets, charts and leaflets about their system, and how to use the remedies on a self-help baasis.

Finding a qualified practitioner in your area should not be difficult either, because the outlets which sell the remedies, in a shop or by mail order, can usually

Focus on the Rider

Edward Bach experimented extensively on himself. He suffered from negative states of mind and would note the physical disorder which followed it, and then wander about the local countryside seeking the plant which had the power to correct the mental condition which he believed had caused the physical one. He eventually identified thirty-eight flowers which he felt possessed the healing signatures which would treat the thirty-eight negative mental attitudes from which people could suffer. These attitudes he placed in seven categories:

- fear
- uncertainty and indecision
- loneliness
- insufficient interest in the present
- over-sensitivity to ideas and influences
- despondency and despair
- over-care for the welfare of others

People who want to treat themselves sometimes find it difficult to admit to themselves what they are really like; so it is often better to consult a qualified flower remedy practitioner who will be skilled at peeling off the various psychological layers and getting to the root of the problem. Also, people often find it easier to open up and talk to a complete stranger, who may subsequently become a regular or occasional counsellor.

give you this information or point you in the right direction. As with other therapies, qualified practitioners sometimes advertise their services in local directories, or contact The Edward Bach Centre (see Useful Addresses, p186).

Top left: Rescue Remedy™ is excellent after accidents or in the event of sudden shock, nervousness, anger and grief

Left: Impatiens is used where irritability and impatience occur

Naturopathy

Naturopathy is an extensive, comprehensive system of treating people and, to a lesser extent, animals with a variety of natural, holistic treatments.

Healing herbs: tools of the naturopath

PHILOSOPHY

The basis of naturopathic practice is founded on the maintenance of health rather than the curing of disease, and the science was originally evolved from Hippocrates and other Greek philosopher practitioners.

HOW DOES IT WORK?

Naturopathists study the mechanisms of health maintenance including nutrition, psychology, exercise, lifestyle and man's place within the environment.

TREATMENT FOR ANIMALS

Although there are recognised qualifications in naturopathy in the human field, we know of none anywhere in the world related to the treatment of animals. In some countries naturopathists can treat animals directly, in others only on referral from a veterinary surgeon.

Cell Injection Therapy

This therapy is usually administered by a veterinary surgeon or, more unusually, by a qualified naturopathist, often working under veterinary referral or supervision (according to the laws of the individual country).

HOW DOES IT WORK?

It involves the deep muscle or subcutaneous (under the skin) injection of cells of foetuses or young animals, with a view to helping the body to repair damaged tissue more naturally and, it is claimed, more effectively than by using, for example, drugs based on synthetic chemicals. It is not a common treatment, but practitioners claim considerable successes.

WHAT IS IT USED FOR?

It can be used to boost the immune system, improve the circulatory system and enhance hormonal function. It may also help to heal injuries, particularly those that are related to repeated work-related stress and strain, as well as generally improving the health and wellbeing of run-down, debilitated animals or those suffering from problems that are age-related in nature, such as degeneration.

Caution

As with many medicines and therapies, there are certain contra-indications (conditions which are not appropriate for its use); these might include respiratory allergies, severe heart problems, certain congenital diseases, advanced cancers and other severe inflammatory and life-threatening disorders.
Cell injection therapy is a very specialised treatment and, if inappropriately administered, can apparently cause serious side effects in horses, including shock; owners must discuss its implications and possibilities with their veterinary surgeon.

Radionics

Often known colloquially as the 'Black Box', this is a form of healing where both the assessment and treatment of a patient's condition is carried out at a distance using an instrument – the 'black box'; practitioners also need a 'witness' – a small piece of hair, horn, skin or a drop of blood, which contains the patient's energy pattern – to help in the procedure, and they then dowse over the witness using a pendulum to assess the condition of the subject. They will then decide on the radionic healing energies required to effect a result.

PHILOSOPHY

Whilst still most controversial, radionics seems to be a very effective form of assessment and healing. Every organ, disease or body system is believed to have its own vibrational frequency by which it can be identified and which can be sent to it using radionic instruments to restore health. It is believed that the natural frequencies of the body are disrupted by the effects of pollution of all kinds and mental and emotional stress, and the result is malfunction and eventually illness. The choice of remedy is down to the practitioner's judgement. Practitioners believe that everything is linked by fields of varying densities – and this is not a new concept by any means, simply that modern scientific instrumentation has only fairly recently been able to identify and measure electro-magnetic fields. Radionics and other complementary practitioners believe that disease or disorder, and any kind of energy disharmony, occurs in the

---

Healing from a Distance

The intuition and sensitivity needed by a practitioner to arrive at some sort of diagnosis is called his or her 'radiesthetic faculty', radiesthesia being detection from a distance. Action (healing in this case) at a distance is called radionics.

---

patient's body or mind if the energy fields are significantly disrupted.

HOW DOES IT WORK?

The radionics practitioner does not need to see the patient, and normally never does so, although a few like to have a photograph. The patient, or an animal's owner as the case may be, sends a witness – most simply a small lock of hair – to the practitioner together with any case history, and the practitioner, using dowsing, then performs a detailed radionic analysis to reveal the disharmonies and energy imbalances represented via the witness. The practitioner mentally asks the pendulum appropriate questions, and these are answered by the movements of the pendulum via the practitioner's unconscious mind. He or she is even more concerned with the patient's underlying causes of disharmony than with the physical or behavioural symptoms apparent, and will treat the whole body/mind/spirit in a holistic way.

Once the various energy frequencies have been determined, the practitioner will select, again through dowsing, the appropriate energy vibration which can be transmitted to the patient by the radionic instruments. These energy wavelengths all have their own individual frequencies or vibrations which are expressed in numerical values known as 'rates'. The calibrated dials on the instrument/s are set to the appropriate therapeutic rate decided by the practitioner. Renowned radionics practitioner Lavender Dower describes how this fascinating therapy works:

'I believe it is all a question of communication. Mind energy patterns are transposed into figures, and these are then set on a radionic instrument and transmitted to different parts of the patient's body through their blood or hair witness, which is placed on the instrument. That energy suggests to tissues in the patient's body the best way for them to repair the damage. How this energy is transmitted to the patient is still a

What is Radionics used for?

The therapy claims to be able to treat almost any physical, mental or spiritual problem, as all are caused by disharmony in the energy fields of the patient. As such, radiesthesia and radionics are an ideal complement to orthodox medicine or other complementary therapies, and there are no side effects to worry about. As with any other therapy, orthodox or otherwise, success is not forthcoming in every case; but horses do seem to be particularly responsive to radiesthesia and radionics. Sometimes the practitioner learns during treatment that some other therapy or a change in general management or work is needed to support other treatments.

mystery. But it works, according to many … that's the main thing.'

Follow-up treatment: The practitioner requires regular reports on an animal's response to treatment so that it can be adjusted if necessary. Although some

dramatic healing effects have been seen by just one treatment, others take longer to respond – but treatment is normally economical. It is often, but not always, the case that the longer a condition has been present, the longer it will take to respond.

SELF HELP

Well, there may be no such thing as DIY radionics (action/healing radionically) because proper training is needed, but there may well be such a thing as DIY radiesthesia (detection of disorders or disharmonies). If you read the section in this book on dowsing, and learn from other books or sources – perhaps a friend who is good at it – you may become adept at this intuitive skill and be able to tell what is wrong with you, your friends or family and your animals (however, radionics should never be used as a substitute for conventional medical or veterinary care). As for actual healing, training is certainly needed for this to be possible radionically, and the contacts in Useful Addresses (p186) will be the next step in learning about this therapy.

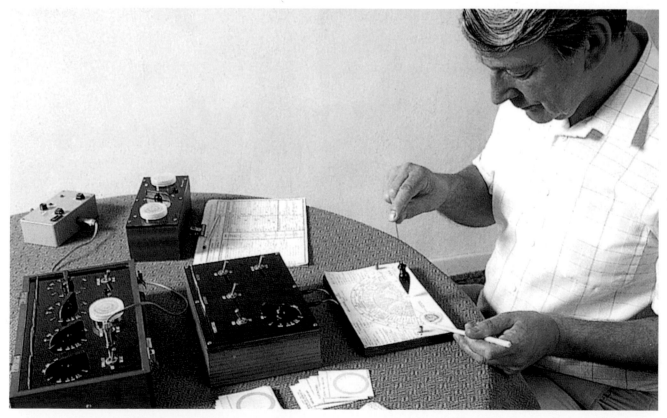

A radionics practitioner 'asking questions' of the 'witness' through the movements of the pendulum

RADIONICS IN PRACTICE

Lavender Dower FKCollR, MRR

Although well into her nineties at the time of writing, it was only at the close of the twentieth century that Lavender Dower retired from her fifty-year career as a radionics practitioner. The second daughter of Sir George and Lady Honor Clerk of Penicuik House in the Lowlands of Scotland, Lavender has, to onlookers, led an extraordinary life. On leaving school she studied sculpture at the Royal College of Art under Gilbert Ledward and Henry Moore; marriage to an MP, followed by motherhood, put paid to her ambitions of fame in this field. Throughout World War II she served as an officer in the ATS (Auxiliary Territorial Service). After the war, separation from her husband followed, and Lavender turned her attention to earning a living for herself and daughter Tilly. She founded the Julip toy company, named after the first horse toy she made, from her London flat, enlisting the help of some of the NCOs she had worked with during her army days. Her training as a sculptor helped enormously, enabling her to devise a method of casting horse models in latex rubber from models she had made in clay.

In the 1950s Lavender was introduced to the Black Box, as radionic therapy was then commonly known, by her good friend Liz Baerlein who was working in this field; together they went on to found the Radionics Association during the 1950s. In later years, after Liz's death, Lavender set up the Institute for Complementary Medicine.

What particularly interested Lavender in this 'energy medicine' was its aim to discover and then treat the root cause of a problem, as opposed to merely suppressing symptoms which could reoccur. Recalls Lavender, 'Practising radionics came naturally to me, I didn't find it difficult at all – but then I'd always been intrigued by "weird things". The instruments when I first started were enormously different from the ones used now. Today, radionics is more spiritual than physical. Original instruments were meticulous in their physical proportions, their wiring and so on, whereas today much of the equipment consists of printed cards.

'My first experience with radionics equipment was with a stick-pad, which comprised a small metal plate covered with rubber. When gently stroked with a finger, it would give a "yes" or "no" answer to your questions, depending on how smoothly your finger passed over it. The stick-pad was later replaced by a pendulum – a quicker and more accurate method of diagnosing.'

One remarkable piece of equipment used by Lavender and Liz was a special radionics camera created by engineer George (Bill) De La Warr, who had introduced radionics to the UK during the war. Basically the camera took photographs of diseased or injured internal organs from a 'witness' of the patient – wherever in the world that patient was – providing the analysis diagnosed from the witness was correct. A 'witness' is a small piece of hair, skin, horn or nail, or a drop of blood, which contains the patient's energy pattern. Photographs of organs/affected areas were shown in varying degrees of clarity and brightness, depending on how severe the condition was.

How the camera exactly worked cannot be explained scientifically. It just did – but only for Lavender and Liz when the de la Warr laboratory physicist, Leonard Corte, helped process and develop their plates. Says Lavender, 'Leonard appeared to have the magic touch which sensitised the emulsion on the plates. It would only work for him. If our analysis was right we got a very good photograph, if it wasn't, we got a blank plate.'

Radionic equipment was instrumental in finding Lavender and Liz a new home for their practice when their business outgrew Lavender's London home: 'Using a pendulum, pointer and a map we found the ideal premises in Gloucestershire – complete with Luke, the friendly resident ghost.'

As radionics equipment and techniques gradually became more sophisticated, Lavender was able to complete an analysis of a patient in only an hour, as opposed to the two days it used to take. This was fortunate, seeing that Lavender's rare talent was becoming well known, and her patient list was growing steadily until it numbered between three and five hundred. Remembers Lavender, 'One day forty envelopes stuffed with horse hair arrived for analysis. I thought ten witnesses a day was a lot, but forty...'

At a 90 per cent recovery rate, Lavender's healing success with animals, predominantly equines, was remarkably high, but with humans it was significantly lower at 80 per cent because, she explains, 'some people just didn't want to get well for some reason or another... perhaps they enjoyed being an invalid too much. Animals are not like that.'

But what about the horses that did not respond to treatment; what were the reasons for this?

Says Lavender, 'I think they were karmic. For some reason those equines unable to become well were hampered by a traumatic happening in a past life affecting them in the present. For example, one horse was terrified of water and I called upon a colleague who was able to take it back in time and asked it why it was

so scared. The horse told him that it had drowned in one life. Other instances involved horses that were frightened of being shut in stables, with the reason being that in past lives they had been shut in places where there had been a fire and they couldn't get out so had been killed. Stable fires were common many years ago. Some horses were frightened of men, and women too on occasion, because they had been ill-treated by them in a previous life.'

From children's much-loved riding ponies to top racehorses, Lavender has treated a wide variety of equines in all shapes and sizes. However, it is usual for people to try alternative treatments, for themselves or their animals, as a last resort when conventional treatment has failed. Did Lavender experience any clients who were sceptical of radionic therapy?

'Practically all of them were the first time. But their reaction when it worked was of surprise and delight. When I retired I had many letters from people saying how marvellous radionics had been for their animals, and how grateful they were that I had been able to help them. That was nice to know.'

Although officially retired, Lavender still keeps her hand in by 'doing the odd one for friends and relations.'

After nearly five decades of radionics work, can Lavender say for certain how this fascinating therapy works?

'I believe that it is all a question of communication. Mind energy patterns are transposed into figures, and these are then set on a radionic instrument and transmitted to different parts of the patient's body through their blood or hair witness which is placed on the instrument. That energy suggests to tissues in the patient's body the best way for them to repair the damage. How this energy is transmitted to the patient is still a mystery. But it works... that's the main thing.'

C A S E   H I S T O R Y

Horse: Rex, a twelve-year-old Arab X hunter-type bay gelding, 16.1hh advanced dressage horse, working and competing at Grand Prix level.

TEMPERAMENT: Described by his owner, Jane Aston, as generally disagreeable in the stable –'If Rex isn't grumpy I know there's something wrong with him!' – but extremely willing and forward-going under saddle. A 'sparky' horse who loves his work.

PROBLEM: Rex's problem began when Jane loaned him to an international dressage rider for competition work. Says Jane, 'After a couple of months, having ridden Rex in Grand Prix classes, this rider rang me and said that Rex was "moving irregularly" and "not up to the job". A vet, after watching the horse compete, confirmed that there was a slight irregularity in Rex's sideways movement. Never having had any problems with Rex before, I felt that he was being pushed too fast, too soon and that any problem in his movement was being caused through a fault in his training.

'To cut a long story short, I sent Rex to a young rider who was competing at Prix St Georges level, and without the pressure to execute half-passes at such a steep angle, as demanded at Grand Prix level, the so-called problem abated. His rider told me that when she "let go of the reins a bit" he moved perfectly!

'However, when I got him back I discovered that whilst he was physically OK, mentally he was a wreck. I took him to a competition and as I rode him up the centre line felt the most weird sensation – I'd never had it before and sincerely hope I never experience it again. It was as if Rex had "left me" and shut himself off into a world of his own. It was as if he'd "chucked life in". Plus he'd been unnaturally quiet at home since his return; like a zombie is the only way to describe him. Normally he's a grumpy old so-and-so to handle in the stable, very "sharp" to ride and absolutely dreadful with tractors, but it was as if I had a different animal. When hacking, or rather, plodding, out he took no interest in things around him, and walked past tractors as if they were not there. It's a horrible feeling when you know your horse is desperately unhappy!'

TREATMENT: A keen advocate of alternative therapies,

Jane called upon renowned radionics practitioner Lavender Dower for help. Says Jane, 'I knew of Mrs Dower's reputation from many ye ars ago via a local hunting and competition yard whose horses she had successfully treated. So I wrote to her, explaining Rex's symptoms and background, and enclosing a piece of his mane as a witness.'

Replied Lavender Dower: 'I have put Rex on treatment. It seems to be mainly psychological as I find fear and resentment as the underlying causes. The only physical things I am treating are the memory centre and the spinal cord and the spinalis dorsi in the withers. It might help to stroke Cabalox gently in over

the area, and a course of Dr Bach's Vervain would help.'

RESULT: Says Jane, 'With her diagnosis, Mrs Dower had hit the nail on the head! I followed her instructions, kept her informed of Rex's progress whilst she continued her treatment of him, and within six weeks I could see a real difference in him; moreover he reverted to his old grumpy self, which was wonderful!

'I used the Cabalox as she suggested; it was a hyperoxygenated massage oil used mainly on horses and racing greyhounds to soothe away muscle aches and strains. Expensive but awfully good, it worked by warming up the muscles as you applied it thereby promoting blood circulation to the area thus helping the healing process. It certainly helped Rex. Unfortunately it is no longer made.

'Mrs Dower also recommended that Rex be given a complete break from dressage work for a season – "let him enjoy himself just hacking about, jumping and generally having lots of fun. He needs a good rest, that's all, there's nothing physically wrong with him" she said, so that is what I did. And it worked a treat. He came back to competition the following year better than ever, and competed successfully.

'Mrs Dower liked to be informed about every two weeks of Rex's progress, and I continued to ask her to treat him as long as I felt he needed it. I did exactly what she suggested, because I had to – I was on a road to nowhere otherwise, and on the point of no return. Nothing else was working, and this did.

'I did have one of Mrs Dower's assistants treat another of my horses once, but I felt that she was unable to help. I disagreed with what she diagnosed, so I wrote to Mrs Dower and asked her to help instead and her treatment worked. I later discovered that the assistant gave up radionics as she felt it wasn't for her.

Dowsing

Dowsing is a method of diagnosis, a way of searching for information, or for substances such as water or minerals. It is not a healing therapy in itself.

It has become more accepted in recent decades: earlier this century, dowsers were regarded as cranks to be dismissed out of hand – though this was less so in previous ones. Nowadays the technique is discussed and shown on both popular and scientific television and radio programmes, and often appears to be successful. Much depends on the sensitivity and intent of the dowser: as with most non-Western-orthodox therapies and forms of medicine, the honesty and sincerity of the dowser is most important.

HOW DOES IT WORK?

It can be done by means of a forked rod or stick known as a divining rod (often seen being used to discover water, minerals, old routes, ley lines and so on), or with a pendulum – a small object suspended from a string or a chain (even a ring on a neck chain has been used with success), most often used to acquire information. The standard pendulum, according to world-famous dowser and radionics practitioner, Lavender Dower, and described in her book *Healing With Radionics*, is a cone of resin containing a seven-coil spiral wound on the Golden Mean Ratio. The pendulum seems to be more difficult to use than the rods, requiring great sensitivity and a completely open mind and lack of tension in the operator. It seems that not everyone has, or can develop, the special art needed to operate a pendulum.

THE DIVINING ROD

This is held in the dowser's hands, which are fairly relaxed and only under sufficient tension to hold the rod level, with the point away from the body. Two separate rods, usually of metal or wood, can be used, with part of them turned to form handles which the dowser can hold. It is believed that the rods respond to changes in the very complex web of natural magnetism and electricity everywhere in our environment and also in ourselves.

How do they 'know' what to search for? The dowser imagines and thinks about what he or she is looking for, and this seems to be sufficient guide for the rods. In any event, it is very often successful, especially with experienced dowsers.

THE PENDULUM

The pendulum as a divining instrument is more difficult to use. The dowser must 'ask in truth', again with no preconceptions. The dowser holds the pendulum chain between finger and thumb and sets it swinging freely, then, being careful not to influence (move) it at all, but letting it 'do its own thing', asks it 'yes or no' questions to which he or she knows the answers, for example 'is today Sunday?', noting in which direction the pendulum moves. Using it then becomes a matter of long practice and development of the sensitivity needed.

Where do the answers come from?

It is said that the answers come from what has been described variously as 'the collective unconscious', 'mankind's pool of subconscious knowledge', and other expressions. Unlikely though this may sound to some people, the fact is that there are countless numbers of people, healers and others, around the world who do use dowsing for many purposes and who constantly experience success with the technique.

Honest, benevolent intent, as in so many complementary therapies, is a pre-requisite of success.

Iridology

Iridology involves studying minute changes in the iris of the human or animal eye to discover the presence of disease in the body. In fact using the individual patterns in the iris as a diagnostic technique has been known in human medicine for some time, but few people are aware that it can also be used to diagnose problems in horses.

PHILOSOPHY

The technique is more widely used in America and Australia, but it is being increasingly applied in Europe. It is believed to have been used by the ancient Egyptians and other civilisations, although in our own times it was rediscovered by a Hungarian doctor, Ignatz von Peczely, in 1881. As a boy Peczely caught an owl, which broke its leg during its struggles to escape. He apparently treated the bird and cared for it until it was better, but during the process noticed a black line forming in its iris; this gradually disappeared as it recovered, leaving just a white mark.

HOW DOES IT WORK?

Peczely became a neurologist, and in the process of his work he realised that every organ is represented by a specific part of the iris, as are other parts of the body. These have been recorded on charts, and iridologists work by noting changes from normal in the eye: in human eyes these occur as pigments and markings on the iris; in horses the changes are usually in the form of lines. The eyes are usually examined in a darkened area, often the horse's stable or a dark building such as a barn or shelter, by means of a small torch and a magnifying glass, and changes from normal noted.

WHAT IS IT USED FOR?

From examination of the eye, a trained iridologist will be able to tell which part of the body is diseased, although he/she will not always be able to identify just what the specific problem is. This is yet another good reason why complementary therapies of any kind should always be used in conjunction with an expert veterinary diagnosis.

SELF HELP

Finding an iridologist: the address of the British Society of Iridologists is given in the Useful Addresses section (p186).

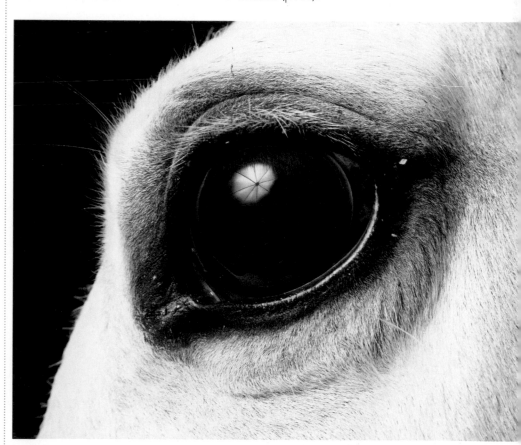

Iridology as a diagnostic technique takes note of changes in colour and pattern in the eye. It is rarely used in horses but is an effective supporting technique to veterinary diagnosis because it often shows up problems before definite symptoms are visible

Kinesiology

Sometimes called 'applied kinesiology' and 'muscle kinesiology', this is a diagnostic technique used to gauge weaknesses within the body which may lead to disease or failure to thrive.

PHILOSOPHY

The technique was devised by an American chiropractor, George Goodheart, as recently as the 1960s when he uncovered the link between Chinese acupuncture/energy meridians and muscles. Basically, the strength or weakness of certain muscles indicates a corresponding strength or weakness in the organ system which shares the same meridian; assessing the muscle can give information as to the state of those organs, and of various related lymph glands involved in the immune system, so aiding evaluation of their condition. Thus a weak organ is detected via its reduced energy flow, which shows as a reduced response in its related muscle.

HOW DOES IT WORK?

It works on the principle that certain muscles share the same acupuncture meridian as particular organ systems, to the effect that if, when tested, a muscle fails to respond by returning pressure against the practitioner's push, then this would indicate weakness in the related organ system. It also incorporates principles of chiropractic and acupressure, and takes into account how muscles respond in relation to foods, and to the essential oils used in aromatherapy.

When using kinesiology on horses, a human surrogate is needed who can touch a particular part of the horse and show up the

What is Kinesiology used for?

Causing reflex points to operate can have several beneficial effects; it can:

- activate and strengthen weak muscles
- relieve muscle tightness and so improve posture, movement and body function
- relieve related pain and stress
- help with nutritional requirements and allergic reactions
- improve the functioning of the nervous system, including the brain
- generally improve co-ordination and proprioception

weakness or strength in the horse in his or her own body. On horses, kinesiology is used mainly in connection with aromatherapy. The principle of this is the same for horses and animals as it is for people, in that specific essential oils, or blends of them, can be tried, and because we are all unique personalities, our responses via kinesiology to the aromas offered will indicate the precise combination of oils that we need to help us, as individuals, combat disease. Thus although the disorder may be the same, the oils required may be quite different because of personality differences and our individual reactions to disease.

This is another example of treating the individual, not the disease.

Testing for muscle strength while a known allergen is introduced

KINESIOLOGY IN PRACTICE

Caroline Ingraham GEOTA

As well as specialising in equine aromatherapy (see p100), Caroline Ingraham also uses kinesiology, on both animals and humans, with great success. Asked how she does it, she replied: 'I use kinesiology in its most simplistic form which is referred to as "muscle testing". This involves using a muscle that relates to an organ system through an energy field, ie a person, in order to determine what imbalances there are. For example I would test a person's pectoralis major sternal muscle in order to check the energy flow in the liver; for kidneys I would test the psoas muscle. I use pressure on the muscle; if it fails to respond by returning pressure against my push, or pull in some cases, then this indicates weakness in the related organ system that can lead to disease or lack of wellbeing.

'However, if an animal or person is very strong, or infirm, or extremely young, it's more tricky to obtain a correct reading.

'Muscle testing is used on humans by chiropractors, particularly in America, as a simple and effective method of placing the legs and arms at such an angle that the supporting muscles are isolated when pressure is applied. The muscle being tested will indicate a strength or weakness relating to the organ system which shares the same acupuncture meridian. A weak organ is detected via its reduced energy flow, which shows as a reduced response in its related muscle. On average, fourteen different muscles are tested.'

When carried out on horses and other animals, muscle testing is done through a surrogate – 'and this is rather difficult to grasp!' says Caroline. 'You really have to experience it to believe it. This sensation is difficult to convey in words, but anyone who comes into one of my workshops finds they are able to do it, and to experience the different strengths and weaknesses for themselves. They might find it tricky to begin with, but usually by the end of a day they have got the feeling for it.

INSIDE INFORMATION

As well as helping to determine the appropriate treatment for an ailment, kinesiology can be used to source the cause of that ailment and pinpoint the exact position of an injury. A 'surrogate' touches the horse on the appropriate meridian. That person has an envelope containing one of the allergens tucked in her belt somewhere else on her. Next to that envelope is a sample of the appropriate essential oil. The kinesiologist touches the surrogate (not the horse), and if the surrogate becomes weak it shows that the horse is allergic to that particular allergen. If the surrogate stays strong, the horse is not allergic. The process is then repeated using other allergens.

Example 1: Pinpointing an injury site. Says Caroline, 'If you are not sure of the actual point of, say, arthritis and therefore do not know where to apply the remedy for maximum benefit, get a kinesiologist to touch where you think the point is. They will work on and around the suspect area, and the resulting weaknesses and strengths felt will guide them to the trouble spot.'

Example 2 – Identifying causes. Kinesiology plays an important role in determining what is causing an allergy. Explains Caroline, 'For example, once you have got a horse's lungs strong again using, in my case, appropriate essential oils, you can discover what is making the lungs weak. Is it the hay, straw, stable dust, pollen...? So you take small samples of each potential irritant and introduce them while continuing with the oils to see if it weakens the oils' effectiveness. If the oils' effect weakens with a test sample of irritant, then you know you have found the cause. You can test different qualities of hay using this technique. If the lungs remains strong, the hay is suitable.

'In the case of a kidney ailment, you can test your horse's water to see if that's causing the problem. Once you have got the kidneys strong, test different kinds of water – bottled, tap, spring – and watch the response.'

Aromatherapy

Aromatherapy is a method of treating bodily ailments using essential plant oils; it is one of the most popular complementary therapies today. It is a discipline well used in ancient civilisations and, indeed, up to this century: scented fresh and dried plants, flowers and herbs were liberally scattered over floors, burned in waxes and oils and used in massage oils, and it became a healing art of both body and mind to choose particular aromas for particular conditions or desired results. Animals, too, readily show their interest in, liking of, or rejection of certain smells, and horses are particularly susceptible to them, having a sense of smell so much more sensitive than our own.

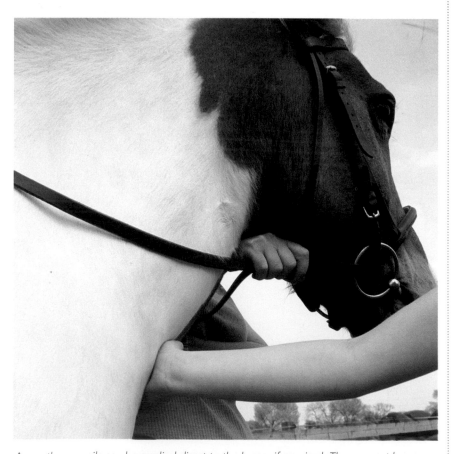

Aromatherapy oils can be applied direct to the horse, if required. They are not heavy and do not leave the coat in a sticky, greasy mess

PHILOSOPHY

Smells are actually physical in character. Minute particles are given off by certain substances, not only from plants but animals, too, and are carried on the air. They are breathed in accidentally or on purpose and often a horse will hold his breath to examine them more fully by means of an olfactory organ called Jacobsen's Organ high up in the nasal passages. The horse will breathe in the aroma, then raise his muzzle and top lip to close off the nostrils, thereby holding his breath so that the particles, which dissolve in the moisture of the natural airway secretions, can be savoured at length, informing him of their nature and possibly their source. This action is the familiar one known as flehmen which always amuses we humans, but which is an important information-gathering action to horses and a valuable survival aid in the wild.

HOW DOES IT WORK?

Today, the formal discipline of aromatherapy is based on the use of pure 'essential oils'. These oils are extracted from plant materials (not only flowers, of course) and are up to a hundred times stronger than the levels commonly found in their source materials. Some aromas are blended with base oils. They are normally applied to the skin or are inhaled, but they can be taken internally, though this should only be on expert advice. When horses are involved, they are usually offered to the horse to sniff, they

What is Aromatherapy used for?

- injuries (wounds, bruises and sprains)
- osteoarthritis
- emotional problems, such as depression, sadness, fear, nervousness, past trauma
- general stress relief
- other minor disorders

For internal use the oils may be dropped on to the tongue, and may be used for a wider range of conditions such as:

- colic
- urinary tract infections
- impotence
- soft tissue damage
- infections
- parasite infestations and other skin conditions

are also often massaged into the coat and skin, or they are simply smeared on.

Scents do have an effect on the state of mind of an animal through being inhaled and 'registered' by the brain, and can pass through the skin and into the lymphatic and blood systems. In this way aromatherapy can be very effective in helping with emotional and stress-related problems, as well as physical ones. Some essential oils also have anti-bacterial properties, and being chemicals, are believed to help adjust the body's biochemistry and so aid healing.

The horse will choose: Just as horses are believed to have a nutritional intuition as to what foods they need, given the choice, similarly they should be allowed to select their own aromas according to their own perceived needs. A qualified and expert practitioner will discuss the horse's condition with the owner and probably the veterinary surgeon in many cases, and will select the oils he or she thinks are most appropriate to treat the condition. The oils are then offered to the horse to sniff: if he shows interest, that is the oil he needs at that time, but if he turns his head away obviously disliking the scent, the oil is inappropriate. Note, too, that the horse's selection and needs may change from day to day, or even according to the time of day.

SELF-HELP

A word of caution: Inappropriate use of the essential oils – in particular, undiluted in another base oil – can be harmful. Unless diluted, commercially available oils are used and the accompanying directions followed, qualified, specialist advice should always be sought from an expert practitioner. Horses may be treated by their owners under the supervision of a practitioner, or treated directly by the practitioner, under veterinary referral in some countries.

Supply and storage: Oils must be kept in a cool, dark place and are usually supplied in dark, opaque, usually glass bottles with the lids

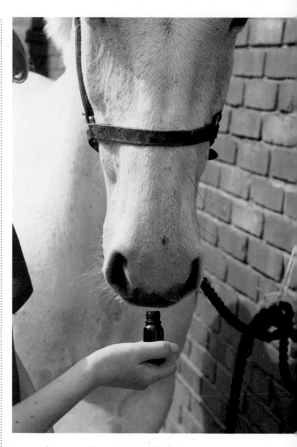

Aromatherapy oils are tested by letting the pony sniff the (securely held) bottle. If he turns away, that is not the oil for him, but if he seems to like it, or even tries to lick or nibble the bottle, his choice is clear

firmly screwed down. They must be kept out of reach of children, animals or the irresponsible. Most users prefer oils which are labelled as being from 'natural', 'organic' or 'wild' sources, and this should be a guarantee of purity and quality.

Using the sense of smell: Natural smells can also be used in the daily management of your horses without using oils at all. For instance, hanging dried lavender in stables is believed to repel flies; cut onions do the same, and are also said to help dispel respiratory infections and allergies.

AROMATHERAPY IN PRACTICE
Caroline Ingraham GEOTA

A member of the Guild of Essential Oil Therapists for Animals, Caroline trained as an aromatherapist in 1984. Her interest in essential oils was sparked after she used them with great success on her own German Shepherd dog, a rescue case, to alleviate fear and encourage appetite. So fascinated was she with the beneficial effects that oils could produce that she worked with a vet in America for two years and discovered that the dramatic results obtained by using oils on horses made them a popular choice of natural therapy.

Following her return to the UK, Caroline found a great demand for her expertise, and as well as writing books on the subject, she now holds courses covering all aspects of aromatherapy for horses as well as other animals.

Caroline Ingraham allowing a patient to lick the oils it wants from her hand

Case History

This case history is a good illustration of smell selection – how horses select the healing oil(s) they feel they need in order to restore mental and/or physical health.

Horse: A 'rescue case' who had been severely beaten with a rake. The rake had become embedded in his hindquarters and he'd bolted, galloping for about a mile with the rake hanging from his side.

PROBLEM: Not surprisingly he was extremely nervous and spooked at everything. His new owner had tried everything she knew to help the gelding overcome his fear and mistrust, but to no avail, so she turned to

Caroline Ingraham for help and advice.

The horse displayed intense nervous behaviour and deep distrust of anything he was unsure of, including people and other animals. This made him extremely unpredictable to handle and ride. Said his despairing owner, 'You name it, he was terrified of it!'

Suiting the individual

Caroline advises: 'I think you cannot label some essential oils as "safe" and others as "unsafe": it's important to consider each oil and animal as individual; what suits one may not suit another.'

TREATMENT: Caroline offered the gelding a selection of five oils she'd muscle-tested him for (see Kinesiology for an explanation of this) and that he had responded to. He chose five: rose, for past trauma; neroli (orange blossom), for depression, nervous disorders and sadness; frankincense, for fear; jasmine, which is quite euphoric; and violet leaf, for nervousness.

He wanted to lick the rose, neroli and violet leaf oils from his owner's hand, and instead of using the top of his tongue, as is more usual, he used the underside of it, which transfers the oils' healing properties into the blood faster. So, even more fascinating to see, the gelding was controlling the speed at which he wanted the oils to go into his body. Explains Caroline: 'Horses can guide their treatment exactly by choosing to sniff or taste oils depending on which curative effect their bodies need.'

Top tip from Caroline

'Never offer too many oils for a horse to choose from because they will lose their identification, and therefore effect, after five or six at any one time.'

The gelding then encouraged his owner to apply frankincense to his nostrils by rubbing his nose into her hand, but he did not want to lick it; and on this occasion he would not allow the jasmine to be applied at all. Says Caroline: 'He kept turning his head away when I offered to dab the jasmine oil on his nostrils, neither did he want to lick it from my hand. He simply wanted to sniff the bottle occasionally, going into a trance when he did so and deeply inhaling its scent for a long time. Once he'd had enough of the oils he told his owner by losing interest in them and moving away. About an hour later

Pour the oil from the bottle into your hand before applying it as directed by the aromatherapist

his owner took him out for a gentle hack with some other horses and riders. Whilst walking down a road, the horses spooked at a plastic bag and shot off, stampeding some cows in a field alongside, but the gelding simply stood still and looked calmly at all the commotion before walking on again. Before using the oils he would have spooked even more violently than the other horses!

'The following day his owner offered the oils again and he didn't want the frankincense – the oil for fear – at all. Interestingly enough, though, he wanted to lick the jasmine and the other three oils originally offered, and continued wanting to do this on a daily basis for a further two weeks. He was guiding which oils he needed, how and when.'

RESULT: The gelding is now a calm horse, showing no signs of his previous problems. Says Caroline: 'If oils are going to work, they do so extremely quickly. Some ailments, such as mud fever or sweet itch, may return to a lesser degree, if they return at all, and the oils that they responded to before can be brought out again; or there may be another underlying cause for an ailment to return and this will need to be checked out.'

Tellington Touch
Equine Awareness Method

The Tellington Touch Equine Awareness Method is a complete physical and psychological system of training horses using a series of carefully devised groundwork exercises and a method of touching or lightly moving the skin over the body in specific ways (called TTouches), and of moving parts of the body, such as the legs, in a non-habitual way, rather like Feldenkrais for horses.

These techniques aim to teach the horse fuller awareness of his own body. The idea is to use the entire method to improve a horse's physical balance and co-ordination, increase his or her athleticism, reduce stress and promote relaxation, and to introduce a new sense of mutual awareness between horse and owner which will improve communication and deepen understanding between the two.

EVOLUTION

The Tellington Touch Equine Awareness Method (TTeam) was devised gradually over the years by Canadian trainer Linda Tellington-Jones. Apart from sound equine physical and psychological training techniques for groundwork and riding, it also employs ways of touching horses which Linda later realised were based on the ancient and traditional principles of acupressure. The technique is based on the concept that many horses resist their riders or simply hold back because of lack of trust, or from physical tension and soreness in the body which affects their behaviour and work.

TTeam around the world: TTeam and the TTouches are recognised

Kathy leads Dessie through the TTeam labyrinth. This is the first time he has done anything like this. A highly-strung horse, he calmed down very quickly when actually asked to think! He follows Kathy's example as she bends down by lowering his head (nearly always a calming influence if not forced) and following where she is pointing with the white TTeam wand. Dessie made it successfully to the end of the labyrinth. At 17.2hh, he negotiated the turns with no trouble

What is TTeam used for?

Some of the problems which have been cured with TTeam include:

- loading and travelling difficulties
- horses who refuse to be tied up
- or who won't leave the yard
- napping and rearing
- pulling and bolting
- competition nerves
- lack of attention ·
- lack of respect for, or 'connection' with the handler

The techniques and whole-method holistic approach teaches the horse to be aware of himself, to calm down, and to listen to his people.

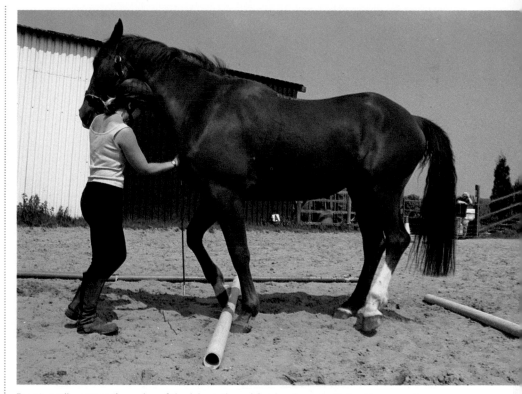

Dessie walks across the poles of the labyrinth and finishes by actually backing over them, helped by gentle pressure on his chest

around the world now, although the method started in the USA, and it is a technique used for any horse from casual pleasure horses to international competitors. It is by no means a therapy or system for training only green or spoiled horses, but any horse which requires a different outlook on life, something different to do, which needs to calm down, to learn to concentrate – or simply for horses and owners who need a closer relationship.

HOW CAN IT HELP?

This method is particularly good for horses who are not living life to the full, such as abused horses, frightened or nervous ones, and those which have chronic injuries or other conditions which affect their body and physical abilities, or which cause them frequent distress or pain.

The special circular TTeam Touches are mainly done with the pads of the fingers and have a beneficial and soporific effect on the horse. There are many variations to these touches

However, it also improves the performance, co-operation and attitude of virtually all horses; thus bossy horses learn manners, and kindly, defensive ones learn to trust, lazy ones learn to enjoy work and excitable ones learn to calm down and relax.

HOW DOES IT WORK?

The TTouches: These are all named after animals and animal movements which Linda felt were most appropriate to the motion or its intention. They can be used on the ground or from the saddle, and really seem to relax horses and get them to concentrate. They particularly appear to help horses think about their own bodies and become more spatially aware.

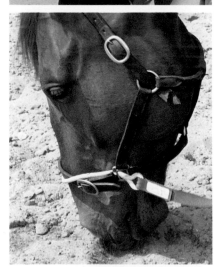

The TTeam Zephyr lead clipped to the offside of the headcollar/halter, passing down through the side dee, over the nose and through the dee on the other side. This gives gentle but significant control for a sensitive horse. There is also a TTeam lead with a chain rather than a rope section (not shown here)

Groundwork: A main feature of the groundwork used is the way horses are led, and the construction of patterns of poles used for teaching them to look where they are going, and to co-ordinate and think about their own movements.

The Tellington lead is a leadrope with a length of chain attached to the end of it which is passed through one of the headcollar side dees, wound once round the noseband, through the dee on the other side and clipped to the top ring on that side. The chain can be changed over when it is desired to lead from the other side. This is an American method of leading horses safely, giving control without pain if used correctly. It is used in conjunction with:

The Tellington wand, a white schooling-length whip which is used both as a guide, and to attract and keep the horse's attention – never for punishment. The leader can adopt various positions to lead the horse, sometimes with a helper on the other side, according to what they are trying to achieve.

Tellington lungeing is carried out with the Tellington lead – shorter than a traditional lunge-rein – and the wand, and is done on an oval with the trainer going with the horse much more, rather than standing in the centre of a circle. A 'body rope' can be used, in a figure-of-eight shape, on the horse to help him feel more 'together', and to encourage resistant or lazy horses to go forwards; and a similar item, but made from soft, stretchy bandages and called the 'body wrap', can be used for more nervous horses who do

not use themselves properly or who tend to rush.

The riding work: This features various techniques including a Western curb training bit with copper roller, specially balanced to encourage a horse to hold his head naturally; the Lindell, a bitless bridle which is good for riders whose hands are not as good as they might be, and for horses who are teething or who have mouth problems; and a stiffened rope loop or circle called the 'lariat', used to steer during bridleless riding.

CAN ANYONE LEARN TTEAM WORK?

Yes: you can learn enough in a weekend workshop with a qualified practitioner to make good, practical use of the methods at home. There

are books and videos about it, too, for home interest and study. However, as with most training methods and therapies you can only go so far on your own and most practitioners would be happy to come to your home to give you private guidance as to how you can use the techniques on your horse. Although not a qualified practitioner Susan McBane uses TTeam regularly with her clients and finds that it ideally complements both Classical Riding and Shiatsu. It really focusses the mind of inattentive, highly-strung horses.

Practitioner training: There are three levels of qualification you can take in TTeam methods if you wish to use it professionally in training or teaching, from Level 1 to Level 3. See Useful Addresses (p186) for contacts.

Left: Pam and Stanley try TTeam lungeing for the first time, using the Zephyr lead and an ordinary schooling whip as Pam does not have a white TTeam wand. The advantage of the white wand is that horses can see it very clearly. Susan McBane uses hers for hacking out: it acts like a blind person's white stick and vehicles coming up from behind seem to take note of it, giving horse and rider more clearance. In TTeam lungeing, the lead is shorter and the handler walks with the horse

Below: At around half Dessie's size, Puzzle makes light work of being ridden through the labyrinth

Centred Riding

Centered riding aims to make riders aware of their bad habits, postures and movements, and then helps them find a way of overcoming them. Imagery is used to improve the body's natural proprioception, and make it aware of its breathing, balance, positional direction or 'steering', and of what is present and going on around it. The rider learns to identify good and bad habits, any particular problems in their riding, and areas of tension in the body and mind, and is enabled to greatly improve them, or remove them altogether.

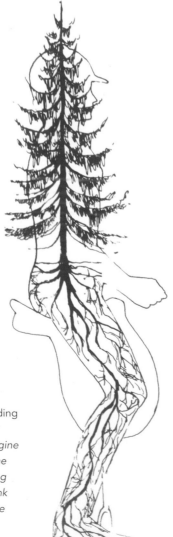

Sally Swift, in her book Centred Riding *provides the rider with this useful analogy. He or she is asked to imagine their body as a spruce tree, with the trunk growing up and roots growing down from their centre. As the trunk grows and becomes more rigid, the roots grow deeper to balance it.*

A partnership therapy

Many faults in riding build up other problems in the rider and actually create problems in the horse, both in his mind and in his way of going, and these are often blamed on him and not on their root cause, which is the rider; centered riding is therefore a partnership therapy, like any other good method of riding – once the rider is improved, the horse improves anyway. The technique sharpens a rider's perception of his own body and environment, improves his sensory abilities, and makes him much more self-aware and so able to correct himself even when the teacher is not present; and this is important in all riding, otherwise one never improves. Moreover this method does seem to produce quite quick results.

EVOLUTION

When American teacher and author Sally Swift devised her 'centered riding' system a few decades ago, it was a revelation in the horse world. At that time most riding teaching was very orthodox, and such subjects as 'mind over matter' were regarded by many as being in the realms of the ethereal. Visualisation, hypnosis, confidence-building and other now accepted techniques were seen as 'a bit queer', and many students considered those who were teaching with the help of these methods to be 'a bit queer' too. However, Sally Swift persisted with her method, and her confidence in it remained unshaken, and because of her determination it first took a hold in the United States.

How does Centred Riding help?

It helps people: Students who suffer from such problems as lack of confidence, competition nerves, inability to perform as their instructors asked, tenseness and so on, have been greatly helped by centered riding techniques; these mainly depend on centreing one's consciousness, developing relaxation and concentration, and visualising certain situations with a view to improving mental and physical performance.

It helps horses: Horses are extremely sensitive animals, and many people believe that those which do not appear to be so, have actually learned to 'switch themselves off' because the instructions and messages coming from their riders and handlers are so inconsistent and confusing. Centered riding may not be a complementary therapy as such, but the authors feel that it is as much a therapy as, say, hypnosis or autogenic training in that it works on the same principles for what are basically mental or psychological difficulties – not disorders, but perhaps problems of perception or confidence – and it has certainly helped many horse and rider combinations around the world to overcome these and improve their partnerships and performances.

HOW DOES IT WORK?

The main aim of centered riding is to make the body aware of itself in space, of what it is doing, and what the horse's body is doing, and to forge a link between the two. It especially emphasises the release of tension which blocks the movements of both horse and rider: the rider cannot feel what the horse is doing underneath him if his muscles are hardened with tension and his joints are not moving in a shock-absorbing way. Centered riding aims to help riders develop the capacity to promote softness and relaxation, so that movement can be felt and controlled. Its four main techniques are:

'Soft eyes': These employ the rider's peripheral vision and awareness of the environment. Riders are encouraged not to focus hard on one place, but to think of relaxing the muscles around the eyes and to remain aware of their periphery.

Breathing: The rider must imagine the inhaled air passing all the way down to the body's centre, level with the pelvis, pushing out the tummy and pushing out the exhaled air in a puff.

Centering: This is the ability to direct your energy or self through the centre of your body, and centered riding instructors teach students to find this for themselves by leaning forwards and backwards until they find a balance which is naturally comfortable for them individually. It is located in the pelvic area in front of the lumbar vertebrae. One suggestion is to think of a single eye in the middle of the pelvis looking in the direction in which the rider wishes to go.

Building blocks: Each part of the body is envisaged as a separate entity placed one on top of the other, and this aids perception and control. Riders are taught to concentrate on absorbing the horse's movements, through their seat from the horse's back via the saddle, more in their hip joints than in the lumbar part of the spine. The technique of 'rotating the hips' in an oval or egg shape – either an upright egg or one on its side – also helps many riders to absorb the movement, and most claim to need much less 'leg' to initiate and maintain movement and impulsion in the horse.

SELF HELP

For those able to use visualisation techniques – and not everyone finds it helpful – centered riding has much to offer. Those interested in it would make a good start by buying Sally Swift's book: this is now a standard text, in which the practical application of the technique is clearly explained. There are instructors who are qualified in her techniques, and Sally herself, now in her eighties, is still actively teaching, mainly in America. If you cannot find a qualified centered riding teacher, the book is so clear that you will be able to apply its techniques yourself, maybe with a sensitive instructor who is also interested in it.

Classical Riding

The spirit of classicism embraces simplicity, harmony and restraint in all things, and is recognised in music and the arts, architecture, in the social graces and in many other aspects of life; in relation to equitation it aims to teach lightness, harmony, and mutual co-operation to the highest levels of technique.

The classical era is thought of as the time of the ancient civilisations of Greece, Rome and also Byzantium. Horse enthusiasts interested in classical riding invariably know about Xenophon, the Greek military commander whose *The Art of Horsemanship*, has survived to this day and can be read with advantage by anyone interested in horse psychology, training, management and riding.

PHILOSOPHY: IS CLASSICAL RIDING A THERAPY?

Classical riding in its truest sense of kindness, lightness and mutual co-operation with the horse can certainly be regarded as a therapy for both horse and rider. Classically trained horses invariably have very strong musculo-skeletal systems due to the gymnastic development of their bodies, and classically trained riders are also fit and flexible because riding makes them so. In fact, good riding is excellent exercise for human and horse, and exercise of the right sort and in moderation is nearly always beneficial – except in cases of some injuries, although controlled exercise is sometimes an important part of the rehabilitation process.

A (w)holistic system of riding: There is an old saying which goes: 'The best thing for the inside of a man is the outside of a horse': but these days, riders (particularly classical) are just as much interested in how their horses tick – in other words, the modern concept of 'body/mind/spirit' relates to the horse as well as to his rider: a (w)holistic system of riding.

Positive physical benefits: The horse's back is the site of many acupuncture points, and non-painful pressure on them from a comfortable saddle may stimulate them, with relevant benefits. Exercise which taxes the body carefully not only promotes strength but, in the Eastern concept of energy flow along channels or meridians, will stretch and stimulate those meridians and promote energy flow, and the production of the body's own uplifting chemicals, the endorphins and encephalins.

HOW DOES IT WORK?

The horse: Correct riding teaches the horse to work with his belly up, his back slightly raised and rounded, his hindquarters and legs lowered and under his body, and his neck and head pushed voluntarily up and forwards from underneath; it develops the musculature of the horse in such a way that he can carry the weight of a rider, and work athletically under him or her, with little risk of injury from stress and strain. This type of work is definitely therapeutic, especially for horses who have previously been worked badly.

The rider: This does presuppose that a rider can assume and maintain the correct position, that well known but often disregarded classical seat, in which an imaginary, vertical straight line may be dropped from the ear, through the shoulder and hip (by which the elbow should usually be) and down the back of the heel. There should be slight tension in the upper body sufficient to hold it in self-carriage, with the shoulders held gently back and down, and the chest lifted slightly. Holding the stomach forwards is also recommended by many experts. The seatbones should be in the central, lowest part of the saddle, the pelvis, lumbar spine and hip joints absorbing and 'going with' the movements of the horse's back so as to harmonise with them, and not block his action and, therefore, his

The late Reiner Klimke, shown here with Ahlerich, was one of the greatest Classical competitive riders of our time, proving that there is no need for a gap between the two fields. Sadly, whilst many competitive riders and trainers praise him, not many appear to emulate his techniques and ethos

willingness and ability to comply with the rider's wishes.

'A good seat', and particularly 'good hands', are phrases which had largely disappeared from modern equestrian terminology; however, they are gradually returning with classical riding. 'Equestrian tact' is also a quality of classical ethos which relates to the rider being willing and able to work with the horse's mind and spirit, and not expecting him to operate like a mere physical automaton.

Working together: When these things are present, the spiritually uplifting and surely therapeutic effect on horse and rider is considerable, the beneficial physical effects on both are marked, and the mental pleasure and satisfaction of working together in the triple harmony of body, mind and spirit is a revelation to those privileged to achieve and experience it.

HOW CAN IT HELP ME AND MY HORSE?

The performances given by the remaining major classical academies of the world – such as the Spanish Riding

School in Vienna, the Cadre Noir of Saumur in France and the schools of Spain, Portugal and the Netherlands – may be considered inspiring or daunting depending on your aims and self-confidence; however, to ride classically you don't have to perform High School airs. Simply riding basic movements well, with the rider sitting and moving correctly, and the horse in the correct classical posture for his level of training, is riding classically and may be all that many riders want to do.

Furthermore, correctly (classically) trained horses at any level of work or performance are known to be able to work to a far greater age than those which are not so ridden, or which are actually abused because the physical stresses on and incorrect development of the latter – not to mention the possible injuries sustained by incorrect ways of going – shorten their physical comfort and abilities – their soundness, in short. In our modern society most horses unable to work (often through no fault of their own) are destroyed for economic reasons.

SELF HELP

There are many books available on pure classical riding of various schools and on 'new wave' horsemanship promoted by what are often called 'horse whisperers', whose methods could actually be described as classical *if* they promote the classical ideals of co-operation and harmony.

A great deal can be learned from these books – and yes, it is possible to learn to ride from books provided you put it into practice. A knowledgable eye on the ground is also invaluable. Learning to ride well is a combination of theory and practice, and although there are classical trainers around to help and advise, regularly or sporadically according to your abilities and pocket, you can certainly help yourself along by reading, watching suitable videos, attending displays, and working on your own.

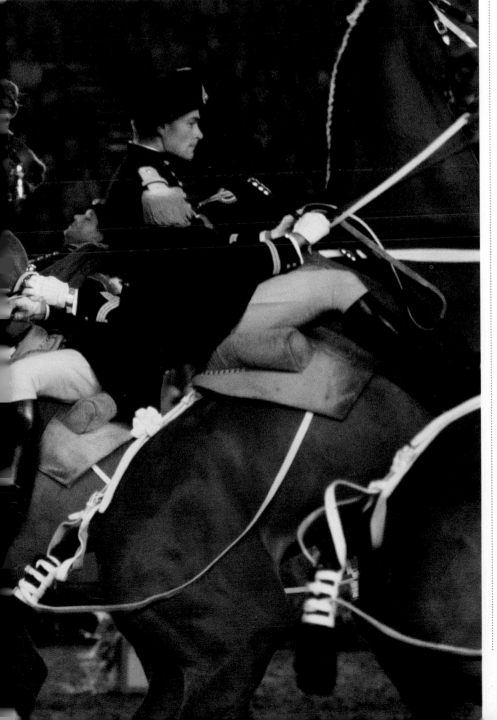

The Cadre Noir of Saumur differs slightly from other classical schools which use Iberian and Lippizaner horses as the French tend to favour more highly-bred blood horses such as their famous Anglo-Arab and Selle Française breeds. Their technique and principles appear to have a stronger military influence than some other schools

Groundwork

Working horses from the ground is an excellent rehabilitation therapy for use after injury or sickness and when expertly done, for improving gait abnormalities.

Some think of it as mainly a training, schooling technique, and as a means of exercising horses when we simply haven't the time and/or the inclination to tack up and ride. These attitudes are perfectly relevant, but they miss a vital and possibly even more important aspect of working horses from the ground: that of building up a horse's strength and technique without subjecting him to the difficulties of carrying weight or trying to obey a human's wishes when hampered by that weight, however expertly controlled.

WHY IS GROUNDWORK OF PARTICULAR BENEFIT?

Groundwork, if well done, exercises muscles in a much more natural way than when we sit on a horse, provided he is not restricted (rather than guided, if essential) by wrongly applied aids and rider movements. Horses feel much freer to go in a strength-building and, at the same time, relaxing way, with 'both ends down and the middle up' – in other words, with the hindquarters and hind legs coming well under the horse providing thrust, with the head and neck pushed forwards and down, and the abdominal muscles (and others) contracted to raise and support the spine from underneath. Without a rider the horse also feels freer to swing along in his back and hips, and to reach out with his shoulders and let his tail follow fluidly behind, creating a beautiful, satisfying picture for the onlooker and an enjoyable physical experience for the horse.

An enjoyable experience: When encouraged to work in this way, nearly every horse takes to it very happily, and seems actually relieved to be allowed to stretch and 'go round'. Many horses appear to want to do this when ridden but, for one reason or another, are prevented from doing so – perhaps by an uncomfortable saddle and girth, or by 'blocking' riding techniques. (A tactful rider will permit the horse just the right amount of forward and downward movement in the head and neck whilst still receiving and controlling the energy created by the hindquarters.) Correct groundwork eliminates adverse influences, and enables the horse to really move and enjoy himself.

A rehabilitation programme: This non-weight-bearing way of working correctly is ideal for building the correct riding muscles, and is the second stage in most rehabilitation programmes. It can be used with advantage at any time during a working horse's routine (two or three twenty- to thirty-minute sessions a week can do nothing but good), and

Horse at liberty showing full expression of movement. Groundwork is essential for allowing the horse to restore and maintain its natural grace and balance without the weight and interference of a rider and their attendant tack and equipment

can be used as a pre-ride warm-up and suppling session; as a gymnastic exercise to work the horse correctly all over; almost as a playtime for him, or at least a very enjoyable sort of activity with his owner or handler; and finally as exercise for its own sake.

WHAT METHODS CAN I USE?

LEADING IN HAND

This is probably the most underestimated and valuable activity you can perform with your horse.

What good does it do him? It allows him to loosen up, stretch out, enjoy a leg-stretch, contract and relax muscles naturally, and gets the blood flowing properly through them. From a mental point of view, it is entertaining for him to be taken out and about in a much more relaxed atmosphere than it would be were he being ridden, allowing him to exercise fairly naturally but in a controlled way without carrying weight. This question of not bearing weight does not mean that the time is wasted: his muscles are working correctly, and the blood is flowing, bringing oxygen and nutrients and removing waste products which, if allowed to build up, create an unhealthy environment within the muscles with subsequent lack of performance – these two factors alone can only enhance correct and healthy muscle development.

Where shall I take him? The work does not have to be done entirely at walk: jogging along beside your

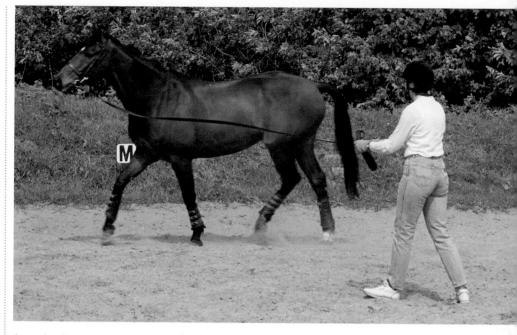

Lungeing is a very common groundwork technique but often done incorrectly, with horses being sent in constant circles at too fast a pace. Here, Stanley and his owner, Pam, show a calm, unhurried trot, although not yet working properly. Stanley wears only headgear, no roller or saddle, and because he panics when lunged with a lungeing whip, Pam does not use one and finds it unnecessary

horse acts as aerobic exercise for you, too! Depending on your environment, you might take the horse out on roads and lanes, or around your premises on tracks, or across uneven ground to help build thoughtfulness, the habit of looking where he is going, balance and agility.

What shall I lead him in? Quiet horses can be led in a headcollar or cavesson, though others may need a nose-chain which offers far more control than a bridle. The lack of a bit

makes it easier for the horse to graze during breaks. A normal-length leadrope is neither comfortable nor safe, and a lead about 3.5 to 4.5m (12 to 15ft) – gives much more leeway should the horse jump around.

LUNGEING

Lungeing is the next step most people would use in a groundwork rehabilitation programme, but again, this should be very carefully monitored if you are not to end up doing more harm than good.

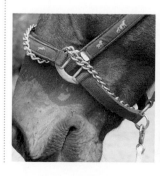

Heavyweight dog choke chain wrapped all round the noseband with the leadrope clip fastened to its rings

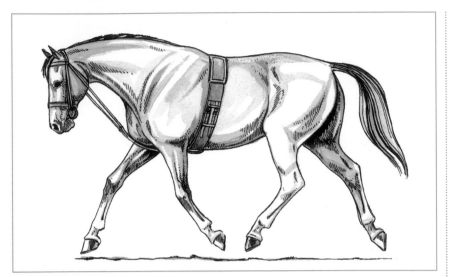

The Chambon promotes a good head, neck and forehand posture but has no direct effect on the hindquarters which are however encouraged to come under and thrust the horse forward from behind

The de Gogue in the independent fitting is another excellent lungeing aid which has a similar effect to the Chambon but with more influence. It is better used for slightly more advanced horses as, if fitted incorrectly, it can cause the horse to become overbent

Equipment needed: You can use a well fitting lungeing cavesson, a bridle, a headcollar with a nose-chain, or just a headcollar with the line fastened to the jaw dee, or combinations of these, depending on the manners and level of education of the horse.

Schooling aids: These should be chosen with very great care, and adjusted likewise.

Side-reins are of absolutely no benefit whatsoever if they are at all tight – and even if they are adjusted so that the horse has just a feel on them (either to the bit or the

cavesson side-rings) when he is standing still normally, when he tries to stretch down and out – usually one of the crucial elements of a rehabilitation groundwork programme – he will be prevented from doing so and will be forced to bring his nose behind the vertical. This can result in strain and injury to t he tissues around the poll – exactly what we do not want.

What schooling aids should do: Probably the best training aids for encouraging a horse to go beneficially on the lunge are the *Chambon*, the *de Gogue* in the independent fitting, the *Tellington bodywrap* or *bodyrope*, and possibly some of the newer aids such as the *Pessoa*. Whatever aid is chosen, it must both encourage and allow the horse to assume the correct working posture of his own free will: it must certainly not in any way force him to go 'in an outline', because then he will not, in effect, be doing so by using the right muscles voluntarily; and as we have said, it must also certainly not prevent him from moving naturally, or from reaching forward and down, or restrict his movement when he tries to do so, forcing him to become overbent. This is not rehabilitation, or even beneficial work, but is positively damaging to his physique and attitude.

Lungeing techniques: A good deal of work should be done in walk to let the horse realise that he can move freely, and that nothing is going to restrict him in any way. Gentle trotting can eventually be introduced, and ultimately canter, with the emphasis always on correct, natural, free, voluntary movement and posture.

The horse should not be asked to perform endless circles: the trainer or handler should walk with the horse much more than is generally the norm, so that he moves in straight lines and large ovals, and really big circles with the lunge rein let out to its full extent – something rarely seen. Work on circles which are too small, particularly during a rehabilitation programme, puts too much stress on the joints, soft tissues, feet, legs and back, and the horse will often then start compensating in his movement to make the work easier, by using the wrong muscles – and you are back to 'square one'.

The attitude of the trainer, of course, dictates whether or not the work is beneficial: if he or she accepts that circles are not *de rigeur* and that the object of the exercise is to help the horse back to health, strength and work, and not to make him perform a perfect circle, then the process becomes much more beneficial.

The Tellington Team method of lungeing: This is a technique something between conventional lungeing and leading in hand, and is much more flexible and accommodating to the horse. Basically, horses are lunged in large ovals on a long lead/half-length lunge-line, and the trainer goes with the horse much more, rather than standing in the middle of a circle with the horse going round and round him.

LONG-REINING

This technique is much more flexible than lungeing; not only can horses be rehabilitated, they can also be educated to a high standard, if the owner wishes – in fact up to High School movements. The long-reins can be attached to a cavesson or to the bit-rings of a bridle if the trainer is sensitive and competent, and changes of direction become easy and fluid once the basic techniques are learned.

Long-reining teaches horses to think for themselves to a greater degree, and they do become more independent if they are long-reined about the place and round the lanes. They do not have such a close contact as with a rider, but they should have an appropriate bit contact and guidance from the

Long-reining is much more versatile and, in practice, interesting than lungeing. This filly's owner is being instructed in the technique by her trainer Tony Hall who in Susan McBane's experience is an absolute natural with horses specialising in traditional methods of backing and riding away (see Useful Addresses, p186). Peggy, the filly, and Shirley, her owner, soon pick up enough basic technique to long-rein on their own

trainer – assuming that he/she is sympathetic and reasonably proficient – who walks or jogs along behind or beside the horse according to the method used (again, walk and trot can be used).

When used as a schooling/ training technique, various school movements and airs can be done on the long-reins.

Long-reining techniques: There are various techniques, and you can always make up your own to suit your circumstances. The standard English/Irish way is to have the near-side long-rein running directly to the trainer's leading hand (the 'inside' rein), with the 'outside' one running down the horse's outside and round his thighs to the trainer's following hand. A saddle can be used, with the stirrups either shortened or run up, through which the reins pass to keep them up, or a schooling or driving roller.

The technique employed in the Spanish Riding School of Vienna for schooled horses during displays uses two half-length long-reins with the handler walking close behind the horse. Then there is the versatile Danish method made known in the UK and Ireland by Miss Sylvia Stanier, LVO, in which a driving roller with rein terrets is used, the reins both passing through these to the trainer's hands.

WORK OVER GROUNDPOLES

There are various techniques involving work over poles on the ground, but this is not the place to go into them all: here we will just discuss the sort of work that a horse being rehabilitated

The TTeam bodywrap is helpful for horses who need to 'get themselves together' psychologically. All TTeam items can be purchased from TTeam offices (see Useful Addresses, p186) and practitioners and are useful additions to more traditional equipment

needs to perform as a therapy. Much will depend on the opinion and advice of the vet, and any other therapist such as a physiotherapist or exercise physiologist who may be helping to restore the horse to strength and fitness.

Why does it help? Generally, work over groundpoles will be included in the exercise regime to encourage the horse to pick up his feet and bring his hind legs well underneath him, so rounding his back properly and pushing himself along from behind, rather than partially pulling himself along from the shoulders, as so many injured horses learn to do (depending on the injury).

Groundwork over poles, with or without some aid to encourage the horse to bring himself together and to round over the poles, also helps to regulate the gait, encourages him to go straight and to move his limbs straight. It is surprising how

polework concentrates a horse's mind, and those who persist in not looking where they are going, or who try to rush or jump groundpoles can be persuaded to lower their heads and concentrate by pointing the way to them with something such as a Tellington white wand: they really look at this, and nearly always end up going straight with their head down and their back end well underneath the body.

Increasing the difficulty: Gradually the number of poles can be increased from one to five or seven and they can be set on a curve rather than in a straight line; they can also be raised slightly on low blocks as the horse becomes stronger and more proficient.

As in all things, it is best to seek the advice of an experienced and preferably qualified exercise therapist when using groundwork as a therapy.

Integration Therapy

'Horse and Rider Integration Therapy' is an individual facet of energy medicine developed by riding instructor and therapeutic masseuse Caroline Dow-Thomas in England. Caroline claims to be able to tune in to the subtle healing energies of horse and rider, which helps her to find the balance and harmony between them, and so help them to overcome their problems and restrictions, and to achieve their aims. She also claims to be able to communicate with the horse, and receive answers to questions about his outlook on life, his routine, his work and his own aims.

PHILOSOPHY

Caroline believes that the whole story of horse and rider is present in their energy fields, and she seems to be one of those few people able to experience the energies of other people and horses. She is also happy to work with other teachers, trainers and therapists because performance and healing are wide ranging and, provided everyone's aims are for the good, there may be much to be gained from other methods and ideas.

Follow our instincts: Many people are more intuitive than they believe, but because they have never really thought about this, they do not use the gift as much as they should, even though they may have hunches and experience intuitive guidance every day. By becoming more aware of ourselves and our horses we can be guided more by natural intuition and gut feelings as to what is right or wrong for ourselves and our horses.

HOW DOES IT WORK?

Busy, modern lives with all their stress and bustle often blank out instinctive messages coming from our inner being: Caroline, with her unique system, spends time with clients encouraging them to slow down, and really consider what their true aims are ('Do you really want to show jump or would you rather just hack around?'); basically she teaches them to reassess what sort of lifestyle would be more fulfilling for them and their horses – who may also in fact prefer a quite different discipline from the one they think he prefers or is good at. Initially, then, she acts as a link between horse and rider, but as the two become better able to tune into each other, she takes more and more of a back seat.

CONTACTING CAROLINE

Caroline's email address are given in the Useful Addresses section of this book (see p186).

What is Integration Therapy used for?

- **To help the rider get rid of stress**: Stress is one of the biggest 'blockers' of communication and performance in the modern world; it automatically causes tense muscles and a closed mind, and this stops everything in its tracks. Horses are exceptionally perceptive and will pick up stress from their rider even though they may not understand what is causing it.

- **To establish balance and harmony**: If the rider can get rid of counter-productive stresses then the true self of both horse and rider can come through, and balance and harmony can be established.

- **To raise your ambitions**: Once people, and horses, realise what they truly want in life, it is surprising how ambitions can change: the truth can give them much more self-confidence and a more relaxed, settled outlook on life, even if their aims have been raised.

- **To resolve physical problems**: This therapy can help horses and riders iron out physical problems and imbalances and psychological ones: body and mind are closely interlinked – clearing one usually frees the other so that balance is restored.

Kinetic Equestrian Training

This is a system of 'feeling riding' developed by Ian Stevenson MS, a sports psychologist whose methods are used by members of the US Olympic team. Described as 'riding with better balance, focus and communication between horse and rider', kinetic equestrian training is a system of being in touch with one's horse at a deeper level of understanding.

HOW DOES IT WORK?

The training teaches riders and owners to use directional breathing as a meaningful communication between themselves and their horses, inviting both to relax and increase the focus between them. By using special breathing techniques when riding, performance can be enhanced, improving transitions, creating and directing impulsion, and maximising contact and balance between horse and rider. In a nutshell, it creates six-legged teamwork between you and your horse.

WHAT DOES IT ACHIEVE?

Owners or handlers experience from the ground ways of working with themselves and their horses. Kinetic techniques are taught which help release stresses and tensions within horse and human: when riding,

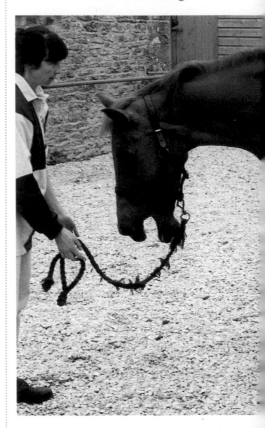

Scanning the energy field of the horse, prior to working hands on. The horse is already starting to listen, relax and respond

these techniques can heighten communication, bringing about a more balanced, focused partnership.

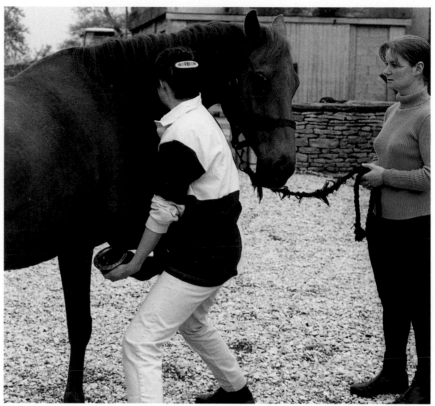

SELF HELP

For further information and training, there is a contact number in Useful Addresses (see p186).

Left: Working hands on with the horse, showing a typical response of lowering the head, stretching, yawning and softening of the eye which indicates calmness and relaxation

Above: Working physically with the horse, by rocking the limbs after energetic hands-on work

Left to right: Sequence showing 'pretzelling' – working homoeopathically with the body to tune into its natural awareness. These exercises act as a warm up before riding

Left: Assessing the rider – noting position to bring awareness of how she's sitting

Centre: Exaggerate how the person is sat for a minute or so, allowing the body to self-organise and bring back symmetry

Right: Unfurl and sit back in a comfortable position. Note the rider's shoulders and chest are more open and even, seat bones are in better contact with saddle and the left foot faces forward more

Faith Healing

Also sometimes called spiritual healing, and 'hands-on' healing, the title 'faith healing' to describe this therapy is probably the most used, and the one that dates back the furthest. It implies that in order to enjoy any benefit, the person being treated must have faith in the method and, presumably, trust in the healer – although healing has been reported in people who were sceptical and tried it out of desperation, often as a last resort.

The late Charles Siddle uses his healing gifts on a pony

A faith healer usually claims to operate not as a healer themselves, but as a medium through which healing comes from other people who have died and passed on to another dimension, but who use the faith healer as a link to this one to enable them to continue to help people still in this life.

PHILOSOPHY

Faith healing (or whatever name you use) is a surprisingly widespread therapy, particularly in human hospitals. Many orthodox doctors and nurses are active, trained healers, and the therapy is actually recognised by the National Health Service in the UK. Unfortunately, very few veterinary surgeons seem to have similar confidence in it, although, as with most complementary therapies these days, they will generally refer a client to a healer, if requested (strictly speaking, referral is unnecessary for such healing).

Human patients have been known to recover against all the odds because they have 'the will to live' and, presumably, 'faith' that a healer is passing on a healing force which will help them. It may well be that, as far as humans are concerned, the optimism and faith they have causes the production of 'feel good' hormones and perhaps other substances which have a strengthening effect on the immune system, thereby creating a chemically hostile environment for pathogens, or alternatively perhaps producing a more favourable environment for healing. But how can this help animals, who have no human-type conception of faith or hope?

Everyone's aura: One theory put forward is that every person and animal has an energy field or aura, a spiritual template, surrounding them which also interweaves with their physical body and is closely concerned with health. If the health and functioning of the body and the mind are in a state of balance, the aura, appearing as colours, will reflect this to those who can see it. If the aura appears unbalanced, weak or congested in any way, the healer becomes a support system for the person or animal, helping to balance the energy field and flow through the body.

If you cannot see auras, this does not mean that you cannot heal. Many people, such as doctors, care professionals, mothers of all species, animal owners, close friends, spouses and partners, can heal those they care about if they have an optimistic and caring attitude.

How effective is it?

One of the authors was told of a clinically depressed person who was asked to hold a glass of water containing seeds before planting. They failed to grow. Another glass, elsewhere, was held by a faith healer before planting. All his seeds (from the same batch) grew well. Traditional Eastern therapies often work on the basis of not only balancing and encouraging the flow of a patient's own energy or life force (Chi or Ki), but also of passing on beneficial energy through the practitioner's own body, when needed, and allowing 'bad' energies to pass out. These therapies are so effective, and practitioners and patients have such faith in, and acceptance of them, that no one can surely be in a position to say that this is not happening.

HOW DOES IT WORK?

Faith healers have different methods of working, and some use more than one method. It is not always necessary for the healer to visit, meet or even speak to a patient, though some feel that healing 'in person' is more effective.

Distant healers: Healers who work from a distance sometimes request a photograph of the person or animal needing help; others do not. Distant healers seem to be able to locate and relate to a human or animal patient they are told about, even to the extent of being able to describe them physically and temperamentally. Writing to a healer, or speaking to them on the telephone, on your own or someone else's behalf, including your horse's, is often sufficient for the healer to be able to make contact.

Code of ethics: Healers almost without exception will not try to heal a human patient who refuses treatment. Where the patient is not in a position to make a decision due to their condition, most healers will try to help. With an animal, some healers claim to be able to ask it whether or not it wishes to be healed, and in most cases it does – except when it truly feels that it wishes to pass on.

What does the practitioner feel during healing? Practitioners describe different states: some say that they simply feel warm and energised; some say that they 'know' that healing rays are passing through them for transmission to the patient, near or far, but cannot feel anything themselves; others claim to feel a slight tingling, or a hot or cold current passing through. Some feel exhausted at the end of a session, whereas others feel invigorated.

A word of caution: Faith healing does not always work, by any means, and the answer one usually gets when this happens is 'perhaps healing is not appropriate for you/your horse at this time'. Illness is regarded by many people in this field – whether healer, assistant or patient – as one of the lesson-burdens we are in this life to experience; but healers will try to assist the process to make the lesson understandable and the burden more bearable.

FINDING A HEALER

Some healers are so well known in a particular field that contacting them is fairly easy. Others advertise in personal columns in regional or national newspapers or magazines, in specialist magazines if, for example, they work only on horses (unusual), in health food shops, and premises offering other complementary therapies, and there are a few in various directories such as the telephone book or local business service directories. Word of mouth is certainly a good recommendation, but not a panacea.

As we have already mentioned, many orthodox doctors and nurses are active, trained healers, and the therapy is recognised by the National Health Service in the UK. And although very few veterinary surgeons seem to have similar confidence in it, they will generally refer a client to a healer, if requested. There is a National Federation of Spiritual Healers which has more than 7,000 members, and many are just as happy to work on animals as people. Many more healers are independent of the federation.

FAITH HEALING IN PRACTICE

The late Charles Siddle, member of the Federation of Spiritualist Healers

Charles Siddle (Photos courtesy of Greenshires Publishing)

The son of a London builder, Charles had a public school upbringing before joining the Marine Commandos. Badly injured during the Normandy offensive of World War II, he spent four years in and out of hospital before settling down to life in civvy street doing what he loved best: working with animals. He owned a string of pet shops until his mid-thirties, and enjoyed breeding dogs, showing and stewarding at Crufts.

As a child, Charles had a gift for talking to animals – 'my teachers at school thought there was something radically wrong with me and took me to see a child psychiatrist!' – but it wasn't until he met eminent veterinary surgeon Buster Lloyd Jones in later years, that he slowly came to realise that he had a particular, and special, gift for helping to ease, and even cure, the ailments and trauma of both people and animals.

Recalled Charles: 'Before he passed over some thirty years ago, Buster said to me, "You are a very spiritualist man – you can heal!" I didn't believe him at the time, but about eight years after he passed over he came to me and told me that as I was such a disbeliever he simply had to come back and make me realise that I could heal. After that he talked to me all the time, guiding me to heal. Buster is my guide – faith healers work with a guide, a spiritual person.'

Charles was adamant that he only saw animals that had previously been examined by a vet: 'Spiritualist healers working with veterinary surgeons have a definite code of ethics; they do not diagnose, nor manipulate, and definitely do not prescribe medicines. I can detect what is wrong, and heal, just by putting my hands on a patient. And I am able to provide distant healing, too.'

But does spiritualist healing effect a total cure? Explained Charles:

'Whatever, there is no pain – healing makes the pain go. Whether the ailment, cancer or whatever, has totally gone I don't know – maybe it's in limbo and will come back if something traumatic happens to the patient later on. I believe many cancers are caused by stress. But so long as the pain goes...

'If healing is not meant to work, then it won't. When an animal is old you can take its pain away, but you

cannot make it young again. Sometimes I have said to owners, "You cannot put this animal through any more pain – its time has come."'

Charles worked all over the UK, and reguarly held clinics at The Natural Medicine Veterinary Centre in Potters Bar run by Richard Allport B Vet Med, Vet M FHom, MRCVS. People who experienced his healing powers are too numerous to list, but the following case history serves well to illustrate his rare gift.

CASE HISTORY

Horse: Jessica, a Thoroughbred brood mare.

PROBLEM: Owned by racehorse breeders Jan and Graham Piper, Jessica was suffering from malignant and untreatable lymphosarcoma (cancer of the blood). The Pipers' vet had advised she be put down on humane grounds as there was no cure. Says Jan:

'Jessica was covered in lumps and open sores, some the size of tennis balls, including one in her throat which meant she couldn't eat. That's when we knew there was no hope of saving her. In fact we had booked the vet to come and put her down, but in a last-ditch effort to save her I called Charles to see if he could help. I didn't believe in this sort of thing at all, but a friend of mine recommended him, having experienced his powers for herself. Anyway, I really didn't have anything to lose.'

TREATMENT: Says Jane, 'Well, Charles came and I wasn't sure what to expect. He simply took off her rug, laid his hands over every inch of her body before re-rugging her and giving us instructions not to take her rug off until the vet came to put her down a couple of days later. The whole process only took five minutes.'

RESULT: 'The morning after Charles' visit Jessica was kicking at her stable door demanding her breakfast – and she ate it all up, too. This was the same mare that couldn't physically eat and was at death's door the previous day! We were dying to take off her rug and see if anything had happened, but Charles had told us not to, so we just had to wait.

'The vet duly arrived, we took off the rugs – and none of us could believe our eyes: all the lumps had gone bar one small mark.' Commented Jessica's vet at the time, 'This is a case I don't talk about as I cannot explain why she is still alive.'

Jessica went on to produce six foals, including the foal she was carrying at the time of her healing, which was born perfectly well. He was named Charlie Siddle and given to Charles as a thank-you gift. He ran under Charles' colours and gave his owner great joy.

Jessica died in 1999, aged fifteen; she'd had six good years of 'borrowed time' which she wouldn't otherwise have had without Charles' healing. Her remarkable story was featured on the television programme *Strange But True* in 1995.

Jessica and her colt foal, Charlie Siddle, born April 1994 (Picture courtesy of Jan Piper)

Reiki

Reiki is the ability to heal and help people by the simple laying on of hands. It is an energy therapy – 'rei' meaning 'universal' and 'ki' meaning 'energy' (pronounced 'rayki') – in that it brings the energy from the environment through the practitioner, who is the healing medium, and into the patient or recipient. It is very calming and invigorating for both practitioner and recipient, and claims to give relief from distressing, uncomfortable and painful symptoms. Reiki can also be sent from a distance, and can be used on both individuals and groups.

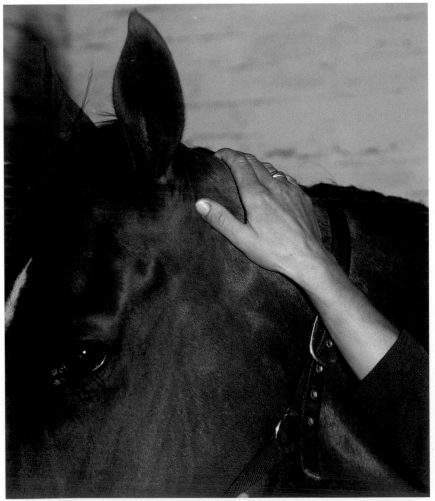

A Reiki practitioner channels energy from the environment into the patient. Horses appear to be sensitive to Reiki treatment, but accept it well the more they experience it

PHILOSOPHY

The ancient healing art of the 'laying on of hands' has probably always seemed a bit of a mystery to most people, something we may have read about in the Bible and similar texts. But what was it, and how did it work? No description was ever made of anything resembling massage or manipulation, or even of the recipient's body being moved at all, just hands being simply laid on. Also there seems to be little mention of it in post-Roman texts, though presumably it carried on quietly in the 'East'.

Then towards the end of the nineteenth century, a certain Dr Mikao Usui, a Christian headmaster of a Japanese university, seemingly set out to discover the truth about the laying on of hands, and also about the miraculous healing powers of Christ and his disciples (and others). By fasting and meditating for twenty-one days on a sacred mountaintop, he finally perceived golden Sanskrit (Indian) symbols, each of which had healing purposes, and he became able to heal, passing on his powers to others. Another version of his story is that he rediscovered the art in ancient Sanskrit literature.

HOW DOES IT WORK?

It is not necessary to place the hands on the painful or sensitive part, because the energy directed by Reiki seems to be attracted to wherever in the body it is needed, almost like electricity going to metal or water. This means that a headshy horse, for instance, does not have to tolerate

What is Reiki used for?

Reiki can be used to relieve distressing symptoms of physical disorders, mental or psychological problems, and simply general unhappiness, tension and so on, in people and animals. It can be used:

- to calm competition nerves in horses and people
- to invigorate them when they have worked hard or been under stress
- to help healing after veterinary or medical treatment
- to relax horses frightened of travelling, those in pain, the generally nervous
- to strengthen the body's resistance to disease
- to help remove and prevent over-stress

In short, it can complement most other forms of orthodox and complementary therapies.

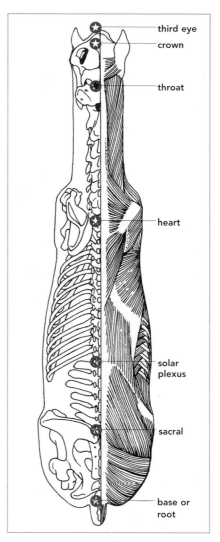

Seven main chakras of the horse

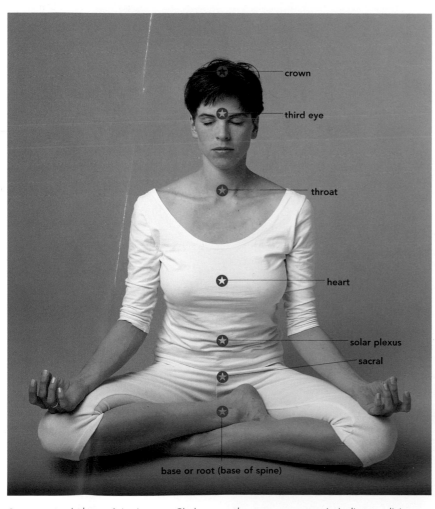

Seven main chakras of the human. Chakras are the energy centres in Indian medicine found along the main meridians

his ears being stroked, because touching him anywhere else on his body will help him. When Reiki is performed on horses, they tend to stand quietly, sensing that this is a different kind of touch.

Can anyone learn it? Reiki is not exactly learnt; rather, an appropriate student is 'attuned' or initiated into it by a teacher. By 'appropriate' is meant that the student must genuinely want to help and heal, and they must be able to 'let go' after a healing session and not dwell on it. There are various degrees of Reiki:

Reiki I: self-healing and helping family, friends and pets;

Reiki II: distant healing and the psychological and emotional aspects of healing; and

Reiki Master: concentrating on spiritual aspects and teaching.

It seems that you do not need to have any special sensitivity to become able to use Reiki; however, the type of people interested in this sort of therapy are normally sensitive, caring individuals anyway, and the more you use it, as in so many things, the more effective your abilities become.

HOW CAN REIKI HELP?

Reiki for humans: Reiki is widely used on humans, not only in hospitals and by professional healthcare workers, but by anyone who has been attuned and educated in its use. A full Reiki treatment on a person may take up to an hour and a half, the recipient being fully clothed and under no pressure or stress of any kind.

Reiki for horses: Horses seem to be very sensitive to Reiki treatment, and sometimes take a little while to get used to it, but they accept it well the more they experience it. A treatment for a horse usually lasts around half an hour. During a first treatment horses sense that something different is happening and, depending on the individual, may be restless at first; but usually they then become calm, and may even become dozy, and 'mouth', yawn and gently chomp – and when they have had enough, they move quietly away.

Coping with stress: Horses today lead very unnatural and often stressful lives: they evolved as free-living creatures, yet today they are all effectively slaves, with no real control over their lives at all, and often kept in totally unsuitable conditions. Although not a substitute for good veterinary or other complementary treatment, or for sound, appropriate management and congenial work, Reiki can help them to cope with their artificial lives.

Preventative Reiki: Reiki also has a preventative role, helping to

Side effects of a Reiki session are the horse at first being restless, but becoming calm, even dozy, often 'mouthing', yawning and gently chomping.

strengthen the body's resistance to disease, and to energise and to help remove and prevent over-stress which so often makes the individual more susceptible to disease because it weakens the body.

Reiki for temperament: Behavioural problems, often caused by insecurity and fear in the horse, lack of a bond or any real communication between horse and owner, or lack of congenial yard or pasture mates, have been greatly helped by Reiki which instils confidence and peace, enables blocked energy to flow evenly, and helps body, mind and spirit to heal and balance themselves.

HOW CAN I FIND A REIKI PRACTITIONER?

Often word of mouth will lead you to someone suitable. You may find a few names and numbers in your local directories, and there are contacts in Useful Addresses (p186) which will help you.

A headshy horse can be touched anywhere on his body in order to help him

Horse Whispering

Horse whispering has become synonymous in the horse world with horsemen and women who seem to have an extraordinary, inborn ability to 'tame' wild and difficult horses. The term is at least a couple of hundred years old, although such people were more usually called just 'whisperers' then. They included the likes of Sydney Galvayne, John Solomon Rarey (probably the most famous of all time – so far) and Dan Sullivan, and they were renowned for their ability to quieten the most vicious and temperamental of animals.

HISTORICAL BACKGROUND

Traditionally whisperers would be asked to give displays in front of royalty and at village fetes and other festivals and celebrations, as well as with circuses and other entertainments. Their techniques have not always been passed down to us, but from perusal of old books, it seems that a lot of them realised the importance of dominating a horse on his own terms in order to tame him. Horses were tied up and down, blindfolded, 'thrown' (brought to the ground), and what Americans and Australians call today 'sacked out' – that is, sacking was flopped and wiped all over the horse to make it submit to being touched anywhere. Some cruel techniques were used, of course, as they are in some societies today; but basically, once the horse realised that the man was 'boss', there was no more trouble – although word has it that many were 'broken' in spirit. It seems that some reverted to their old ways once the whisperer departed. The old-time whisperers, it seemed, were loathe to instruct their clients and audiences in how to carry on the good work, unlike today's variety.

The horse's 'friendly charm': There were exceptions. One of the early revivers of classical equitation in the seventeenth century, Antoine de Pluvinel, is famously quoted as having said: 'We shall take great care not to annoy the horse and spoil his friendly charm, for it is like the scent of a blossom – once lost, it will never return.' How *very* true this is: even if we manage to 'reform' a horse through kind treatment, if he ends up once again in rough hands, he will revert to his 'vicious' behaviour.

'WHISPERING' TODAY

So what about today's variety of 'horse whisperer'? Probably the best known name is that of Monty Roberts, but there are many more, such as Pat Parelli (*Natural HorseManShip*), Michael Peace (*Think Equus*), John Lyons, Kel Jeffrey (*The Jeffrey Method of Horse Handling*), Ray Hunt (*Think Harmony*), Buck Brannaman, Mark Rashid, Tom and Bill Dorrance (*True Unity*), Richard Maxwell, Richard Shrake (*Resistance-Free Riding*), Frank

---

What is Horse Whispering used for?

Most psychological and behavioural problems experienced by horses and their owners can be alleviated, if not resolved, by a horse whisperer. He/she would almost certainly be able to:

- improve communication and understanding between an owner/rider and his/her horse
- help handling difficulties: loading, travelling, leading in hand, stable manners
- resolve a horse's behavioural problems: nappiness, rearing, bucking, bolting, shying
- calm down a difficult/temperamental/highly strung horse
- start a young horse: teach it to accept the handler's touch, right through to being ridden
- discover, through communication, any physical problems, so a solution/cure can be arrived at

Michael Peace (Think Equus) with foal and dam. The natural approach to relationships with horses is increasingly based on understanding and using the horse's body language

Bell and others. Most of these are American, though not all, but unlike their predecessors they claim no mysterious aura, no magic, no secret tricks in dealing with horses, but a logical approach using the horse's own outlook on life, his own language (which Monty Roberts christened 'equus'), and with the emphasis sometimes on dominance, as in the herd, and sometimes on an equal, mutually respectful partnership – but always with humane treatment and kindness tempered by discipline when necessary, usually for safety.

A psychological therapy: Most of these trainers have built up successful businesses training horses, retraining miscreants, and educating their owners and handlers to think like a horse, not a human, like a prey animal, not a predator – which is why

most of us have problems relating to our horses, it seems. Logical! We have to stop projecting 'boss', 'hunt', 'attack', 'pain', 'submit', and start projecting 'horse', 'safe', 'friend', 'respect', 'family' – and in practice it does work. As a psychological therapy this approach is brilliant, provided the owner keeps up the good work.

BEHAVIOURISTS

It will be noticed that most of the above are men, but women are often as successful as men, and sometimes even more so: Linda Tellington-Jones, Miranda Bruce, Heather Simpson and Kelly Marks. In fact they are regarded more as behaviourists, although certainly Kelly was taught by Monty Roberts and uses many of his systems, now, having her own called 'intelligent horsemanship'. We apologise sincerely to those we have omitted.

COMMUNICATORS

There is another type of horse whisperer which could perhaps more accurately be called a horse or animal communicator: those who claim to be able to tell what a horse is thinking, what it is trying to say to its human connections, and to be able to transmit to the horse whatever its owner would like it to know. In effect, they claim to act as a medium for a two-way conversation between horse and owner; in this category we have Nicci Mackay, Beatrice Lydekker, Peter Neilson, Stefanja Gardner and others.

HOW DO HORSE WHISPERERS WORK?

Certainly those in the first category, who might be termed enlightened trainers or even horse-language experts, work by using assertive (even aggressive) or submissive body language, the sort used by herds of *equidae* the world over from time immemorial, to establish a relationship with the horse. Some prefer this relationship to err slightly on the side of the human, so that the human is seen as higher up the herd hierarchy and the relationship is, say, a 60:40 partnership or wider; others prefer it to be on a 50:50 basis, with mutual respect (personal discipline) being shown by each partner to the other.

Think like a horse: What all these trainers have in common is a desire to persuade owners to think like a horse, as described above; this can also be said for the behaviourists, who urge us to understand why our horse might be behaving as he is, and help us work out ways of changing his outlook towards us, and ours towards him. The behaviourists often use scientifically classic ways of coping with behaviour problems, although many use specialised equine techniques, too. Again, today the emphasis is on kind effectiveness rather than brute domination.

Communicators – mind-to-mind contact: It is perhaps the communicators who are the most mysterious of the genre. The fact that so many of them are uncannily accurate with horses they have never met, do not know, or from which they may be hundreds or even thousands of miles distant, surely indicates that they have a special something that the rest of us do not. 'She told me things that have happened between me and my horse that no one could possibly know…' is a common remark after a 'meet-up' with a communicator, '… and she told it to me from my horse's point of view, not mine!' indicating that clearly the communicator was getting some message from, or having some type of conversation with the horse.

Think in pictures: Members of the Equine Behaviour Forum have for years sporadically reported on experiences with their horses which involved mind-to-mind contact. The most common way of communicating with horses mentally is to think to them in pictures, and given practice, concentration and good intent, this really does seem to work – even when you don't intend it to sometimes.

Sadly, some can never achieve any success now matter how hard they try, and in this case all they can do is learn to observe the horse's most minute physical signs of how it is feeling and what it could possibly be trying to say.

FINDING A 'WHISPERER'

The horse world is full of trainers. Some are conventional, some are kind, some are cruel, some are true experts, others are not – and the one that works for your friend and her horse may not suit you. So just where do you go, and whom do you believe?

Word of mouth is often, but not always, a good way of finding a trainer, whisperer, communicator or behaviourist.

Application to some professional body which trains instructors and practitioners in its techniques will produce a list of appropriately qualified people.

Attending lecture-demonstrations given by likely sounding people is also a good plan, because you can sit in the audience anonymously and just absorb the general feel of how they operate, or watch them giving a private or class lesson in your area.

Communicators, however, do not normally operate in this way. Here, they may be listed **in directories**, often those compiled by specialist-interest groups such as the Classical Riding Club or, occasionally, commercial magazines. Sometimes they are the subject of **articles in the press**, and again, **word of mouth** may bring someone to your notice.

Caution

If a trainer, whisperer or any other therapist (or teacher) does anything to your horse which your conscience tells you is wrong, stop the procedure immediately. He is your horse, not theirs.

Any procedure, healing or training, must be safe for horse and human.

John Lyons comments: 'the horse must be calmer and more trusting at the end of the session than at the start'. This is an excellent yardstick.

Frank Bell and Pierre. Sadly for UK readers the talented Frank Bell has not yet worked in the UK. An American with a Western background, his methods are unique, emphasising both safety and relationship-bonding

Phototherapy

In winter, with its short days, many people suffer from a condition known as 'seasonally affective disorder' (SAD): this is brought on by too little light, and a shortage of the hormones that light stimulates. Too much melatonin may also be a contributory factor: this is a hormone which is produced in darkness, and it has a direct affect on horses in that it is responsible for depressing breeding desire and condition in 'long-day breeders', such as they are. Phototherapy involves managing the intensity and duration of light in order to cure this condition; and it has several other benefits, as we shall see.

WHY FULL-SPECTRUM LIGHT IS IMPORTANT

Sunlight is essential for life: without the sun, this world as we know it could not exist. Sunlight is the energy source for plant growth and, therefore, the food source for every creature on earth whether it is herbivorous, carnivorous or omnivorous. Artificial lights are used to stimulate plant growth in greenhouses and aquaria, and these give out full-spectrum light: that is, they contain the artificial equivalent of natural sunlight with all wavelengths or spectra of light, from the ultra-violet to the infra-red and all points in between. Similar lights are used to treat people suffering from SAD, although this has to be done under expert supervision because the ultra-violet and infra-red ends of the spectrum contain certain potentially harmful rays to which some people – and animals – may be particularly sensitive.

PHOTOTHERAPY AND HORSES

BREEDING AND SHOWING

It has been known for some years that exposing breeding stock to bright, preferably full-spectrum light from immediately after the winter solstice (usually the 21 December in the northern hemisphere) for sixteen hours a day, accompanied by eight hours a day of darkness, will trick their brains into suppressing the release of melatonin, and will stimulate the release of other hormones, so that the breeding cycle is triggered and horses come into breeding (or showing) condition early, shedding their winter coats, growing their summer ones, and becoming sexually active. This is far more effective than grossly and unkindly muffling up show horses and ponies and increasing their feed – although warmth and food do play a part, though a much smaller one, in the process.

PREPARING YEARLINGS FOR THE AUTUMN SALES

Interestingly, a friend who manages a Thoroughbred stud insists that, when preparing yearlings for the sales, it is noticeable that those exposed to full-spectrum light and wearing no rugs have even better-looking summer-type coats out of season than those exposed to the light but which wear rugs as well; furthermore the former also appear healthier and in better general condition, presumably

---

What is Phototherapy used for?

- To trigger a mare's breeding cycle
- To delay, in summer, the growth of a winter coat, prior to the autumn sales
- To encourage, in spring, a horse to cast his winter coat, in preparation for the early summer shows
- As a therapy for horses that are stabled all the time, particularly in indoor barns and therefore possibly suffering from SAD
- As a treatment for convalescent, or sick, or very tired horses
- To dry off, and warm up horses after swimming

Light also boosts the immune system, helping the horse to fight off infections (obvious or not), and it may also help reduce allergic reactions in some cases.

Caution

A word of warning: A bright (200-watt) ordinary domestic lightbulb in each stable works fairly well; however, note that the cheap, blue-spectrum fluorescent lights (the sort normally sold in shops) actually seem to make matters worse in many cases, often causing headaches in humans (and possibly in horses, too), irritability and being much more difficult to see by, apparently because of the specific light wavelengths they emit. They also have nothing like the beneficial effect on coat and breeding condition of candescent bulbs or, certainly, of full-spectrum lights.

because their whole bodies, inside and out, have the benefit of the light.

In the case of yearling preparation, the light treatment is started immediately after the summer solstice (21 or 22 June in the northern hemisphere) so that the horses' brains do not register the shortening of the days which triggers the casting of the summer coat. It may not be really noticeable till the end of August, but the process is going on nevertheless, and maintaining the length of day and the intensity of daylight certainly keeps the yearlings' winter coats at bay for the autumn sales.

THERAPEUTIC EFFECTS FOR HORSES

As far as therapy is concerned, who is to say that horses, too, do not suffer from 'the blues', not only in winter but at any time when they are short of full-spectrum light? In winter, we are all probably short of light, even though not everyone shows it, and as far as horses are concerned, even when they *are* turned out, the rugs they often wear prevent the biochemical action of sunlight on their skin which helps the body to make vitamin D.

For those denied turnout: Many unfortunate horses are denied significant turnout these days, even in summer, and they, too, are almost certain to be short of the benefits of exposure to natural light. It must be well worthwhile installing full-spectrum lights (such as 'Daystar' or 'Activa') in their stables, not to mention turning them out more – without clothing when the weather permits.

For those in barn-type stabling: Adequate turnout is important for all horses, which means that those living in barn-type, indoor stabling are particularly badly off when it comes to getting enough light. Those in loose boxes can at least put their heads out and receive exposure to natural light through the pupils of their eyes and via the skin of their heads and necks, but those in indoor stabling or indoor covered yards get hardly any, as glass and plastic windows also usually filter out many wavelengths of light. Studies have shown dramatic improvements in the condition of these horses when an area of full-spectrum light has been installed in covered yards – all the horses tried to congregate near or under it, and their health and behaviour improved noticeably.

SELF HELP

Install a solarium: One way of giving horses daily doses of light, albeit for restricted periods, is to install a solarium in your yard in a specially designated area or box. These provide heat and/or light, depending on what bulbs are fitted, and are commonly seen in hydrotherapy centres to dry off and warm up horses after swimming; their other beneficial effects, of light exposure and warmth and relaxation, are significant for convalescent or sick horses, not only cold, wet ones, and rehabilitation and remedial yards often offer this welcome service to their residents. (See also Chromotherapy, p134.)

Focus on People

People who always wear spectacles and contact lenses may be short of full-spectrum light because lenses often (depending on their type) filter out some wavelengths, and not just the potentially harmful ones. As in all things, moderation is usually the key, and some exposure to full light every day without wearing spectacles or contact lenses may be a good idea – half an hour a day minimum in winter is recommended. Your optician or doctor may be able to advise on this.

Chromotherapy

Chromotherapy, or colour therapy, sounds a most unlikely way of 'curing' the problems of either a horse or a human: however, it is known and accepted that colour can affect a person's mental state; equally colour can have a psychological effect on animals. On a day-to-day basis, we all know how we are affected by our surroundings and by the colours we see: thus a pleasing colour scheme makes us feel uplifted, relaxed, happy or invigorated, whereas one we do not like can certainly make us feel depressed, miserable, tense and generally unhappy.

Focus on the Rider

Chromotherapy is used a good deal in hospitals, particularly mental hospitals and rehabilitation centres, and it could probably be used to good effect in schools (which are usually very bland and unimaginative when it comes to colour), workplaces and shops, and in business and marketing.

Colour therapists use colour to improve overall health and also specific disorders, and attribute different qualities to each colour, although these tend to differ slightly according to varying sources.

THE PHILOSOPHY BEHIND IT

WHAT IS COLOUR?

Scientists tell us that there is actually no such thing as colour, simply that our eyes perceive differing wavelengths of light as colour; indeed, the dictionary definition for colour is 'the sensation produced when light of different wavelengths is reflected from surfaces having different reflective properties, and falls on the human eye'.

If the colours of the rainbow (red, orange, yellow, green, blue, indigo and violet – known as the visible spectrum) are painted in equal segments on a white disc which is then spun on a pin like a Catherine wheel, it will appear white. Sunlight (daylight) is known as white light because of this – yet it contains all the colours of the rainbow, from the red end of the light spectrum to the blue end; and it is the intensity of daylight that dictates when horses come into summer condition, critical for breeding (if you are a breeder) or for coat appearance (if you are involved in showing).

Each chemical element gives off a characteristic colour wave, identified by scientists by means of a device called a 'diffraction grating' which gives each wavelength and chemical element a colour wave.

WHAT IS CHROMOTHERAPY?

When colour in the form of light reflection enters the eye it is split into different elements of colour, including colours/wavelengths from the invisible spectra (ultra-violet and infra-red) as well as the visible described above. By means of a special light-emitting instrument, chromotherapists can apply the different colours through polarised filters to apply the colour representing an element a horse is felt to be lacking, or which is felt to be needed to promote a particular response, to restore the body's natural balance.

WHAT EFFECT DOES EACH COLOUR HAVE?

In general, colours from the red end of the spectrum tend to be invigorating or irritating, and those from the blue end calming or depressing.

Red: The colour of warning and poison in nature: it is said to cause hyperactivity in children, and anger, aggression and violence, although it can be cheering and stimulating. It is claimed to relieve catarrhal conditions, to be pain relieving, and to boost certain hormonal secretions as well as the circulatory system. It is a marketing colour used to draw attention to advertisements, posters and so on. It can irritate patients

What can Chromotherapy Treat?

In both humans and animals, chromotherapy claims to be able to treat a whole host of conditions:

- degenerative joint disease (osteoarthritis)
- varied soft tissue injuries such as muscle strain and spasm
- tendon and ligament problems
- skin diseases, ranging from ulcers to mild irritations (including mud fever and sweet itch)
- nervous conditions
- respiratory disease
- allergies
- bruising
- some heart conditions
- general failure to thrive

with heart conditions or who are over-emotional.

Orange: Said to be uplifting, and to draw attention for advertising. It is claimed to stimulate some hormone production and depress others, improve respiratory function, help repair and build tissue, and calm down over-active nervous tissue, relieving muscle spasm.

Yellow: Believed to enhance learning ability and to promote cheerfulness, as well as encouraging objectivity and judgement. It is said to stimulate the lymphatic system and the motor nervous system, and to generally promote the passage of cellular fluids; however, it apparently restricts the action of the spleen.

Green: In the middle of the light spectrum, and regarded as a neutral colour. Horses seem to perceive green as white (they see reds,

oranges, blues and purples well, however). It is felt to be a 'cleansing' colour for humans – or at least calming and anti-pathogenic, being instrumental in killing off 'germs'. It is claimed to be tissue-building, but can apparently be depressive if overdone. In marketing it is said to encourage us to spend money.

Blue: A calming, cooling colour, also said to encourage the desire to buy. Like its near relative, green, it is apparently anti-pathogenic and also promotes anaesthesia, and has a pain-killing effect. It helps disperse bruises, inflammation and tension, including reducing blood pressure, and it promotes the growth of new cells.

Purple: Said to be highly depressive or very calming, depending on the temperament or condition of the patient. Thus it can have a generally toning-down, repressing effect on

several body systems, yet it is claimed to be a mild analgesic and effective against bacterial infections, and it can stimulate the spleen, and boost white cell production; it can also help treat shock and regulate body temperature.

The above shortlist takes account of only the main 'rainbow' colours. Other, in-between colours have their own effects: for instance, pink is said to be very relaxing and 'happy-making', brown gives a feeling of stability and warmth, grey tends towards lack of confidence and is preferred by those who like to remain in the background, and turquoise is said to strengthen the immune system.

SELF HELP

From the above list, you may already have some ideas of what colours to use in your own and your horses' environment. We have heard of an aggressive stallion who refused to travel, but who improved vastly once the inside of his horsebox was painted pink! Perhaps horses would like the lower halves of their stables painted grass green and the upper halves sky blue, to simulate an outdoor life. The use of calming colours should presumably help excitable, highly strung horses, and the use of stimulating ones perk up those of a more phlegmatic nature.

There are only a very few professionally qualified colour therapists working on animals, but a consultation may well be informative and helpful.

Feng Shui

Feng Shui (pronounced 'fung shway') is the ancient Chinese practice of arranging your home (or your horse's home) or other premises to encourage health, happiness and prosperity. Practitioners use such aids as crystals, mirrors, water or colour schemes, as well as the lie of the land in positioning new buildings or altering existing sites where applicable, in such a way as to encourage the flow of good energies. Positive or negative energies coming from the earth (such as ley lines) can have major effects on our lives. Many people whose premises have been given a Feng Shui makeover report an improvement in their lifestyle, fortunes, health and happiness.

PHILOSOPHY

Feng Shui practitioners tell us that we are all affected by our environment, and that it can actively work against us if objects are positioned incorrectly, or if our premises are sited in a 'bad' place; conversely, it can help us to experience a happy, prosperous life if good energies can be encouraged by placing and arranging objects and areas favourably.

Like many Eastern therapies, Feng Shui, in its various schools of thought, is an ancient one, but in recent years it has blossomed in the Western world as well. The words mean 'wind and water' and relate to the Yin and Yang of other therapies such as acupuncture, the balancing opposites of energies and characteristics positive and negative, male and female. If these energies are out of balance our fortunes, health and happiness are adversely affected. Small but carefully thought out changes in our environment can divert, block or encourage good and bad energies or influences, and so improve matters.

HOW DOES IT WORK?

What not to do: In general, Feng Shui eschews dirt, clutter, sharp corners, flat landscapes, past influences from previous inhabitants or people, draughts, darkness, stuffiness, excreta, drains and lavatories, and miserable colours – and that's not all there is to it. Bad energies are attracted by all those things, but good energies can be attracted by their opposites, and the bad energies can be banished or at least diverted or counteracted.

What to do: Rounding off corners, siting muck heaps on the eastern borders of your premises, hanging Chinese coins tied in red ribbon in your horse's stable or in the prosperity part of your house, hanging wind chimes in the stable yard or garden, putting photographs of your loved ones (human or animal) in your relationship area, strategically siting mirrors and taking other measures – all these may improve health, happiness and prosperity.

Feng Shui principles hold that every home (and your stable yard is your horse's home) is divided into areas relevant to your (or his) life: for

---

What is Feng Shui used for?

Feng Shui has its place when used correctly in promoting health, wealth, career and relationships; so how can 'feng-shuing' buildings help horses?

- It can help the relationship between the rider and his horse and so advance their mutual careers
- Poor equine health may be caused by bad Feng Shui
- If the premises where the horse is kept has had generations of bad luck they may need 'cleansing' to 'clear the air'
- It can help improve your horse's concentration and learning abilities
- It can help physical problems such as sleeplessness, rheumatism and even cancer

Feng Shui fact

It is said that, in life, equines, people and other animals are born with 'heaven's luck': your 'start in life'. Then when you 'hit the earth', you have 'horse luck' or 'man luck', meaning karma, the theory of inevitable consequence – fate, destiny. However, it is possible to make your own luck, and Feng Shui is all about bringing opportunity and clearing the way forwards for yourself. Basically, employing Feng Shui can help make life better.

Complementary or Alternative Therapies; sometimes they advertise in the 'Personal Services' columns of local newspapers. Feng Shui can be done on a DIY basis, but it is quite a complex art, and in the end, you will probably get better results by engaging a consultant, particularly if the philosophy is new to you. He/she will usually work around existing premises, first assessing the history of the inhabitants, human and animal, and their personalities, and also the premises, plus the 'feel' of the place – and horses are more sensitive to good and bad spaces than humans often are – then give a detailed, personalised consultation as to what can be moved, what can be changed slightly, and what other measures can be taken such as using plants, colours and other objects to ameliorate your circumstances and encourage beneficial influences and energies.

A Feng Shui consultation: This may last anything from an hour to half a day, depending on individual circumstances; and whilst some Feng Shui factors will have a very quick effect, some may take a few weeks or even up to six months – although most work more quickly than that.

instance health, contentment, achievement, relationship/marriage (involving people and animals), money and so on – and these areas should be set out or positioned in a certain way for the good energies to flow into them. They can also be arranged, and objects placed in and around them, so that bad energies will be banished or at least diverted from them.

Even if you keep your horse in premises you do not own and so feel helpless to change, you could make minor changes to your horse's stable, your area of the tack room, his tack and clothing and so on, and these can make a significant difference to his circumstances.

WHERE TO GO FOR ADVICE

Local directories will give details of Feng Shui consultants, often under

Ley Lines Theory

Earth comprises physical properties (geophysics). Basically, ley lines are lines of energy that correspond to underground streams of water or small electrical currents produced by pressure on quartz crystals in the ground. Further, they produce lines of geopathic stress, which is why they have bearing on animate and inanimate bodies regarding health and wellbeing. Where humans and animals are concerned, ley lines can affect health in all sorts of areas, with problems such as sleeplessness, rheumatism and even cancer attributed to them. Ley lines are said also to affect the sound structure of and/or atmosphere in buildings, which is why Feng Shui experts are called in on building sites, particularly Chinese, to ensure buildings are constructed so that they are in harmony with the natural flow of energy in the air and ground. Structures such as railway lines, roads, water courses and overhead power cables may interrupt the natural pattern of ley lines, causing further geopathic stress to humans or buildings. Makes you think about the 'sick building' syndrome that office workers complain of, doesn't it? Now equate that to equine housing...

Says practitioner Charlotte Bradley: 'It's no coincidence that Hong Kong is also called the Feng Shui Capital: no one does anything there without calling in a Feng Shui practitioner first – and business is booming!'

FENG SHUI IN PRACTICE

Charlotte Bradley

Having trained under two of the world's leading experts Dr Michael Oon, and Lillian Too, and studying the ways of Master Yap Cheng Hai in true and authentic Feng Shui , Charlotte is an authority on this ancient Chinese art of promoting health and wellbeing. Says Charlotte, who is based in the New Forest:

'Sometimes we have to look at our surroundings and a little further than a horse's anatomy to find the cause of a problem – horses are extremely sensitive beings.'

In addition to practising traditional, as opposed to Western, Feng Shui, Charlotte is a respected writer on this ancient art for newspapers and business magazines. There are many areas in which Charlotte believes Feng Shui can help, and explains:

'Feng Shui is similar to acupuncture and works on buildings as opposed to bodies, harmonising the energy-lines or pathways through the body or building along which life energy flows. Acupuncture progressed from Feng Shui.'

So how can 'Feng Shui-ing' buildings help horses? Says Charlotte:

'Employing it can aid the relationship between you and your horse and therefore help both your careers, or simply improve an existing one. Poor equine health may be caused by either bad Feng Shui or ley-lines under the ground. Alternatively the premises where the horse is kept may need "smudging" – meaning cleansing – to "clear the air" if it has generations of bad luck and bad Feng Shui.

'Sometimes, moving your horse to different premises can result in financial difficulties for one reason or another. This may be down to the new premises having bad Feng Shui. Or perhaps your horse has problems concentrating or learning? Maybe you want to learn more about a particular discipline? Feng Shui can help both of these aspects.'

Sceptics might perceive Feng Shui to be 'the ancient Chinese art of extracting money from gullible people', but Charlotte has a more considered approach: 'Don't knock things until you have tried them. If something works for you and your horse and makes you both happy and contented, then that's the important thing. There's a lot more to this therapy than the popular belief that keeping the toilet seat down will prevent your wealth flushing away.'

Some people have discovered that when they have moved their horse to a new yard, the animal's temperament has changed drastically, or it has become continually lame or has suffered constant illness and bad luck. But is it luck or bad Feng Shui?

Compared to more readily accepted therapies – such as aromatherapy, homoeopathy and acupuncture – Feng Shui is a comparatively new concept in the UK, therefore viewed with suspicion in some quarters. However, as Charlotte explains, it has been around for thousands of years in China, but kept secret for centuries so that others could not benefit from it. In fact one of the first Ming dynasty (1368–1644AD) emperors banned his people from using it as he didn't want them to become more powerful and successful than himself – and the ban wasn't relaxed until Mao Tse-tung came to power in the twentieth century. It is only in recent years that its concept has filtered through to the West.

Says Charlotte, 'There has been much misleading information written about Feng Shui in the press, so many people misunderstand it totally. Unsurprisingly, therefore, they think it a joke and view it with scepticism. Mind you, it wasn't that long ago that other forms of now-accepted "alternative" therapies were viewed in the same way. Feng Shui isn't going to win you the Lottery, nor is it magic, but it has its place when used correctly in promoting aspects of your life such as health, wealth, career and relationships.

'In the beginning of my involvement with Feng Shui I came across the Westernised version, and that's how I became interested in it, but I found it never, ever worked so became disillusioned with it. Then I met an oriental man named Dr Oon, who introduced me to an oriental lady practitioner Lillian Too, and that's how I got to learn the authentic way, which was a lot more complicated – and interesting. And it worked.'

So how does it work? Explains Charlotte:

'You actually practise Feng Shui on the building or yard a horse is housed in, as opposed to the horse itself. Firstly you start with the shape of the yard; I get clients to post me a layout of their yard and surrounding site so that I can see a bird's eye view of a yard before I visit it and know exactly what I'm dealing with. The ideal shape is either a square or a rectangle, but many are horseshoe or L-shaped which can create bad Feng Shui.

'Feng Shui is made up of five elements – water, wood, fire, earth and metal – and each of those elements take on negative and positive energy (Yin and Yang respectively) which, when situated around or in a building correctly, make up a creative cycle of life. These five elements represent different types of landscape which provide us with good Feng Shui, and we take appropriate steps in placing in a particular way objects which are symbolic for certain elements, which provide more harmony for particular things, in such a way that the cycle is completed satisfactorily.'

What sort of objects? Explains Charlotte:

'Each element has a direction – north, south, and so on – so I take my compass to a yard and define where the directions are and work out a map. Once I've worked out the compass points I mark out existing elements on my map, such as trees, water and so on. If a yard is L-shaped, for example, it means that a corner is 'missing' in a certain area; it does not make up a total square. Depending on what that corner represents, its absence could affect a money area, or relationships or health, so

I'll place an object which is complementary to that element at the relevant point.

'If there is a fast-flowing watercourse running behind the yard, or your horse's stable, this is considered inauspicious because its energy is too fast – good Feng Shui is gentle – so I'll place a relevant object between that and the yard or stable to balance the water element's

Feng Shui practitioner Charlotte Bradley

effect; otherwise you'll carry on having financial problems and missing out on opportunities.

'Everything in Feng Shui is based on the elements of Yin (quiet; feminine; dead; dark; cold; passive; negative) and Yang (positive; masculine; light; warm; active): Yin and Yang influence destiny and govern nature. If Yin and Yang are unbalanced, then problems can occur. For example, if there is too much Yin energy on a yard, you won't be doing so well. So to improve this energy I would have to put in more Yang objects or Yang colours.'

CASE HISTORY

Horse: Gem, a nine-year-old mare.

PROBLEM: Explains Charlotte, 'Gem had so many problems, particularly hormonal. She thought she was a stallion in the field and her owner, Susan, had to take great care in handling her as she was so unpredictable. This occurred before herbal supplements for hormonally imbalanced mares could be bought. Susan had had to move Gem from several yards because of her behaviour – not many people could cope with her. Gem became very bad at two yards in particular. She'd kick out, pull people over, round up other horses in the field and not let anyone near them. Being a hefty sort of mare she could be extremely formidable when in a "strop"!'

Gem also became distraught when stabled. Charlotte realised that the ground behind the stable sloped downwards, which was bad Feng Shui as it wasn't 'supporting' her – the energy was too Yang.

TREATMENT: Says Charlotte, 'Susan wanted to sell the mare and had nothing to lose, so decided that Feng Shui was worth a go. I placed objects in her stable and under her bedding to create a complete life cycle.

'For the earth element – there are many types of earth elements for different directions – I placed a crystal wrapped in red cloth to energise it under the straw bank in the south-west corner. This is for relationships. In the west "projects" corner – representing competitions and suchlike – I hid some Chinese coins up in the wooden rafters to correspond with the metal element. At that point Susan thought that if anyone saw what she was doing they'd think she was barmy!

'In the north-west corner I again placed a metal object; this is for drawing to you people who will help you. And after this Susan found herself being approached by other people on the yard who offered advice and help with the Gem. One person lent her a saddle, because in one of her incidents with Gem her saddle had been wrecked.

'In Gem's "career" corner, at north, I placed a black stone for support. In the north-east corner, which relates to knowledge and learning, I buried another earth

A crystal wrapped in red cloth to energise the south-west (relationships) corner

element, a crystal, under her bedding. The east corner is a wooden element, for health, and here I didn't place anything because her stable was made of wood. In the south-east corner, which is the prosperity side and Susan wanted to sell her, I placed her water bucket.'

RESULT: Says Susan, 'I didn't know how using Feng Shui might change Gem, but her whole attitude altered for the better almost immediately. She became much quieter and gentler, and didn't try to devour you when you walked into the stable. Training-wise she began to listen and try her best, fulfilling the potential I knew she possessed.

'Pre-Feng Shui I could not sell Gem for love nor money. Every time I tried there was a problem – she had an accident, or she became unwell when a potential buyer came to try her. I just could not understand what was going on. After Charlotte employed the treatment I sold her immediately – people were queuing up to buy her, and I got the full asking price. Feng Shui, I believe, helped make the most of our opportunities.'

Top tip from Charlotte

'Feng Shui isn't just for "problem" horses: it can be used to bring further opportunities to you and your horse, whether you want to compete seriously, or simply feel more fulfilled. And if your landscape – the surrounding buildings or land at your yard – is not giving you and your horse "good" Feng Shui, it can be corrected!'

Saddling

It may seem strange to see the subject of saddling in a book on complementary therapies, but we have included it because of the great damage which can be done to a horse's body and mind by an uncomfortable and painful saddle, and because of the huge improvement evident in his attitude and way of going once he is wearing a saddle and girth which fits him, and which is correctly put on and adjusted.

The horse's back is also the site of many acupuncture/acupressure points which can be unintentionally stimulated by uneven pressures from ill-shaped, badly fitting saddles or simply those in poor condition, with hard, lumpy stuffing in the under-seat panels and a panel shape which creates very uneven pressure on the back. Conversely, even comparatively gentle pressure on those points and on the energy meridians which run down the horse's back and sides can, some believe, promote gentle stimulation of the points and meridians to the general benefit of the horse.

NATURE'S HORSE

Whether we are happy for our horses to go naturally, or whether we wish them to go in a way which we think is an improvement, we ultimately have to accept the fact that, if we study the typical equine way of going, every horse's movement will change (deteriorate?) from what is natural to him as soon as we put a rider on his back – in fact, even as soon as we just put a saddle on him, and work him riderless in it. Therefore, the practice of saddling horses is always going to be a damage-limitation exercise or, at best, one of damage prevention.

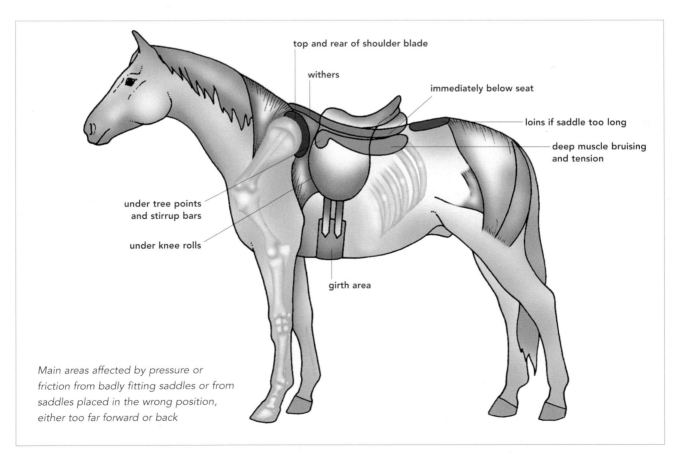

top and rear of shoulder blade

withers

immediately below seat

loins if saddle too long

deep muscle bruising and tension

under tree points and stirrup bars

under knee rolls

girth area

Main areas affected by pressure or friction from badly fitting saddles or from saddles placed in the wrong position, either too far forward or back

WHAT ARE WE LOOKING FOR?

Most of us have been taught that the basic principles of fitting saddles are that there must be no pressure anywhere down the spine, and that the saddle tree (the framework around which it is built) must not be so narrow that it pinches, nor so wide that it rocks from side to side. But over the last decade or so, our curiosity regarding equine studies and equine science has increased, and many of us are now aware that there is a very great deal more than that to the art and science of saddle fitting.

Whatever type or school of saddle you use, be it English, Western, Iberian, show-jumping, dressage and so on, the most important points are these:

■ The saddle and girth must not cause the horse pain or discomfort.

A well-positioned dressage saddle (not too far forward so that it interferes with the shoulder blades) with a central seat and the stirrup bar far enough back to allow the rider to easily assume a classical leg position with the heel below the hip

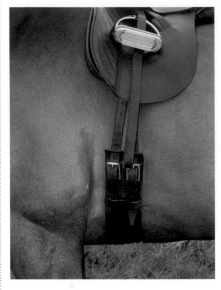

A conventional short dressage or belly girth. An Atherstone pattern, tapering behind the elbow, would allow more room in action

■ The saddle and girth must not directly or indirectly interfere with the horse's movement.

■ The saddle must be comfortable for the rider, and encourage him or her to ride in the correct seat for the discipline undertaken, otherwise he or she will not be able to ride well and will then cause the horse pain and/or discomfort, and/or will interfere with his movement.

In practice, this means that:

■ The bearing surface of the saddle must be generous so as to distribute pressure over as wide a surface as possible, as evenly as possible.

■ The bearing surface must be smooth, comfortable and pliable so that it will mould to the shape of the horse's back both when he is still or moving, and so that the horse's back muscles can work

comfortably into the padding without discomfort or interference.

■ The gullet must allow a clear channel of daylight all the way down the horse's spine when the horse's heaviest rider is in the saddle, and when he or she leans forwards and backwards.

■ The gullet must be wide enough all the way down (6cm/2½in) so that the inevitable slight sideways movements of the saddle in motion do not bring the panels into contact with any part of the spine, but not so wide that the bearing surface is reduced and concentrated on the weaker area away from the tops of the ribs.

There should be a clear tunnel of air all the way down the spine

■ The top of the shoulder blade, which rotates back towards the saddle when the horse extends his foreleg, must not contact the front edge of the saddle (except possibly in some designs of saddle which have flexible under-seat fans or panels which purposely lift on contact).

■ The saddle must sit on the horse's back so that the rider is placed centrally in the seat with even weight distribution. If the rider is

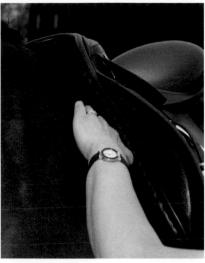

Right: If the saddle is placed too far forward on the shoulder the action of the shoulder will be hampered

Far right: Here, the saddle fitter checks the front of the saddle for the amount of pressure exerted behind the shoulder. She should be able to slide the flat of her fingers down the front of the saddle fairly easily

pushed forwards the weight will be too much over the front of the saddle over the tree point/stirrup bar area, which already is the one which exerts most pressure on the horse's back; and if the rider is pushed backwards, the weight will be too near to, or even on the cantle area, pressurising the weaker part of the horse's back where the false ribs are.

■ The saddle must, therefore, sit

The saddle fitter slides the flat of her fingers beneath the panel along the back to check for even contact

well behind the top of the extended shoulder blade (by the width of the edge of your hand) and well in front of the loins to avoid pressure on, or contact with, these two vulnerable areas.

■ The girth must be able to be fitted sufficiently far back so as not to interfere in any way with the free movement of the horse's foreleg around the sensitive elbow area. Horses who have the desirable conformation point of a natural girth groove in this area are far easier to fit in this respect.

■ The girth must be wide enough to spread pressure comfortably, though a good point is for it to be tapered in the elbow area to prevent interference, trapped skin and injuries here.

Ideally it should have either a central elastic insert at the breastbone, or an elastic insert at *both* ends to allow even 'give' around the ribcage during movement and breathing. An insert at one end only produces an uncomfortable twisting effect

which also tends to tilt the saddle slightly to the opposite side every time the horse breathes in.

GETTING THE RIGHT ADVICE

Saddles should be fitted to horses by qualified saddle fitters, not simply by qualified saddlers who may be superb craftsmen but who normally do not know enough about equine anatomy, physiology and the biomechanics of the horse's back.

The horse's stance when he is just standing, and his way of going at all gaits including jumping, if appropriate, must be minutely studied, and his facial expression and movements compared under different saddles in order to find out which one he really finds most comfortable.

Many countries now have professional associations governing saddle making and fit, and run courses in this important and fairly complex subject. Appropriate addresses for guidance are given in Useful Addresses (p186).

Dentistry

Maintaining the good condition of the teeth is fundamental in the management of a horse. Many behavioural problems are related to pain in the mouth or teeth. As with other therapies, dental work is differently regarded in different countries: in some, anyone can work on a horse's teeth, but in others, horse dentists may only rasp teeth and remove hooks, other procedures such as extractions are seen as strictly surgical and the domain of a veterinary surgeon. We are now encouraged to call equine dentists 'equine dental technicians'.

INSENSITIVE BITTING

For the horse, having a bit put in his mouth is just an additional problem, and although it is not supposed to contact the teeth in any way, sometimes it does, either because of incorrect adjustment or harsh use. If the bit is too low it can bang on the tushes or corner incisors, and maybe even wear, chip or break them; and if too high, it can do the same to the front premolars. If the bit is harshly or even just firmly used, it can damage the premolars quite significantly and, depending

BASIC TOOTH-RELATED PROBLEMS

Horse owners should have their horses' teeth properly attended to at least once a year. We all know how distracting, uncomfortable or painful even a minor mouth problem can be, particularly one caused by a tooth that is sharp or broken, decaying or abscessed – and, of course, it is just the same for horses.

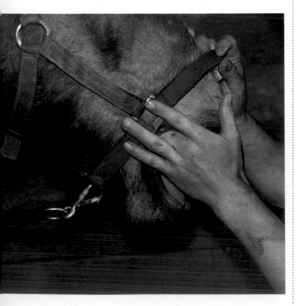

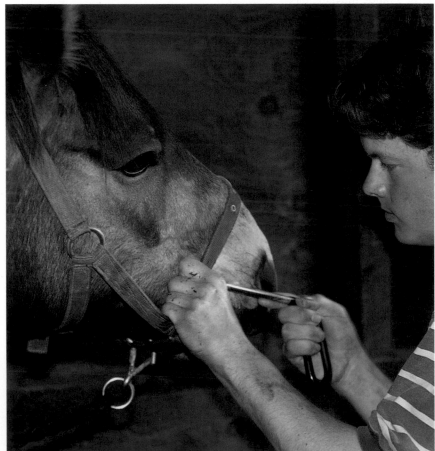

Left: Feeling for sharp edges and hooks
Above: A simple rasping operation which may be carried out by equine dental technicians (commonly but incorrectly called horse dentists) but anything involving surgery must be performed by a veterinary surgeon in the UK. This may not apply in other countries

How often is treatment needed

A mature horse's teeth should be checked, and if necessary treated, once a year; for young and old animals this should be twice a year, or even more often. They should also be checked if you notice any untoward or unusual behaviour which could stem from discomfort or pain in the mouth, such as:

- head tossing
- difficulty in eating
- strange movements of the jaws or head when eating
- restlessness when eating
- dropping food out of the mouth
- undigested food passing out in the droppings
- refusal to accept the bit when used correctly and humanely

on the type of cheek the bit has, it can trap the horse's cheek between the teeth and the bit cheek, with the most excruciating pain – imagine it yourself – and injury to the cheek. In some cases the tongue can be injured, particularly if the horse, in trying to avoid the discomfort, gets his tongue over the bit and the underneath of it is torn by firm bit pressure.

UNEVEN WEAR

Horses are herbivores, and should therefore be spending at least sixteen hours a day eating suitable food, mainly roughage such as grass, hay, haylage or other forage feeds. This length of time spent struggling to eat tough food with inadequate teeth or a painful mouth is most distressing and can result in loss of weight, unhappiness, worry and anxiety. Unlike ours, a horse's teeth erupt continuously; furthermore, the normal upper jaw

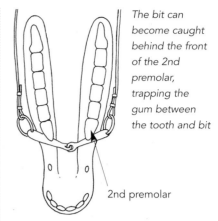

The bit can become caught behind the front of the 2nd premolar, trapping the gum between the tooth and bit

2nd premolar

is slightly wider than the lower jaw, with the result that the outsides of the upper molars and premolars can become sharp due to lack of contact with their opposite numbers; the inner edges of the lower teeth may also become sharp.

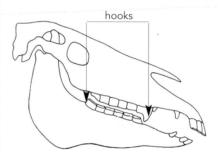

hooks

The hooks which form on cheek teeth shown here interfere with normal chewing movement and can affect the action of the bit. They should be removed during rasping. It is essential that the vet or dental technician checks right to the back of the mouth and most would prefer to use a gag to keep the horse's mouth open during this process because it is a potentially dangerous situation

This means the insides of the cheeks and the tongue, can become cut. Hooks can form on the front, upper premolars and on the back, lower molars due to wear patterns.

These sorts of disorders can be put right by anyone competent to

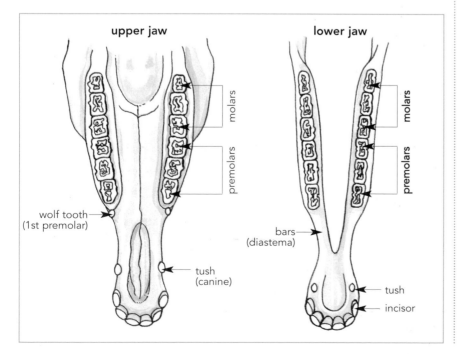

upper jaw lower jaw

molars

premolars

molars

premolars

wolf tooth (1st premolar)

tush (canine)

bars (diastema)

tush

incisor

perform routine dental work, but anything more serious such as a broken, decayed or abscessed tooth that needs extracting, should be dealt with under anaesthetic by a veterinary surgeon or a qualified dental technician, depending on national laws.

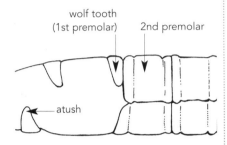

Wolf tooth

OTHER PROBLEMS

Other problems which can occur are the growth of small premolars, called wolf teeth, at the fronts of the upper premolars; malocclusions, where teeth do not meet properly and so create uneven wear patterns which can greatly affect eating; and incisors which are either undershot or overshot so that they do not meet, making grazing difficult or impossible.

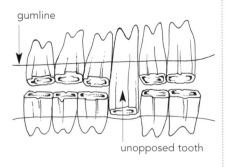

When a tooth grows into the space created by its missing opposite number it needs to be rasped down frequently to prevent serious interference with the jaw movement and painful gums

Age-related problems

Young horses: Like other mammals, young horses have 'baby' – milk – or deciduous teeth, and 'adult' or permanent teeth. When the permanent teeth are erupting, the deciduous teeth sometimes become jammed on top of them (when they are called 'caps'), making eating very difficult, and these must be removed by a vet or a dental technician.

Old horses: In old horses, the teeth may reach a point where there is little or no actual tooth (dentine and enamel) left, but only the softer, root part of the tooth, and this will make chewing ordinary food very difficult. Such horses must be fed a nutritious, soft diet such as soaked sugar-beet pulp and high protein/energy cubes, mixed to a mushy, though not wet, consistency. Grated roots such as carrots, and fruits such as apples – you could chop these in a food processor to make the task quicker – can be added as well, and other wetted cubes and pellets such as dried grass and alfalfa can be used to provide nutrients in a form the horse can cope with. He will find it very difficult to chew up hay, haylage, chopped forage feeds and maybe even grass. A vet's or nutritionist's advice should be sought as to an appropriate diet and, if necessary, a supplement. The horse must be given plenty of food, including overnight, so that he is not hungry, without actually overloading him with nourishment.

WHERE WOULD I FIND AN 'EQUINE DENTIST'?

Any qualified veterinary surgeon is trained to perform all dental work. Other people working as 'equine dentists' may or may not be qualified or legally able to carry out a full range of dental operations: this will depend on the law of the country in which they are practising. For example, in the United States of America, the Worldwide Association of Equine Dentistry runs training courses and qualifies its students, but unfortunately its qualification is not recognised in the UK where only veterinary surgeons may carry out a full range of treatments including extractions. Also, some countries do not permit anyone other than a qualified human dentist to use the word 'dentist'. In the UK, the British Equine Veterinary Association and the British Veterinary Dental Association are establishing training courses to allow trained, examined and certified 'equine dental technicians' to perform 'certain other oral manipulations' as well as basic rasping.

In most countries, 'equine dentists' are free to rasp teeth, and to advise owners when the attention of a vet is needed. Although vets will certainly come along and attend to your horse's teeth, and some owners prefer a vet to do this, many owners find that 'equine dentists' do a superb job, too.

Farriery

Maintaining the good shape and healthy structure of the horse's foot is of tremendous importance to his overall ability to move naturally and, therefore, in a balanced way. It is also important because it can prevent so many disorders if performed correctly from foalhood onwards and because it can help heal other disorders which develop later in life.

FARRIERY FOR THE FOAL

The most influential time in a horse or pony's life from the point of view of shaping his feet, legs and action for ever, for better or for worse, is from birth to six months, most foals needing their first balancing trim at two or three months of age unless there have been previous problems. Up to about six months old, the bones in the legs are soft enough to be influenced fairly easily by any corrective trimming or, exceptionally, shoeing which may be needed to rectify congenital or hereditary faults of conformation, stance or action. Properly balanced little feet provide a sound, even base of support for the legs and joints to form against and grow naturally.

On the other hand, if they are left to grow on their own on poorly conformed and poorly balanced feet, the joints and limb bones can grow and develop in a compensatory way and may easily become crooked, overstressed, unevenly weighted and so on. By the time the youngster is six months old, the owners will be worried and the farrier will be cursing that they did not call him in earlier when matters could have been

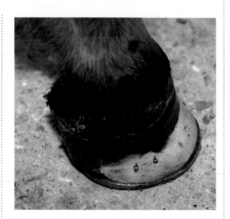

The skills of a competent concerned farrier particularly when surgical or remedial shoeing is required – as in the case of this foal – are crucial to the future performance potential and value of a young horse. Farriery should begin early enough in a horse's life to make a real difference if problems are not to arise later

corrected, and problems avoided, so much easier. From six months to about two years of age, the farrier can do a certain amount to help correct limb and foot alignments, function, and the animal's action; but after that there is little that can be done.

FARRIERY DURING THE EARLY YEARS

With adult horses, great skill and judgement are needed in a farrier to enable him to know just when to alter a foot balance with a view to

correcting a limb or action fault, and when to leave it for fear of causing unaccustomed stresses on mature bones and joints which may create more problems than they solve.

A really competent, caring farrier, given the chance to trim and shoe a horse or pony during the early months and years of its life, can affect that animal's comfort, performance and prospects for a long, useful and comfortable life to the extent that it may be happier and much more valuable than if faults had been allowed or encouraged to develop by neglect or poor shoeing. One remedial farrier told one of the authors that far too many owners pay hardly any attention to their animals' feet until the time comes when they need shoeing at about three years of age, by which time some problems are extremely difficult or impossible to correct.

FARRIERY FOR OLDER HORSES AND PONIES

Many problems with feet and legs stem from poor farriery practice and technique. However, once the horse comes into the hands of a really good, conscientious farrier, certain problems can be corrected.

Balancing the foot: The basis of all good orthodox farriery comes down to shaping the horse's feet so they conform to the classic correct foot balance as detailed in the accompanying diagrams, as nearly as is possible for him as an individual, taking into account his conformation and action. The

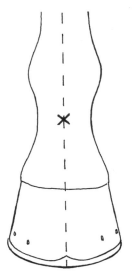

The balanced foot – an imaginary vertical line down the centre of the fetlock joint to the centre of the toe should divide the foot evenly

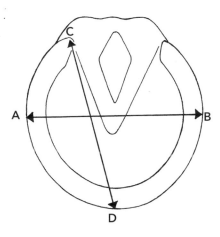

A balanced forefoot – the line A–B should equal the length of line C–D

hoof/pastern axis has to be correct and also the side-to-side balance, and he should be shod appropriately for his work, and so that the heels have adequate support with the toes sensibly short. Feet which have been carelessly trimmed often have excessive horn here and there, not to mention complete 'false' soles which have built up; however, these can all be removed during balancing, with

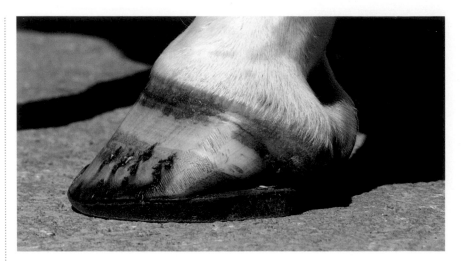

Wedges, heel pads or eggbar shoes are helpful in supporting low or collapsed heels. A common fault is to allow horses to have long toes and low heels which causes multiple problems

immediate improvement in the horse's comfort and action. Conversely, feet which are badly worn, broken, split and chipped need careful trimming and building up, maybe with synthetic materials and glue-on shoes, to improve balance whilst new horn is growing.

The importance of remedial shoeing: If problems are allowed to develop unchecked and the farrier shoes the horse to accommodate rather than to correct the problems, they can become chronic and cause uneven stance and action, vastly affecting the horse's comfort and ability to work and

In the unbalanced foot the left side of this leg will be subject to stretching forces which will injure the soft tissues. The right side of the leg wil be subject to crushing forces and pressure on joint cartilage and bone and encourages the formation of splints, corns and other injuries

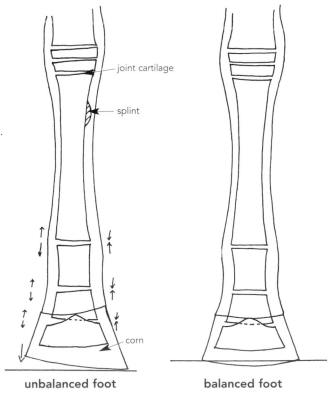

unbalanced foot   **balanced foot**

Sandcracks, as shown here, and generally chipped and broken feet can be caused not only by poor horn quality but also by allowing feet to be unbalanced which creates uneven stresses on the foot

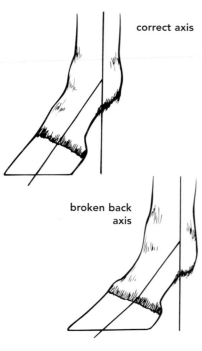

correct axis

broken back axis

broken forward axis

The Natural Trim

  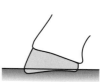

The feet of feral horses are often found to wear quite unlike the standard, level trim most farriers carry out. In particular, the toe often wears square and the quarters (sides) wear, too. Some farriers now purposely trim and shoe horses in this way

Research and observation of feral horses and ponies in recent decades has shown that, depending on ground conditions, most wear their toes off 'rolled' and squarish, and sometimes also wear them at the quarters (sides); all this makes for a more square-shaped foot than the classic rounded front-foot trim or more oval hind-foot trim. There is currently much controversy as to whether or not this shape is appropriate for domestic horses. It is an inescapable fact that many horses who do not have problems of action or conformation still do wear their shoes rounded off or actually squared at the toes (though not particularly from dragging the toes), and this must speak volumes for the validity of this theory.

It will be interesting to see how farriery, which became much more accommodating of new ideas and research during the latter part of the twentieth century, progresses in the twenty-first. One thing is certain: it will retain its crucial role as a remedial and complementary therapy of the greatest importance.

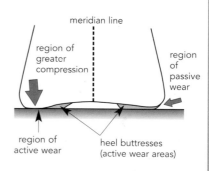

maybe eventually causing lameness. The constant discomfort is also a stress on him which will deplete his energies and gradually affect his general health.

Once the foot is rebalanced, and support given with appropriate shoes, the difference can be amazing. The foot will be encouraged to grow normally and in the right places, and uneven pressures caused by faulty shoeing and action will be removed.

Left: In the leg with the correct hoof/pastern axis stresses will be evenly distributed in the foot and leg. The broken back axis creates strain on the ligaments and tendons running behind the leg and pressure on the sesamoid bones in the fetlock and on the navicular bone. The broken forward axis makes the foot more prone to concussion and uneven forces in the foot and leg

THERAPIES FOR

THE RIDER ONLY

Ayurvedic Medicine

An all-embracing, truly holistic system of health maintenance, this is the traditional system of medicine practised in India, Sri Lanka and some adjacent cultures. It is a way of life aimed at promoting good health and resistance to stresses and diseases of the body, mind and spirit, rather than a repertoire of treatments for specific and obvious illnesses which are often the end of a line of encroaching disorder.

Ayurveda promotes the belief that everything in the universe is composed of energy: this is called 'prana' and is the identical life force to the 'Chi' of China, the 'pneuma' of ancient Greece and the 'Ki' of Japan. By balancing that energy in relation to the world we live in, our health and wellbeing will be enhanced.

PHILOSOPHY

It is believed that our energy constantly changes its flow within us, and Ayurveda teaches us how to persuade it to be balanced, so encouraging the optimal functions of every cell in our bodies. This relates to our entire being and affects our emotions, thoughts, actions, our diet, sleep, personal habits, relationships and our views of the past, present and future – every aspect of our existence. By achieving a balanced life in every way we shall function optimally and achieve spiritual fulfilment and emotional happiness. Quite an aim, but one on a par with other Eastern philosophies.

Principles: These are based also on the belief that we consist of

What is Ayurvedic Medicine used for?

When things go wrong and our prana (life force) is thrown out of balance, Ayurveda can help to restore that balance and to heal individual disorders: it is said to be particularly effective for dealing with stubborn, chronic conditions, especially:

- high blood pressure
- distress
- skin disorders
- respiratory problems
- sleep difficulties
- headaches and migraines
- depression (clinical or otherwise)
- anxiety
- digestive disorders
- allergic conditions

combinations of five elements which are slightly different from those of Traditional Chinese Medicine (see p154) and from our own, Western view of the elements as being earth, air, fire and water. In Ayurveda, the elements are air, fire, space, water and earth, plus three other influential forces which Ayurvedics call vata, pitta and kapha, in which the other elements are manifest.

HOW DOES IT WORK?

Some of the elements employed in Ayurvedic medicine are a special type of aromatherapy, breathing techniques, detoxification of the body, nutrition, exercise, medicines from herbal, mineral and other vegetable sources, meditation and relaxation, music as therapy, techniques for enhancing physical and emotional wellbeing, and Yoga. Manipulation of energy points called 'marma' is also a significant element of this system; whereas in Traditional Chinese Medicine fifty-nine energy meridians are recognised, in Ayurvedic medicine there are several hundred. There is also a form of massage aimed at helping the release of toxins from the body.

Ayurvedic practitioners often work on the immune system, as that is the basis of physical health and, therefore, mental and spiritual wellbeing. They try to re–balance the prana and keep it flowing strongly and evenly so that it can resist the invasion of 'germs' and other aggressive and harmful agents such as toxins, often secreted by our own bodies when under stress.

WHAT DOES TREATMENT INVOLVE?

The practitioner will first ask questions which will reveal the patient's constitutional type; he or

Ayurveda for horses

Although far from widely used yet, it is possible to ask any practitioner to treat an animal, as with any therapy. Veterinary referral or permission is needed in some countries, including the UK.

in this and related philosophies, and these may also be advertised locally in newspapers, magazines and health and sports venues.

Where can I find a practitioner? It is true that there is nothing to compare

with personal treatment and education, and local and regional directories often carry advertisements and listings for Ayurvedic and other similar systems of health maintenance and medicine for those wishing to pursue them further.

she is then given a set of guidelines to follow which are carefully prepared for the patient as a unique individual, aimed at promoting their health and wellbeing, physical and mental. Treatments will be geared towards the specific condition(s) present, and although Ayurveda is a safe treatment, some conditions are not apparently effectively treated by it, such as cancer, mechanical, locomotory problems, and some types of hernia. Children and pregnant women will be given slightly different treatment from that given to other people because of their unique sensitivities.

It will probably be necessary to visit a practitioner at least three times, and maybe ten or more, the more persistent and severe conditions requiring the most attention.

SELF HELP

Where can I learn more? There are now several good books and videos on the subject of Ayurvedic medicine as a whole, or on specific aspects of it such as Yoga. Local and regional educational authorities often run non-vocational classes and courses

Ayurvedic medicine teaches the body to balance its natural 'prana', or energy, making it more resistant to stresses and disease

Chinese Medicine

What we now call Traditional Chinese Medicine (TCM) is a system of health maintenance and restoration which is truly holistic in nature and is itself an intricate web of action and interaction of its various elements, rather like the body itself. The main aspects of it are acupuncture and herbalism (Chinese herbalism includes mineral and animal substances as well as vegetable), the others being diet, meditation and specifically structured static and moving exercises as in Chi Kung (Qigong) and Tai Chi (Taiji). Although seemingly different, the same underlying principles are accepted for each regarding the nature of the human body and its place and purpose in the universe.

HISTORY

TCM was already a sophisticated, highly effective and firmly established system of health maintenance and restoration at the time of the Shang Dynasty of China in about 1000BC, and ancient texts dating from around that time and later contain material, information and philosophies which are obviously much older. The theory of Chinese medicine evolved to be used, with all its elements used as appropriate, to enhance the functions of each of them synergistically – like two plus two equalling eight instead of merely four.

The principles behind it: The Chinese view the body as a microcosm of the universe, and TCM is founded on the holistic concept of the universe as set out in the principles of Taoism or Daoism, which holds that everything in it is interdependent. As far as Western cultures are concerned, the increased popularity of this system is proof of the basic dissatisfaction in our own societies with much that Western

allopathic medicine has to offer.

Those patients who have given themselves over to a TCM practitioner may find it hard initially to understand what possible benefit there is in being pricked with needles, for example, or in performing strange-looking exercises, or consuming herbal potions which all our senses tell us to avoid, or in sitting motionless in 'contemplation of one's navel' when probably they have so many more pressing things to do – but the proof of this pudding really is in the eating of it.

This school of medicine has proved over thousands of years that it is highly effective – though not always, as with all others, in every case – to such an extent that it is now widely accepted in the West.

HOW DOES IT WORK?

TCM sets out, as do so many Eastern therapies, to balance and harmonise

Every part of a massive variety of plants can be used in Chinese Medicine

What is Chinese Medicine used for?

Chinese medical practitioners aim to use all the well established techniques at their disposal to give the patient a self-maintenance programme of therapy and life-management aimed at balancing their energy and their body/mind/spirit unit towards a good life. The herbs, for example, all have their own aspects of Yin and Yang and will be prescribed according to the patient's imbalance: if he or she is lacking in energy (a Yin condition) a Yang-type herb will be prescribed to make up the balance. Acupuncture can be used to stimulate either the production of energy in Yin conditions or to disperse it in Yang ones, and restore an even flow, and so on.

the flow of energy, life force or Chi within the body. Chi is believed to flow evenly on a twenty-four-hour cycle (which accords with the Western scientific acceptance of the body's roughly twenty-four-hour circadian or biological rhythms). It flows along channels or meridians, probably easiest thought of as directions, and has opposite qualities which must be balanced, called Yin and Yang. These are the eternal opposites of male and female, light and dark, full and empty, low and high, wet and dry and so on.

Other remedies: As well as relying on the five main principles of TCM, a practitioner may also recommend other remedies, such as a Feng Shui consultation to balance the Chi in the patient's home or workplace, all with the overall aim of balancing vital energy in an interdependent, reinforcing and supportive way so as to help the patient exist more harmoniously in the environment in which he or she finds him- or herself.

Of course, one does not have to be ill to seek a consultation: Chinese

medical practitioners are as happy to carry out check-ups as to treat disease, because the overall aim is to prevent disease occurring and to create a fulfilling, purposeful and happy life.

HOW DOES A TCM PRACTITIONER WORK?

The practitioner uses looking, listening, asking and feeling or palpation to diagnose disorders or imbalances. He or she will then consider all the modalities or therapies available within the whole concept of Chinese medicine and, like any other doctor or therapist, will prescribe accordingly from those, along with giving general advice on lifestyle and attitude.

The Five Element theory: The concept of earthly elements has been mentioned in connection with Indian Ayurvedic medicine. TCM recognises five elements: water, fire, wood, metal and earth, and these play a vital role in balancing Chi, in addition to Yin and Yang. The Five Element theory stems from observations of the various types of

dynamic processes, functions and characteristics in nature. Some TCM practitioners use the Five Element theory to decide how they will treat a patient, whereas others use the basic Yin/Yang perspective and develop their understanding of the patient's deficiencies or excesses of energy in order to treat him or her.

This whole concept is extremely complex and cannot possibly be covered here: there are many excellent books available for those who wish to pursue their knowledge of this vast subject.

WHERE CAN I FIND A TCM PRACTITIONER?

Word of mouth is a good way, but advertisements and leaflets are often found in clinics and hospitals (particularly in multi-cultural localities), in health food shops, in 'ordinary' Western hospitals, clinics and surgeries, on the premises of other complementary therapy practitioners, and in local and regional directories.

Traditional Chinese Medicine for horses

It is possible to ask any practitioner to treat a horse, as with any therapy, under veterinary referral in some countries. Acupuncture and acupressure, part of TCM, are practised fairly commonly on animals by trained veterinarians or other practitioners. Chinese herbalism may also be used.

Yoga

Yoga is an aspect of ancient Indian Ayurvedic medicine, and was probably one of the very first Eastern therapies to take a significant hold in the West. Yoga has several schools of thought, but all have the same basic aims.

PHILOSOPHY

As with other Eastern therapies, Yoga works on the premise that all the systems of the body, the mind and the spirit work best when they are in harmony and balance. The basic tenet of Ayurvedic medicine is that the body's energy, life force or 'prana' flows round many channels or meridians in the body, and that these channels and associated energy points – called 'marma' – can be stimulated and manipulated by specially structured stretches and postures: the essence of Yoga.

Prana apart, gentle stretches and movements are an excellent form of physical exercise, assisting muscles to regain their tone and 'realign' themselves, releasing knots of cramp and tension, and generally helping flexibility and mobility. The back is an important focus of attention since it contains the crucial spinal cord, and provides outlets and inlets for motor and sensory nerves.

HOW DOES IT WORK?

Physical Benefits: The purpose of Yoga is to counteract stiffness from tension by gently flexing and lengthening the muscles, tendons, ligaments and joints to get the prana flowing by stimulating the channels and marma points. The circulation of blood and lymph is improved, the spine gains in flexibility and resilience and the back muscles become stronger and more elastic.

Yoga to alleviate back pain: Those of us who have not developed good

Yoga for Horses

So far we have not heard about a formalised system of Yoga for horses, but the basic principles can certainly be applied to them. Because the basic essence of Yoga for humans consists of careful stretches, the practice of performing stretches with our horses is already applying a Yoga of sorts to them (see Stretching, p60 and Shiatsu, p24). However, in order to stimulate specific energy channels and/or marma, these would have to be transposed from a human Yoga chart to an equine one, and for this the expertise of an holistic veterinary surgeon and/or equine physical therapist versed in Yoga would be necessary. Shiatsu has been successfully transposed to horses by Pamela Hannay and others

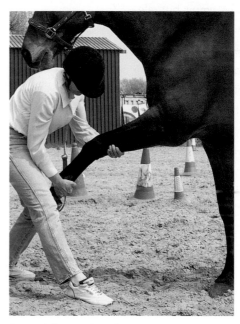

so why not Yoga? As things stand, careful stretches for horses will be beneficial to them and have similar benefits to Yoga for humans, in particular with regard to alleviating back pain.

Horses readily develop back problems simply because we sit on them, and then make them work whilst we do so. Their spinal structure was certainly not evolved to carry weight from on top in addition to the considerable weight of their abdominal contents slung beneath, and asking them to perform non-voluntary movements under our weight is almost bound to cause them injury of some degree. Yoga-type stretches should help alleviate their discomfort, and strengthen their back structure.

posture generally experience tension and discomfort in the muscles involved. Yoga will help us to develop a relaxed, yet gently tensioned and balanced upright posture when standing, moving and sitting, and of course when we are riding, too.

Psychological benefits: Inevitably Yoga will also have a significant and beneficial effect on the mind and spirit. We cannot operate at our best when stressed by stiffness, discomfort, restricted movement or muscular contraction and pain, and are bound to feel short-tempered and grumpy; but release from these physical tensions will clear and free the mind, and enable us to make more balanced judgements, and behave towards people and horses with greater equanimity and patience. Yogis (Yoga teachers) believe that physical tension causes psychic energy to be trapped in the spine, and that the practice of Yoga releases it and channels it through the vertebral column and associated soft tissues to the brain.

Maintaining a balance: Again, we come to the Eastern concept that if the balance of this energy – or, in this case, prana – is out of kilter we become sick, injured or in some way mentally or physically disadvantaged. Yoga balances the prana, whether from a therapeutic or maintenance viewpoint, to help keep us in optimal health.

SELF HELP

There is a plethora of books on

One of the most common health problems experienced by riders is back pain. Yoga can help to promote better posture when sitting, walking and, of course, riding

Eastern therapies and philosophies in which Yoga will be discussed. Also, because Yoga is a well established therapy in the West, classes and courses are frequently run by education centres, night schools and non-vocational educational establishments. Doctors' surgeries often display details of classes, as do other health and fitness centres and clinics; and Yogis (Yoga teachers) are often listed in local and regional directories.

Chi Kung (Qi Gong)

Chi Kung is one of the Traditional Chinese Medicine therapies: it is a way of banishing worry, stress and nervousness, all of which can upset the digestive and urinary systems and, therefore, the entire health of the body. It is a gentle form of exercise and posturing which promotes a healthy body and mind, and is used for health maintenance, disease prevention, and the rebalancing of the body/mind/spirit unit, in common with most Chinese therapies.

CHI KUNG IN THE WEST

As with many Chinese therapies, Chi Kung is extremely wide-ranging and can take a lifetime of study. Western practitioners understand the difference between the two cultures, East and West, and have succeeded in adapting Chinese practice to our rushed and overstressed Western lifestyle, with the aim of strengthening our immune systems (often weakened by over-protection from pathogenic organisms – too much hygiene!) and overcoming disharmonies of Chi in our bodies, minds and spirits.

A concept of gentle exercise: To many Westerners, the word 'exercise' means something that we do not want to do – hard effort, wasted time and a depletion of our energy sources, far from an enhancement of them. In practice, exercise can be as effortless as lifting a little finger! In China and other Eastern countries, the concept of regular, gentle and structured exercise is seen as crucial to health and a long life, and anything more stressful is undertaken with caution.

In sports physiology and therapy: It has been recognised for decades now that human athletes who push themselves to their limits are likely to live shorter lives than people who take things easier; they are also likely to suffer from other chronic diseases later in life. Examples quoted are poorer immune systems and osteoarthritis in particular. Although Chi Kung is a therapy offered in this book for riders, it is reasonable to suppose that overdoing things, even though it may not seem like it at the time, also adversely affects the lives and long-term health of our horses.

A philosophy of caution: It is not tough, either, to exercise ourselves or our horses in bad weather conditions without wearing appropriate clothing – thus Chi Kung is another Chinese philosophy which recommends sensible, reasonable and more gentle treatment of our bodies, minds and spirits, which will gradually build up energy and strength. As regards our horses, it can only be to their benefit to adopt these sensible philosophies of caution, which also means treating them with the consideration that should be accorded to any living being whose ambitions may be different from our own.

What is Chi Kung used for?

The term Chi Kung or Qi Gong loosely means 'energy cultivation', which indicates that it can help to maximize the way we store, move and use energy to maintain and improve our health and wellbeing. There are thousands of exercises for different purposes, such as reinforcing depleted energy; moving on or dispersing blocked or excess energy; and strengthening energy for defensive purposes.

Practitioners study for many years and regard their learning as never finished, and can display amazing feats of muscle strength which enable them to withstand tremendous blows and wounds. Other methods of Chi Kung help the practitioner strengthen the internal energy of the body and spirit, and promote the excellent health and longevity for which the Chinese are famous.

HOW DOES IT WORK?

Small, effortless exercises and 'rounded stillness' teach the student to co-ordinate body, mind and breathing to encourage the body's 'Chi' or energy to flow and encourage self-healing. These exercises are part of daily life in China where they are performed, along with their related therapy Tai Chi, in public and private, alone and in groups.

The idea of the exercises is that they activate energy meridians and acupoints according to how the body moves and is positioned, and the length of time the position is held.

CHI KUNG HEALING

Chi Kung as a form of healing involves a practitioner guiding his or her own Chi or energy, via acupuncture points, into the patient to enhance the flow in an unbalanced or diseased body. According to the practitioner, the patient may stand, lie or sit, and there is little or no physical contact, which makes the therapy hard for many Westerners to understand. It is essential that the practitioner himself (or herself) has a strong, vibrant energy system, encouraged by regular practice of the Chi Kung exercises and positions.

Chi Kung massage or 'hands-on' treatment again claims to facilitate the transfer of energy from or through the therapist to the patient, and seems to be highly effective when it takes place between practitioners and patients with the right attitudes for healing and belief in the system.

For maximum benefit choose a class which only allows a small number of pupils

The intent of the mind: It is important to believe that the Chi in one's body follows the intent of the mind. If the practitioner does not truly want to heal, and the patient does not truly want to get better, it will not, cannot, work. Where uncertainty exists, the energy is weakened. It is also difficult to achieve healing when the patient or practitioner is embarrassed or 'uptight'. 'Centring' is a crucial process in many Eastern therapies: it is vital to draw one's 'existence' down into the body's centre, a point about 4cm (2in) below the belly button inside the body. Settle and calm the mind and focus on your true intent, and the energy will flow! There are Chi Kung meditation practices which facilitate this process. Meditation, dealt with on page 174, does not necessarily mean that the practitioner goes into a trance or even remains still: it is possible to move and be in a meditative state at the same time.

SELF HELP

Chi Kung can be taught to a basic level by simply studying some of the many good books and videos available on the subject. This will get the student going; then, once some benefit is seen, many students will want to find a teacher – and this is not always easy. As with any 'new' idea, many teachers have jumped on the bandwagon and are taking Chi Kung classes when they themselves have little real knowledge of Traditional Chinese Medicine and are mainly interested in making some money. It is best to look for a teacher via word of mouth, although some good ones do advertise in local journals or can be found through local councils' leisure departments. Look for one who takes small groups and is willing to spend time not only showing and explaining the moves and postures, but also discussing the philosophies of Chi Kung and Chinese medicine.

Tai Chi (Taiji)

Tai Chi or Taiji is an Eastern art and therapy – not just a Chinese one – related to Chi Kung (Quigong); however, it involves graceful, flowing movements, which is different from the purely stationary postures of Chi Kung.

HISTORY

Tai Chi is believed to have come about from a dream experienced by the Taoist monk Chang San Feng in the fourteenth century AD, in which he saw a fight-dance between a snake and a bird; from their actions he developed thirteen movements. These have developed and changed somewhat over time, into the different schools of Tai Chi thought which we know today, and which all, nevertheless, share the same basic Taoist philosophies connecting them with Chi Kung (to which readers are referred, p158).

There is a powerful and effective martial art form of Taiji called Taijiquan which means 'supreme ultimate fist' and which demands a level of commitment in terms of personal discipline, time and regular training which is probably well beyond the ambitions or needs of the average student, who is simply looking for the best way to keep fit in body, mind and spirit without having to experience the stress of working out, jogging and so on. Through its Taoist roots and its links with Kung Fu, the fighting art of the monks of the Shaolin temple, Taijiquan probably goes back over 2,000 years – so in terms of most Eastern disciplines and therapies, it is comparatively new!

CAN I TEACH MYSELF TAI CHI?

There are many books and videos which claim to teach this art, though both of these formats have their limitations because of their static nature. As with anything involving movement, books and pictures can only give an overview or basic understanding of its actual practice. Videos are much better in that they can illustrate the motions themselves, though invariably they cannot give as much verbal information as books.

The best way to learn Tai Chi is definitely to find a good teacher, either for individual lessons or for classes. Advertisements for classes and lessons can be found in local newspapers, non-vocational educational supplements and establishments, regional directories, health food outlets and, of course, by word of mouth among those interested in health and fitness and oriental philosophies. Advertisements for Tai Chi videos for riders sometimes appear in equestrian magazines.

What is Tai Chi used for?

Both Tai Chi and Chi Kung enhance the development and maintenance of our health and wellbeing, regulating the system and preventing disease. The word or words 'Taiji' or 'Tai Chi' mean 'supreme ultimate', and most practitioners and experienced students of the art agree that it is probably the supreme ultimate as a form of exercise, maintaining internal and external health, and strengthening body and mind. It certainly seems to fulfil its promises of balancing the energy (Chi) flow of the body, calming the mind (Shen) and promoting ultimate internal and external health.

Alexander Technique

The technique of using the body to best advantage was devised by F. Mathias Alexander late in the nineteenth century; great interest is now being generated in its philosophies, and it is being applied to various artistic and sporting disciplines as well as to business and everyday life. As far as riding horses is concerned, the technique has been found to improve co-ordination, performance and wellbeing in the rider and, consequently, the horse's performance and attitude.

PHILOSOPHY

The body is born with an innate knowledge of how to function. It is said that a child learns over three-quarters of the things it needs to know in order to survive before it is five years old, one of the most important being how to hold and use its body – how to maintain and control its locomotory system. It probably learns fairly early on that injury causes pain, and by the same token learns that in order to avoid pain the body can be used in a different way, a compensatory way, to take the stress of the injured part. There are two problems with this, however: first, the new way of standing, sitting and moving may well be unnatural so the body is actually working at a disadvantage; and second, even when the injury has healed, the new way may become a habit.

When compensatory movement becomes a habit: Unfortunately, it is not only injury which causes problems, but also basic misuse of the body, and once misuse or compensatory movement has become habitual, it can take more than simply telling ourselves, or being told, to move properly to enable us to do so. Good posture involves what we casually refer to as reflex responses, 'automatic' responses, which we normally do not even think about; when they are working well and normally, the body works within normal limits with little apparent effort.

HOW DOES THE TECHNIQUE HELP?

The Alexander Technique can help us to learn to stop interfering with these reflexes so that we can restore their effectiveness and, therefore, normal movement. We feel able to move more easily, to breathe, speak, and even to think with greater ease and freedom, and when on a horse, to adopt an appropriate seat or position and to go with his movement more naturally, so enhancing our performance together.

Learning the technique: Lessons in the Alexander Technique, which is a hands-on experience, will teach the pupil to think about the movements of his or her body and how they affect muscle activity. The teacher will both tell and show the pupil how to achieve and recognise the right quality of muscle tone, which will help to release inappropriate

---

What is the Alexander Technique used for?

As far as riding horses is concerned, the technique has been found helpful in the following ways:

- it improves co-ordination, performance and wellbeing in the rider and, consequently, in the horse's performance and attitude
- it improves self-awareness and productive or creative thought
- it resolves chronic injuries or their effects, such as neck and back pain, shoulder tension
- it helps improve poor breathing techniques or disorders
- it helps to resolve stress-induced conditions and lack of energy

The Alexander Technique will be of benefit if these sorts of situations have been brought about by poor postural and movement techniques.

The Alexander Technique in the saddle concentrates on making riders aware of what their bodies are actually doing and enables them to assume the correct posture

tension, so freeing the body to become better and more naturally balanced and aligned.

HOW DOES IT WORK?

The effect on the horse: As far as riding is concerned, poor performance in the horse, 'difficult' behaviour, vices such as napping, rearing, bucking, refusing to 'go' properly, running away and even shying and jogging, may well be caused by poor riding technique stemming from a poor seat or position in the saddle, stemming, in turn, from poor posture both on the ground and on a horse.

A poor and unstable position unbalances the horse who, in carrying a rider is, remember, carrying about a sixth of his own weight and maybe more – a considerable burden, particularly when it is moving around. Because many riders do not learn how to actually school and train their horses properly, many horses are themselves moving unnaturally and wrongly; and because they have never been taught how to move safely and to their own advantage under a rider, it is even harder for them to cope with such a burden.

The effect on the rider: A rider must be straight and fully aware of how he or she is sitting – not crooked, or lopsided, or too far back or too far forward. A great many riders do have these faults, but do not have the remotest idea of it; they genuinely think they are riding straight and well. Alexander

Technique lessons will equip the student with body-awareness and resultant control, but for maximum benefit they need to be applied to riding by someone who is both expert in Alexander, and can also teach good riding: then the rider will be made fully aware of just how his or her body is positioned, how it is moving, and therefore how it is affecting the horse. It is not simply a matter of correct application of the aids, but of full mind and body co-operation with the horse.

SELF HELP

Although there are books on the Alexander Technique, and on its application and value relative to riding, it is not a technique that one can learn alone beyond the basics. As with so many modalities, there is nothing like personal experience to learn about it, and it is strongly advised that anyone interested in it has lessons from a qualified teacher. A course of lessons (a minimum of twenty is recommended) is obviously far more effective than just a few to start the pupil off on the right track – although even a few will bring about a noticeable improvement in the pupil's thought processes, bearing and posture, movement and wellbeing. It should be remembered that, unlike learning to ride, lessons in the technique are not an ongoing process which one needs to continue indefinitely: once proficiency is attained, the pupil is very much in control of his or her body, and good, correct movement and posture become habitual, not the injurious or

Many riders are rather lop-sided. This common fault is greatly helped by Alexander Technique training

compensatory kind. Once lessons have been taken, their benefit remains for life – provided, as with so many things, one keeps up the practice.

Riding and the Alexander Technique: Unfortunately there are very few people who are both qualified riding teachers and qualified Alexander Technique teachers: for instance, in

the UK at the time of writing there are only two. There are, however, numerous people teaching riding – and doing it well – who are not qualified, and it may be possible to find one of these who is also an Alexander teacher. On the other hand, becoming a proficient pupil of the technique by having lessons in it oneself may enable you to apply its techniques to riding.

Feldenkrais Method

How can you possibly control your body's movements when you don't really know what your body is doing? The Feldenkrais technique is based on educating students to achieve 'postural awareness' through slight and gentle, non-habitual exercises which aim to achieve efficient movement using the least effort. Participants learn to become aware of how they are actually moving, and learn, through experience, new and better ways of moving, with awareness and better control of their bodies.

Feldenkrais is an ideal method for removing blockages and raising awareness in the rider and, therefore, preventing resistances in the horse which cause battles or disappointing work. It teaches riders to feel and know when they are interfering with a horse's movement, so enabling them to 'free' their horse to give his best performance.

HOW IT EVOLVED

The method was devised by a physicist, Dr Moshe Feldenkrais, who, after a serious knee injury, began observing his own habitual movement patterns and, through considering different ways of moving, found that, as a result, he could move more easily, which lessened the impact of his injury. His system teaches people to understand how they are moving and to stop using poor movement patterns which become 'ingrained' into the nervous system which, in turn, causes them to keep on moving in the same way. Students learn to feel how they are moving and how poor movement patterns actually prevent them moving efficiently: the teacher will then help them to discover new, more efficient ways of moving, and to absorb the feel of these new types of movement which, in their turn, will become familiar to, and so habitually utilised by, the nervous system.

HOW IT WORKS

It is a particularly beneficial technique for riders because of the importance of their being in correct balance with their horses and, in order to enable the horse to perform optimally and free from discomfort or even pain, enables them to stop unwittingly giving the horse confusing messages. Because the rider is working with nature and moving correctly, certain uncomfortable or painful postures experienced by some riders can be lessened or eliminated.

The importance of posture: Many riders are crooked or unbalanced and genuinely do not realise it. As teachers, the authors have many times tried to correct students' postures, only to be told: 'But that's how I *am* sitting!'. Riders also say that initially they feel most peculiar when the teacher places them in the correct position and shows them how to move appropriately – but once they and their nervous systems become used to it, it feels so much better. The Feldenkrais method helps riders to feel right when they are correctly balanced, and to recognise what their bodies are doing so they only give a horse an aid when they

Feldenkrais for Rehabilitation

Within the method, there are two techniques: 'Awareness Through Movement' is used in groups, and 'Functional Integration' is for private, individual sessions. Feldenkrais is ideal for rehabilitation after illness or injury, or for congenital or hereditary problems which prevent a person moving normally and naturally. It has helped many people with emotional problems as it gives self-confidence and self-reliance, and is especially valuable for those involved in movement and physical technique such as riders, swimmers, musicians, craft workers, dancers, skaters, athletes and the like, both amateur and professional.

mean to do so; thus they avoid giving the horse involuntary aids, causing unwanted reactions. It is also surprising how many people move well on the ground but immediately adopt incorrect movements and imbalances once they sit on a horse: these, of course, subsequently unbalance the horse, and so a vicious circle is set up.

Riders are taught, among other things, to use their spines correctly in guiding the horse and absorbing his movements. They are taught to stop blocking their own natural movements, and thereby those of their horse, too.

Riders often have poor movement and self-carriage of the head, neck, shoulders and arms – and the hips and knees can be problems, too! Some feel pain and tension in the ankle, and especially running up the outside of the lower leg, due to poor leg and foot position, and inefficient weight absorption – although the rider's own make and shape can cause problems. All these difficulties can be helped significantly by Feldenkrais tuition and experiential learning.

SELF HELP

Although there are books and videos available for those wishing to learn about the Feldenkrais method and they are very helpful, there is no replacement for personal experience and tuition, either in a workshop or a private session. Increasingly, rider-related Feldenkrais days, weekends and other events are being held, not that they are not widely advertised

in the ordinary commercial equestrian press because of the high cost. Specialist groups with a holistic interest in horses, management and riding are the best sources of information, also classical riding groups, complementary therapy outlets – retailers selling

herbal and homoeopathic products – enlightened training centres, groups concerned with equine behaviour, and the training and rehabilitation of injured or 'problem' horses, are all probable sources of rider-related Feldenkrais tuition.

The Rider's Influence

Horses do not adapt naturally to having a weight, and especially a moving weight, on their backs. Their natural reaction when they feel a weight on their backs – and this applies as much to experienced, trained horses, if less than to younger ones – is to tense against it and brace (stiffen) their muscles. This alone is enough to hamper their movement. No horse moves as freely under even an expert rider as he does when loose.

The key to the horse's comfort, so that he can carry his rider with as little interference to his movement as possible, is that the rider must move in close sympathy with his movements – and riders can only do this if they are able to fully control their own body, and be completely aware of how it is positioned and moving. This is no simple matter – and it is the riders who cannot do this who complain most often that each time they ride, their horse resists them, either actively, or by simply withdrawing into himself and not responding to their requests or demands. Sadly, many riders then beat the horse out of anger and frustration, or 'to teach him a lesson' – which is, of course, totally useless, stupid and cruel.

The Feldenkrais Method makes it much easier for riders to be able to feel what they are doing and to be able to correct it

Exercise & Posture

The human body, as the equine, was meant to move, and it has been well established by the medical profession that moderate, appropriate exercise is one of the best health-giving remedies possible. The field of exercise and posture is vast, and specialised disciplines encompassing both are discussed in this book, such as dance therapy, the Alexander Technique and Feldenkrais. Other complementary therapies are based on movements, postures and exercises, such as Chi Kung, Shiatsu and Yoga.

PHILOSOPHY

Going for a walk before dinner or 'taking one's constitutional' was a regular part of most people's day until recent decades; even people

A common misconception among riders is that they cannot flex their hip joints. If you can walk you can flex your hip joints

who had a hard physical job realised the benefits of walking and exercising their body in different ways. Today, however, although there is increased interest in formalised walking such as rambling, it seems that shorter walks for fresh air and mental relaxation, including walking to and from work where practicable, have gone out of fashion – we appear to be more short of time, and less active altogether

because of the increase in sedentary pursuits, and perhaps we are lazier than previous generations.

HOW DOES IT WORK?

Avoid excesses: People who do not exercise are known to be generally less healthy in mind and body than those who gently tax themselves by taking moderate, regular exercise, whether this be in the form of a walk, or as dancing, running or some kind of sport. Too much exercise, though, can be as damaging as too little, and high level athletes do tend to suffer from such diseases as degenerative joint disease or osteoarthritis later in life, and to deteriorate more quickly physically (even if they maintain gentle exercise after their competitive careers), even to the extent that they might not live as long, according to some doctors, as people who are easier on their bodies.

A middle way: It is far better from a general health and strength point of view to make oneself fit gradually,

How does exercise benefit us?

The benefits include:

■ an increase in the heart and breathing rate, and so an increased supply to the body of oxygen and nutrients, and the quicker removal of waste products

■ the strengthening of body tissues

■ a more active mind, as we concentrate on how our bodies feel, and on what we observe around us

■ an increased secretion of beneficial hormones, including endorphins and encephalins

■ the psychological release of feelings such as stress, tension, anger, depression, helplessness, poor self-esteem and others – all of which are greatly reduced by exercise, according to therapists

and to maintain a moderate level of fitness, than to aim to reach peak performance – although many athletes want this so much, and want to succeed, that possibly in their cases not performing to the highest level of which they are capable might produce psychological problems based on feelings of disappointment, deprivation and frustration.

SELF HELP

There is so much information available in the field of exercise and posture that whole books have been written on it! Perhaps here it is sufficient to say that anything which keeps us healthily active is beneficial, whether this is simply going for regular walks, dancing, playing some kind of sport, practising Tai Chi, Yoga, Chi Kung, aerobics (with caution), swimming, skating or, of course, riding.

So whether you believe in using up energy in exercise, or using exercise and posture to get the energy flowing, there is no doubt that, carried out wisely, exercise is good for you.

Regular, moderate aerobic exercise both in the saddle and out of it will increase fitness and stamina

Zero Balancing

Zero Balancing is a technique based on both Eastern and Western principles of healing. It is a very gentle method which aims to achieve a balance between the body's energy and the musculoskeletal system using finger pressure and stretching exercises.

Its aim is to release accumulated tensions deep in the body, and it is said to effectively relieve stress, discomfort, pain and emotional problems. It is said to be applicable to a range of circumstances and is appropriate for health maintenance and personal development as well as therapeutic purposes.

PHILOSOPHY

The technique was developed in 1975 by Dr Fritz Smith, an American doctor, osteopath and acupuncturist who also studied rolfing (a somewhat 'energetic' and deep form of massage) and yoga. The body has several joints which have only very slight movement (such as the sacroiliac joints between pelvis and sacrum), their main purpose being the transmission of energy or force within the skeleton. If these joints become misaligned or imbalanced, the body moves in a compensatory way, setting up other imbalances and tensions which can have widespread and unexpected effects.

TECHNIQUE

A Zero Balancing practitioner will use particular finger pressures and sustained stretches which aim to create a stillness in a specific area, enabling the body to relax and 're-organise' its tissues around that area, so re-establishing normal structure and function.

Zero Balancing for Horses

The principles of Zero Balancing are gradually being transposed to horses – they too, like us, can suffer the physical manifestations of tension. Unfortunately, there are currently very few practitioners in the UK who can do this kind of specialist work. As a therapy it is more common in the USA.

Dance Therapy

It is said that anything we enjoy is good for us in moderation, and millions of people the world over enjoy dancing. It makes us feel good even if we are not particularly talented dancers but just like fooling around on the dance floor; and as purely physical exercise it provides a mental release and satisfaction.

As a therapy, it is surprisingly accepted and common. It is used to 'release the natural flow of bodily expression', as one leaflet put it: in short, it aims to help participants express their feelings through individual, spontaneous movements, as opposed to their learning a routine and performing set steps in a structured way.

Any release of emotion and tension, and any correct movement and 'loosening up' of joints and strengthening of tissues benefits riding: in particular, learning to use the body parts separately yet in co-ordination greatly improves and facilitates riding technique.

HOW DOES IT WORK?
Students are usually taken in groups, and therapists differ in their personal approach: often their treatment will include breathing techniques, slow, studied movements, rhythm practice, and often visualisation – in which they may discuss, for example, how the patient would like to move, and scenes which they find calming, exciting or helpful, particularly copying animal movements; some encourage the use of the voice during dancing.

The sheer sound and beat of music, whether it is slow and relaxing or more invigorating according to the patient's or participant's needs and preferences, is a very powerful encouragement and guide, said to stimulate the release of negative emotions and encourage the dancer to feel an involuntary surge of energy not experienced by, say, simply going for a walk.

Internationality: Used worldwide, some therapists prefer to use the music and rhythms of a particular country. Latin American music can be particularly effective, and Native American drumming and singing, African, Russian, Greek and oriental music are all suitable; other people may like pop music better, or the classics, rock, country music and so on. If the dancer is capable of expressing an opinion, he or she is often asked what they prefer, and what will make them happy.

SELF HELP
You can find classes through health food shops, local councils and libraries, civic centres, schools – especially those used for adult education classes – doctors' surgeries, clinics, and by looking for advertisements in local papers, regional directories or colleges of education.

Of course, you can simply put on your favourite music and dance away at home on your own or with partners, friends or family, although from a therapeutic point of view for those with specific emotional problems, classes with a therapist are the best option.

What is Dance Therapy used for?

It helps to treat emotionally disturbed patients by both invigorating and calming them in a beneficial way, and by giving them the benefits of plain physical exercise which they would otherwise not take. Emotionally disturbed people frequently perform non-productive movements (like horses with stereotypies or vices) such as rocking, excessive nail-biting, self-mutilation, walking or running aimlessly around, and flapping the arms for no apparent reason, all believed, again as in horses, to provide an emotional release for distress, however caused. Dance and movement therapy is used in mental hospitals, and patients do seem to improve after attending classes.

Pilates

The Pilates method is an exercise technique which works in a specifically individual way according to the mental and physical needs of the receiver. Developed early in the twentieth century by a German, Joseph Pilates (pronounced Pi-lah-tees), the method provides both physical and mental training, and its major principle is to strengthen the postural muscles which stabilise the torso – an essential element of good riding!

PHILOSOPHY

Pilates aims to realign and rebalance muscles, and is gentle yet highly effective, avoiding any sort of soft tissue injury which can sometimes actually be caused by other less subtle exercise techniques and fitness régimes. As well as being used to enhance the fitness and function of a healthy body, it is also used in rehabilitation programmes after injury.

It is becoming increasingly popular with athletes, dancers and other performers, from those who are already commited to bodywork of some kind, to others who have never exercised in their lives. Elderly people and those recovering from injury find it particularly rewarding, as do those suffering from stress-related and eating disorders, and many other hard-to-treat conditions which themselves debilitate an already malfunctioning body: for instance, M.E., osteoporosis, repetitive strain injury and weight disorders.

TECHNIQUE

Clients of a Pilates practitioner will have a carefully devised exercise régime worked out specifically for their needs, to retrain the body to work effectively with minimal effort and no tension. It is claimed that the body will come into 'perfect balance', resulting in the stimulation of the immune system and improved general health due to the internal organs being enabled to position themselves naturally and so function correctly. Posture, strength and co-ordination are all improved, to the overall benefit of the client.

Pilates is a gentle form of exercise, which not only improves fitness of the body but also relieves mental stress

Hypnotherapy

Hypnotherapy does not work for everyone – but nor is it some weird entertainer's trick to get people to do things they don't want to do without having any idea of what is happening to them. It is a valid therapy fully recognised by the UK's National Health Service and those of many other countries, and it can be a regular part of the treatment and rehabilitation of mental patients, as well as just those with mild psychological difficulties. Hypnosis has been described as a naturally occurring condition akin to day-dreaming, but it is structured and guided rather than random.

HOW IT WORKS

Do practitioners really swing a pendant in front of your eyes, chanting some clichéd phrase? Well, the pendant part might apply with some practitioners as a method of getting you to concentrate, but rest firmly assured, no practitioner can 'make' you do anything you would not normally want to do.

The client will usually be encouraged to relax either by sitting in a comfortable chair, or lying or half-lying on an inviting sofa or couch. The use of a pendant is known as a 'fascination technique', but not all practitioners use it. Some ask you to concentrate on something marked on the ceiling, a particular picture on the wall, or an attractive object in their line of sight. Others do speak quietly to you, but quite normally, and not particularly in a sleep-inducing monotone because they don't want you to go to sleep: you have to be conscious to respond and benefit, but

deeply relaxed and, according to some, almost in a trance.

The therapist usually asks the client about his or her background, things they have enjoyed in their life, and unpleasant things which might have brought on the current problems, and does an assessment of possible reasons. He or she then brings the conversation round to ways of correcting it, all in a gently reassuring and gradually progressive way.

PROGRAMMING YOUR MIND

Imagine you are having problems performing lateral work (it does help to have a therapist who can ride here!): the therapist will talk you through a schooling session and tell you to vividly picture yourself riding perfect movements, putting into practice everything you know you should be doing but can't seem to get together when riding, and to visualise glorious success, perfect

What can Riders use it for?

Hynopsis as a therapy is perfect for riders who have problems relating to confidence, co-ordination of movement, adapting to their horse, competition nerves, or just getting-on nerves. It truly involves mind over matter, and is said to be a most enjoyable process.

movements, a willing horse going perfectly – and so on. In other words, you programme your mind, mentally rehearsing and living the moves, and your mind tells you that you can and will do it.

You can make all your mistakes under hypnosis and get them out of your system, rather than doing it on your horse and upsetting him. You can think clearly, give aids perfectly and at exactly the right time, take off at a jump smoothly at the ideal distance and get away with barely a disturbance in your position, achieving clear round after clear round – all in the comfort of the practitioner's cosy consulting room.

There is no suggestion of the hypnotherapist having any sort of power over the client. As with most complementary therapies, intent is the crucial factor: thus the client must really want to overcome her problems, and the therapist must be fully trained and in tune with this type of work so that he or she can really help the client.

FREEING THE BRAIN

Hypnotherapy obviously works by influencing and 'freeing' the rider's brain. The brain's right side, which governs the irrational side of our nature and our unconscious and subconscious functioning, often takes control just when we do not want it to do so. The left side, which controls the conscious and logical functions, must learn to take precedence when we ask it to. This is particularly important to riders because horses are extremely sensitive to our thought processes and also to minute movements, voluntary and involuntary, made by our bodies. We, therefore, have to control ourselves most effectively in order to control our horses. It takes two to ride, and this is not true of any other sport in quite the same way.

OVERCOMING LACK OF CONFIDENCE

When we make a mess of something, all too often the right side of the brain keeps reminding us of how stupid we felt, what a failure we are, and what a waste of time it is to keep trying, despite the fact that we may have made only one

People who take up the sport at an older age often feel nervous about a number of things: how will the horse react? will I fall off and hurt myself? These fears can result in the rider abandoning their chosen sport almost as soon as they have begun. Hypnotherapy may help the rider to cope with these worries

mistake. In a sensitive or susceptible person, this can easily lead to lack of confidence next time the occasion arises: you keep remembering what you did wrong, not what you did right, and this affects your horse's mental approach, too.

Hypnosis can help the left side of your brain to overcome the right side's 'run-you-down' attitude. The therapist will promote relaxation in the client, and lead him or her through a successful riding experience, in minute detail, getting everything right, and often making it so vivid that the recipient almost thinks it was real.

WILL IT WORK?

Therapists quite often tape a session, or provide a client with a tape to play at some time when they can concentrate and relax in peace and private and when they have plenty of time to visualise and 'live' the good techniques and experiences. Some take longer than others to improve, but if you are receptive to hypnotism, the technique is almost bound to work sooner or later, after which you should be in a position to 'treat' yourself whenever a problem arises, perhaps with occasional consultations, if necessary.

FINDING A THERAPIST

Try looking in your local directories, or contacting equestrian organisations for a 'horsey' hypnotherapist. The information in the Useful Addresses section of this book should also be helpful.

Self-Hypnosis

Before trying the techniques on yourself, it is strongly advised that you have some sessions from a specialist therapist, ideally one who rides because of the technical nature of our sport, although this might be difficult to arrange.

Self-Help Tapes

Your therapist could probably give you a general self-help tape to listen to, ideally every day or, more probably, in the evening when you are slightly tired, relaxed and have finished all your chores. You do have to concentrate on the tape and visualise everything as described on it with sincerity and good intent. When you get into it, you will realise afterwards that you were, indeed, in a mild, self-induced trance even though you had no sensation of losing control and were certainly not unconscious. You experience deeper breathing, relaxation and a slower heart rate. Some do fall asleep part way through, but the messages on the part of the tape they 'miss' do go into the brain – and, of course, you can always replay it later to make sure there is nothing amiss on it – if you are that cynical!

Rest assured, also, that unless you are actually asleep, you can bring yourself out of your trance at any time just by opening your eyes. You are in control, not a voice on a tape or some induced process in your brain.

Hypnosis for Riders

Riders invariably live very busy lives, and finding the energy to do anything other than essential chores is difficult. However, many people who experience self-help tapes report increased energy and enthusiasm for life's daily routine – yet they often say they feel calmer about everything and more confident about themselves, their ambitions and their lives. And as long as the whole procedure is done correctly, this calmness carries over into the crucial riding activities, and people usually say that their riding and handling of their horse, coping with spooks and so on, is much more effective and enjoyable.

Riding is almost always improved by increased relaxation in the rider, as this transmits itself to the horse, and this is one of the keys to truly effective riding in a partnership.

Relaxation Techniques

Controlled relaxation of mind and body is generally the key to good riding and horse handling; however, it is something that some people find very difficult to achieve.

WHY IS RELAXATION USEFUL?

If there is one thing that horses can sense immediately it is tension. They are normally fairly laid back creatures themselves, but because they are prey animals, there is always a certain guardedness and an awareness of possible danger just beneath the surface of their relaxed appearance. They pick up any tension in a fellow member of their group or herd straightaway, and because of the way the herd alarm system works, become alert, tense, and on their toes themselves. This is not always a helpful characteristic for riders and handlers, who may be feeling an element of tension themselves, because a horse will immediately sense this and, by his very nature, become somewhat on edge, too, less willing to 'listen' and more likely to spook, and will certainly not be in the mood for close, mutual communication.

Horses can also tell the difference between 'horsey' and 'non-horsey' people, and between 'animal' and 'non-animal' people, and will react to them accordingly.

Helpful tension: There are times when a certain amount of tension may be considered useful. If, for example, you are hacking across a field and are charged by a bull or a herd of bullocks, it is no good remaining relaxed – you want to get out of their way as quickly as possible, and a little tension here may just help you remove yourselves speedily from an unpleasant situation.

Similarly, in a competitive situation, some riders feel that a little tension will stir up their horse and encourage him to make that extra effort.

LEARNING TO RELAX

Learning how to control tension can only help your relationship with your horse – and with other people, too. There are all sorts of methods of promoting relaxation: perhaps at present you find stretching out in front of the television a good way to relax, or maybe with a good book and a glass of wine. However, formal relaxation techniques taught in company and with a good teacher who can focus your mind and teach you how to do it properly are often a really enjoyable way of learning to 'let go' – and of making new friends at the same time. These might include autogenic training, hypnotherapy and Yoga.

As a rule there is also no shortage of general relaxation classes of various types; these are usually advertised in health food shops, doctors' and other surgeries, clinics, night school and other educational premises, 'learning' supplements in local newspapers and magazines, and in sports gymnasia.

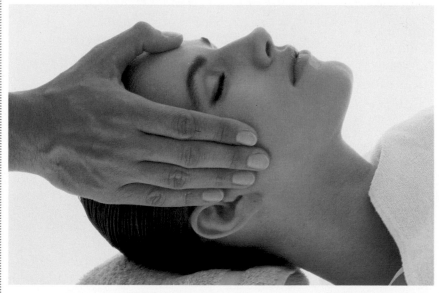

A good teacher can help focus your mind and release tension, with a variety of different relaxation techniques now widely available across the country

Meditation

Meditation has been an important part of Eastern, oriental medicine for thousands of years, and like many other therapies and medicine systems of that nature, it has increased in popularity in the West in the last half century or so. A simple definition may be that meditation is a means to exercise the mind in contemplation. It is not going to sleep, it is not self-hypnosis, it is not letting the mind wander randomly around, and it is not switching off completely from yourself: quite the opposite. It is guided contemplation, initially by a teacher and later by yourself.

Benefits of Meditation

Competent 'meditators' are always adamant about the benefits of meditation. They regard meditation as an essential part of their day and feel:

- stronger
- less vulnerable to life
- clearer-headed
- more decisive
- independent yet able to help others
- healthier

PHILOSOPHY

Chi or Qi follows the intent of the mind: when this becomes confused, unable to concentrate, stressed by happenings in one's life or suffers from sickness, its Chi is dispersed and the body Chi becomes weakened. The overall balance of body, mind and spirit is disturbed. To restore the balance, the mind must be settled and re-focused on the mind intent. The various Eastern cultures, religions and practices all differ in just how to do this, and many complex books have been written on the subject of meditation.

HOW DOES IT WORK?

In the Western world, meditation classes, tapes, books, videos and study circles have brought to other cultures the undoubted benefits of being able to concentrate the mind and 'tune out' external influences, even if only for a few minutes each day. Half an hour a day is recommended. Some schools of thought require participants to adopt certain postures, as in Yoga, others promote meditation during movement such as Chi Kung and Tai Chi, some teach chants or mantras as a means of concentrating the mind, whilst others preach silence. Meditation is even taught on distance-learning courses with manuals, audio tapes and videos as learning materials. Most people, however, prefer to experience the techniques in company or at least during private lessons.

Students are encouraged to feel, to listen to and concentrate on their breathing. Fresh Chi enters with each inhalation and stale Chi is expelled with each exhalation to be refreshed by the universe. It is not essential to have your eyes closed – in fact, if you meditate when you are tired you are not likely to obtain full benefit from it as you will probably fall asleep. Insomniacs, however, could benefit from this!

Other techniques: Other techniques will be taught in classes, such as feeling the strength of your Chi, feeling or imagining it flowing strongly and evenly through your body, perhaps concentrating on areas where you have an injury, a disease, or the feelings of an emotional problem of any kind. Sometimes

Guided comtemplation takes discipline

vizualisation of light is taught.

Very often, new students cannot manage more than a few minutes, if that, of meditation, no matter how sincere they are. Those who try it for a giggle usually cannot manage it at all, not surprisingly. But if you persevere it does become easier.

FINDING THE TIME

Horse owners, particularly those with other pressures and commitments such as a job and family, nearly always moan, understandably, that they really haven't time to spare half an hour a day meditating! First thing in the morning, the ideal time, is too rushed, they are working or coping with domestic and family matters all day (try your lunch hour), and in the evening they are so exhausted after seeing to the horse(s) that their single hour

relaxing in the evening is so precious they don't want to switch off from their favourite television programme, music, book or conversation with their partner. If you meditate in bed you go to sleep.

A Daily Routine

The benefits of meditation are undoubted. Although few of us would wish or perhaps have the ability to become so tuned out of the physical world that they can withstand extreme pain, as can some Yogis, half an hour a day on most days should be within reach of most people. The effects and value of your personal body clock should not be ignored. Try to give the same part of the day every day to meditation. Be comfortable and wear loose clothing. Try to meditate out of doors if possible in fresh, unpolluted air; make sure you are warm enough; and do not meditate within an hour of eating – your breathing co-ordinates with your flow of Chi, and a full stomach can interfere with this; Chi (and blood) are also diverted during digestion to the important task of extracting nutrients, rather than centreing your mind.

However, competent 'meditators' regard it as an essential part of their day, and consider it is tremendously worthwhile to sacrifice something else to make the effort.

Metaphysics

Metaphysics is a formalised therapy which illustrates perfectly the concept of mind over matter. Its guiding principle, or mission statement in today's parlance, is 'Your life is the mirror of your mind'.

WHY DO WE NEED IT?

It is often somewhat galling for people who are going through an extended run of misfortune to be told to snap out of it, that it can't last for ever (when it's already lasted for twenty years), or to think positively. Many people need help to do those things, and qualified metaphysicists can certainly help. It is not the same thing as counselling

which, in its worst form, simply involves talking to someone who only listens and offers no counsel at all.

HOW DOES IT WORK?

Metaphysicists help and guide their clients to look at things realistically and to get at the truth of situations, to put past experiences into perspective, and as far as

horsepeople are concerned, to tune into a far better relationship with their horses to the benefits of their lives and futures as a whole.

WHO CAN HELP?

In the UK, riding instructor, metaphysicist and Reiki practitioner Wendy Price has developed 'reflective riding' which she describes as a 'thought-provoking tool for healing the mind, body and spirit'. Her system is proving very popular with riders and their horses, whether they have problems or just want better relationships out of life and, perhaps, a more balanced view of it.

For further details, see Useful Addresses.

Neuro-Linguistic Programming

We are all familiar with the concept of 'the power of positive thinking', and neuro linguistic programming (NLP) is an effective way of thinking ourselves competent: it is a way of teaching the human brain that there is more than one way to react to circumstances, and it aims to change negative responses ('I can't jump that!') to positive ones ('That's easy!').

By making your mental approach to a situation positive, NLP can actually help to improve your physical performance. Visualisation techniques in many therapies get us to vividly imagine or 'see' ourselves doing something we really want to do, and to experience it mentally so

Many riders experience a mental block when it comes to jumping lessons. NLP can help to overcome their fears

that we are confident of its actually happening.

PHILOSOPHY

The learning process: Anyone who has ever learned to do anything has experienced NLP to some extent. The brain communicates to the body, which responds by doing what is asked of it – and the more often this is repeated, the easier it becomes, until it is taken for granted – like learning to walk or write, driving a car, tacking up a horse, typing a letter, playing an instrument, speaking a language and so on. When we are first learning it usually seems strange and difficult because our neural pathways have never experienced it before and have to work out ways of doing it; this applies to mental or emotional tasks as well as physical ones.

A bad experience: If we have a bad experience our brain similarly stores it (the smallest thought is an experience) and establishes it in our minds as the norm, sometimes quite

firmly. So whenever a similar situation arises in our lives, our subconscious mind instantly flashes these picture-memories up to the conscious mind as a warning: 'This is what happened last time you were in this situation. Don't do it again.' And very often we don't, or we become very negative and nervous about it, which again, often results in stopping us even if we *were* willing to have a go. This can also result in our performing badly, maybe hurting ourselves and actually reinforcing the negative memory.

PROBLEM AREAS

Anticipating trouble: People can become nervous of an activity, such as jumping, even if they have never been hurt when actually doing it, simply because they know that it is possible to fall off, and then they just imagine falling off and getting hurt. Falling off can also result in our responsibilities having to be met by others, if there are any others: if we are incapacitated or killed, who will look after our families, what will happen to our animals, and so on? If we knew for certain that falling off was not painful or dangerous, we should not be frightened of it.

Lacking in confidence: Another area of problems is during competition: some people who seem full of confidence become seriously nervous once they are actually in the arena 'being criticised' (judged). Perhaps this is because they care too much what other people think of them; or perhaps they are trying to prove to themselves, and not to others, that they are good at something, but the mere presence of some unknown judge undermines their self-esteem.

Frightened of lessons: Some people are similarly frightened of having lessons, even though they want desperately to improve; this may be because they are afraid of showing up their inadequacies to their teacher; or because they know that what they will be asked to do will be difficult because they could not do it previously; or because it is a new movement or idea and they have never tried it before, and might make a mess of it and 'show themselves up'.

HOW DOES NLP WORK?

NLP turns around all these negative thought-pictures in our minds and replaces them with positive pictures. It is all about confidence and believing (even knowing) that you can, realistically, do what you are aiming at, once sensible goals are set. A practitioner may get you to remember an occasion when you did well and really enjoyed yourself; he/she will then designate 'anchors', small physical actions or postures to adopt whenever you think of that good time: then, when you are trying to do it again, you adopt the anchor which is associated in your mind with the good time, and you experience again the brilliant feeling of success and enjoyment – and gradually you will find that you perform much better. There are various other techniques which a practitioner can use to help establish positive thoughts and images, and to banish negative, bad ones.

Memory association: The basic principles of neuro linguistic programming are inbuilt into our minds. Everyone has good times in their lives as well as bad ones. When we hear a particular song, especially if performed by an artiste or group associated specifically with it, we often instantly go back to the time in our lives when that song meant something special to us, and this can make us feel happy or sad, embarrassed or pleased with ourselves, and so on. Association is very strong: for instance, many can remember what they were doing, where they were, and who they were with, when the deaths were announced of President Kennedy, John Lennon and Diana, Princess of Wales. And most people will always remember how they spent the millenium New Year's Eve in 1999, even though they may forget others.

Using 'anchors': By devising 'anchors' to associate with particular feelings – such as pressing your fingers together for confidence or scratching your nose for happiness – you can eventually, perhaps with the aid of an NLP practitioner or just a friend who understands the technique, bring those feelings to the fore simply by using the anchor. Other anchors include imagining vividly an occasion of great success and confidence, and also allocating a specific word or phrase to associate with it. Basically, repeating the process of conjuring up your anchors along with the picture will reinforce them all in your mind, so that ultimately the anchors can be used to serve up the feeling you want. This biological process works!

My Horse and NLP

Horses, of course, have to be retrained to overcome fears, and cannot be taught NLP: however, scientific research in the USA has shown that by repeatedly giving a horse its favourite titbit and praising it during something unpleasant, the horse will willingly come to tolerate it, and may actually seem to enjoy it, or will at least learn to ignore the unpleasantness, and to associate the procedure with the titbit instead. Gradually the titbit can be dispensed with, verbal praise being enough.

Biofeedback

This is a technique which claims to inform people of specific internal physiological states; it was pioneered by Maxwell Cade.

HOW DOES IT WORK?

It uses electronic methods, and claims that particular physiological states correspond to certain types of activity. For example, a change in skin resistance (measured electronically) from low to high is felt to correspond to a feeling of calm and relaxation, as does an increase in the temperature of the fingers.

WHAT IS IT USED FOR?

Biofeedback is used to help people control and change how they feel, to help them affect their own physiological responses to emotions; it is therefore often used to help prevent and control stress-related disorders such as migraine, indigestion, muscle tension, nail-biting and so on. The patient receives information about their state, and learns to control a condition by imagination.

Autogenic Training

Autogenic training is a self-suggestion technique that deals with a rider's general tension and irritability. Usually a six- to eight-week (part-time) course is needed for the pupil to learn its technique effectively, after which he or she should be able to use it alone, to help with psychological and resulting physical problems as they arise.

HOW DOES IT WORK?

Like other self-suggestion techniques, the student learns how to visualise situations that she wants to occur (such as being relaxed and confident during a show-jumping round) and how to convince herself that she is capable of performing at the desired level. On a general basis, the technique involves practising mental images which the student finds relaxing and which can be transferred to specific situations.

It can be used to treat a variety of both psychological and physical conditions, such as insomnia, depression and stress, and irritable bowel syndrome, headaches and peptic ulcers.

SELF HELP

With the reassuring presence of a calm, confident teacher, the classes are a great help and, certainly for those new to the technique, set the student on the right track to be able to use autogenics alone and effectively.

Therapeutic Touch

Therapeutic Touch is a healing therapy devised by an American nurse, Dolores Krieger. She has always had a great interest in healing from the holistic point of view, despite working in a conventional medical environment, and followed the subject of faith or spiritual healing avidly.

Dr Grad's experiment: She knew about the experiments of a Dr Bernard Grad at McGill University in Canada who wanted to find out if faith alone was the main cause of healing, and the reason behind the placebo effect. He asked a successful healer to hold in his hands one of two identical glass containers of water. Dr Grad then sowed barley seed in two batches, one being watered with the water the healer had held and the other with the untreated water. The seeds from the first batch grew bigger and greener and were found to contain higher levels of chlorophyll – plants' source of energy through the process of photosynthesis – than the seeds/plants watered with the untreated water. Several repeats of the experiment produced the same results.

A healer's touch: Dolores Krieger believed that if healing could produce higher levels of chlorophyll, it should also be able to produce higher levels of haemoglobin, which is closely related chemically to chlorophyll and is the blood's oxygen carrier and, therefore, energy 'enabler'. In 1971, she assisted with an experiment involving twenty-eight patients suffering from various diseases, some of them serious, in which nineteen were treated with hands-on healing from a noted healer and nine had no healing treatment. As Krieger suspected, haemoglobin levels rose in the treated patients but not in the other nine, and some of the first group also reported that the symptoms of their diseases either became less, or even disappeared altogether.

Healing worldwide: Further study of healing led Dolores Krieger to learn more about it, and to teach it to many other healthcare professionals, including other nurses and also doctors. Aware of the traditional scepticism of the medical profession, she named this healing Therapeutic Touch – which, of course, simply implies therapy by means of touch. Under that name, healing is now widespread worldwide, mainly in hospitals and clinics.

Glossary

This glossary has been devised as a general list of words commonly used in the context of healing and mainly of complementary therapies. Not all the words it contains are used in the book, but they may be useful for those readers wishing to increase their knowledge.

abduction: movement away from the midline or median plane of body.

acupoints: specific points usually on the energy channels or meridians of the body where energy flowing close to the body surface can be adjusted to promote healing.

acute: a condition which occurs suddenly and lasts a short time.

adaptogenic: herbal medicine term to describe a substance which helps to restore the body's homoeostasis and improve its adaptability and, therefore, the functioning of the immune system.

adduction: movement towards the midline or median plane of body.

adhesion: fibrous tissue abnormally joining together other tissues, normally after injury.

adjuvant: a substance enhancing the activity of another.

aerobic: needing the presence of oxygen for its function (aerobic exercise, growth of aerobic bacteria etc).

allergy: abnormal or over-reaction of the body to a substance.

allopathic: medical system which aims to treat a disease process by bringing about another process of a different kind; medical system which uses counter remedies to induce an effect opposite from the symptoms present, eg administering anti-inflammatories, antibiotics, painkillers etc; allaying symptoms.

alterative: substance which enhances health by gradually 'cleansing' or detoxifying the body and improving the uptake of nutrients; improves metabolism.

anaerobic: not needing the presence of oxygen (anaerobic exercise, growth of anaerobic bacteria etc).

analgesic: relieving of pain.

anaesthesia: state of completely losing consciousness and physical sensation.

anodyne: painkilling.

antiopathy: medical system which uses medicines to suppress symptoms, a policy many believe does not address the root cause.

aperient: mild laxative.

arterial: relating to arteries.

articulate: unite by moveable joining, to join with when in movement.

astringent: substance which contracts cell walls and stops unwanted discharge.

asymmetry: lack of symmetry, evenness or balance.

ataxia: loss of muscular co-ordination.

atony: absence of normal muscle tension.

atrophy: wasting away or decrease in size of an organ or muscle resulting from poor circulation or lack of use.

auras: the layers of energy around the body perceived by some in colours, and by others as feelings of strength or weakness, good or evil.

auscultation: listening to a patient's body sounds without a stethoscope.

avascular: lack of blood vessels.

balsam: scented plant fluid.

benign: not harmful.

biodynamics: study of the movement of the body and the forces acting upon it.

bioenergy: the biological energy in all living creatures.

bitters: group of chemically related herbs with a bitter taste.

'black box': radionics/radiesthesia.

bursa: a cavity filled with lubricating fluid (synovia) enclosed by a sac of tissue and sited to protect against friction, such as around a joint, on top of vertebral spinous processes etc.

bursitis: inflammation of bursa.

calcification: becoming hardened by calcium deposits.

callus: a toughened, fibrous or bony area protecting against and formed as a result of friction.

carcinogenic: causing cancer.

cardiac: relating to the heart.

carminative: easing of cramp-like stomach pains and flatulence, mildly sedating the intestinal wall.

carpal: relating to the knee (wrist) on the foreleg of an animal, but the legs of a human.

catalyst: a substance which enables

a chemical reaction or process to happen more quickly.

cathartic: substance acting as a purgative, 'clearing out' (usually) the intestines and 'cleansing' the system.

cell: the body is composed of individual, microscopic 'containers' of various substances and structures; these have different purposes – namely skin cells, blood cells, cartilage cells or bone cells – and they are the basic units of living structures, plant or animal.

cellulose: major part of the equine diet; carbohydrate forming plant cell walls.

chakra: one of several energy centres of the body, as perceived by Indian medicine.

Chi: energy or life force (Chinese), believed fundamental to all aspects of life. Present throughout the universe and concentrating, in the body, in the meridians.

chronic: gradual in onset (disease), long-lasting.

Circadian rhythm: periodic rhythm or cycle of the body governing functions, particularly sleeping, energy levels and alertness, and synchronised with the day/night cycle of slightly over twenty-four hours.

cognitive ethology: a branch of biology involving the study of character and suggesting that some animals do have an innate sense of right and wrong and are able to judge situations and act accordingly.

collagen: fibrous protein tissue in bone, cartilage and soft tissues.

complementary nutrition: the art of

feed supplementation; the use of feedstuffs which are incomplete in themselves but which can make up a balanced, complete diet when used with others of appropriate analysis.

congenital: a condition present at, and usually before birth, not necessarily inherited.

connective tissue: the fibrous soft tissue which binds together, strengthens and stabilises other tissues.

constitutional remedy: a remedy which encompasses the whole body/mind/spirit of the patient.

contraction: narrowing, shortening or tightening.

contra-indication: condition present which makes the application of a particular therapy or medicine inadvisable.

Dan Tien: energy centres of the body as perceived by Chinese medicine.

debility: weakness, being 'run down'.

decoction: herbal remedy made by boiling vegetable material in water, particularly woody material, allowing it to cool, and offering it to the horse to drink.

demulcent: a substance which soothes and protects irritated or damaged mucous membranes, especially the intestines.

diagnosis: discovering and identifying a disorder by assessing its charactistics and the symptoms or signs present.

dilation: widening or expanding.

distal: distant from the centre of the body.

diuretic: increases the production and flow of urine.

dorsal: towards or sited on the back surface, the surface facing away from the ground, opposite to 'ventral'.

dorsal spinous processes: projections from the tops of vertebrae.

electrolytes: mineral salts such as sodium, magnesium, potassium, chlorine and calcium which regulate the conduction of electricity in the body; they are lost in sweat.

encephalins/endorphins: the body's own opium-related substances which help to reduce pain and induce euphoria or the 'feel good' factor.

energy bodies: the layers or 'sheaths' of energy believed in Chinese medicine to surround the body.

energy medicine: healing system which stimulates the body to heal itself by evening up or balancing its energy flow, rather than simply providing back-up with additional medicines such as antibiotics, anti-inflammatories and painkillers.

enteric: relating to the intestines.

enzyme: a protein which acts as the catalyst of a biochemical process or reaction.

essential oils: volatile oils obtained from plants, each with a characteristic scent and, it is believed, often with therapeutic properties, used in aromatherapy.

eugenics: homoeopathic term for the treatment of the foetus in the womb.

expectorant: substance which stimulates the expulsion of mucus from the lungs.

fascia: sheet or band of tough, fibrous tissue, around and supporting the body structures below the skin.

fibrosis: formation of fibrous tissue, of a type that is poorly supplied with blood.

flaccid: weak, soft, without 'tone'.

generic: term used in pharmacy to indicate the name of a chemical substance instead of its brand name, eg paracetemol (the drug) instead of Panadol (the brand name).

haemoglobin: the oxygen- and iron-carrying protein colouring matter of the red blood cells.

haemostatic: the ability to stop or control bleeding.

'heating': term used to indicate excess energy obtained from feed, usually cereal concentrates; it can also be the result of non-organic additives in feeds such as preservatives or even synthetic vitamins in some cases. Processed sugars can cause 'heating'.

heroic remedies: 'strong' medicines which can be risky and have unpleasant side-effects.

holism: the scientific theory and principle of holism was first published by philosopher Jan Christian Smuts (1870–1950) who stated that holism is the creation and maintenance of wholes, of complete biological systems; any lack of completeness or imbalance and disharmony can interfere with the body's naturally holistically structured systems.

homoeopathic: curing a disease process by administering medicines which, in the healthy individual, would cause that disease. Based on the concept that 'like cures like'.

homoeostasis: state of physiological balance, within certain limits, of the internal systems of a body; tendency of biological systems to self-adjust to maintain themselves within optimal functional balance for survival, regardless of external environment and influences.

hormone balancer: herbal remedy which rebalances the hormonal system.

hormones: the body's 'chemical messengers' secreted by many glands of the body, according to purpose.

hydroponic grass: grass and its relatives, usually barley, grown by means of liquid nutrients, mainly water, and no soil; it is ideal for winter use.

hyperthermia: excessive heat in the body.

hypotensive: in herbalism, a remedy which reduces blood pressure.

hypothermia: insufficient heat in the body.

immune enhancer: herbal remedy which improves the function of the immune system.

immunostimulant: stimulates the immune system.

indication: prevailing condition/s which strongly suggest a specific remedy.

inflammation: the natural reaction of the body to injury; there is heat, redness, pain and swelling.

infusion: herbal preparation, in which boiling water is poured over plants to extract the active ingredients; it is drunk when cool.

inhalation: herbal preparation, in which boiling water is poured onto ingredients, and the vapours inhaled.

involuntary: outside the control of the conscious will.

isopathy: the treating of a disease by the administration of the agent which caused it, as in homoeopathy, vaccination.

jing: in Chinese medicine, the vital essence which is the source of all life and individual growth and development; an aspect of Chi.

Ki: Japanese pronunciation of the word indicating the body's energy or life force.

lateral: towards the outer sides of the body.

lateral spinous processes: sideways projections of vertebrae.

lesion: tissue damaged by injury or disease, so that it no longer functions as well as it did originally.

lumbar: relating to the loin area, between the thorax and the pelvis.

lumbo-sacral joint: the joint between the lumbar vertebrae and the sacrum; the point at which the hindquarters 'flex' to tilt the pelvis and hindlegs beneath the body in engagement.

luo: system of channels linking the main meridians in Chinese medicine.

lymph: straw-coloured fluid containing mainly white blood cells; it helps the blood to 'cleanse' the body and fight disease. Contained in vessels/tubes and kept moving by the pressure of adjacent tissues and structures.

lymph glands: masses of tissue in the lymphatic system which 'deactivate' disease organisms.

malignant: harmful, invasive.

materia medica: study of materials used as medicine.

medial: towards the midline of the body.

median: related to, or very near the midline of the body between the left and right halves.

meridian system: energy channels or directions along which the body's life force or energy flows; the meridians are linked and influence each other, and also body parts and organs.

metabolism: the sum total of all the chemical changes which occur in the body.

miasm: infectious agent or emanation; sometimes used to imply a 'jinx'.

modality: a factor which makes symptoms better or worse; changing symptoms by natural means such as movement, weather, time, temperature, diet etc.

mother tincture: homoeopathic undiluted solution of plant extracts in alcohol from which other remedies are prepared.

moxibustion/moxabustion: the burning of the herb moxa on the tops of acupuncture needles to enhance their action by warmth and to release the herb's aroma as part of the treatment.

mucilage: slimy substance in plants used to soothe and protect irritated and inflamed tissues; it has mild laxative properties.

mucopurulent: mucus containing pus.

nadis: energy meridians linking the chakras through the body in Indian medicine.

narcosis: deep sleep or unconsciousness usually caused by a drug.

necrosis: death of tissue.

neoplasia: new cancerous growth.

nervine: herbal substance which calms nerves.

neurosis: mental state involving inappropriate behaviour.

nosode: an homoeopathic medicine or vaccine containing disease material, and administered to treat or prevent that disease.

oedema/edema: an accumulation of unusually large amounts of fluid between the tissue cells.

olfactory: relating to the sense of smell.

opiate: drug obtained from opium, or one with similar qualities.

oral: relating to the mouth.

organic: growth of crops, including grass, without the use of artificial pesticides, weedkillers and fertilisers.

osmosis: movement of fluid through the cell membrane from a concentrated solution to a less concentrated one.

ossify: to change into, or to develop bone.

palpation: examination by feeling; the use of the sense of touch.

palliative: treatment giving temporary relief of symptoms.

panacea: universal cure-all.

pathogen: a parasitic or disease-causing organism or substance.

pathological: relating to, or resulting from disease.

pectoral: relating to the chest.

percussion: diagnosis by means of tapping various parts of the body, usually the abdomen, and gauging the different sounds produced.

phyto-prevention: the use of plant materials in disease prevention.

phytotherapy: the use of plant materials in medicine.

pneuma: the ancient Greek word for the body's life force or energy.

potency: in homoeopathy, the strength of a substance based on its ability to cause changes in the body; the necessary dilution of a homoeopathic remedy.

potentise: to 'activate'/give strength to a homoeopathic medicine.

prana: the Indian word for the body's life force or energy.

precursor: a substance needed before another can be formed.

probiotic: in nutrition, a feed additive containing live micro-organisms, to boost their presence in the hind gut and improve digestion in cases where they have been depleted.

prognosis: outlook; the prospects of recovery.

progressive: worsening condition.

prophylactic: able to protect or prevent the body from succumbing to disease/illness.

proprioception: the body's sense of its own physical position or state.

proving: in homoeopathy, the administration of a remedy sufficient to cause the expected disease symptoms in a healthy body.

proximal: close to the centre of the body.

pulmonary: relating to the lungs.

purgative: strong laxative.

pyrexia: high body temperature, fever.

qi: another spelling of the Japanese word pronounced 'kee', meaning the body's life force or energy.

reflex action: a nervous reaction which does not need conscious thought to bring it about.

remedy: in homoeopathic parlance means 'medicine', used to treat a particular condition. A means of curing or treating.

restorative: in herbalism, a substance which restores the body to normal function.

Rolfing: a vigorous system of massage and manipulation aimed at realigning the body's soft tissues after injury or psychological trauma; it can be somewhat painful.

rotation: in manipulative-type therapies, the careful turning movement aimed at improving the mobility of a joint, and at promoting energy flow in adjacent meridians.

rubefacient: substance which gently warms and reddens the skin, ie some liniments.

sacroiliac: relating to the sacrum, and one or both ilia, or wings, of the pelvis, eg sacroiliac joints and ligaments are those between the front top of the sacrum at either side and the underneath of the two ilia, either side of the croup.

sacrum: five fused vertebrae forming a triangular bone below or behind the lumbar vertebrae; in horses the part between the point of the croup and the root of the tail.

saponins: toxic substances found in plants which break down fats; in remedies, some are expectorant and some diuretic.

scar tissue: fibrous tissue formed by the body after injury; it is weaker than the original tissue.

sedative: in acupuncture/acupressure and related therapies, dispersing excess energy. A substance which reduces nervous function and induces sleep.

sepsis/septic: destruction of healthy tissue by infective bacteria; it can be systemic or topical.

shen: an aspect of mind and spirit in Chinese medicine.

similimum: homoeopathic remedy producing symptoms closely matching those shown by the patient.

soluble: dissolves in water.

solution: liquid preparation of one or more solid chemical substances which will dissolve (are soluble) in water.

spasm: involuntary contraction or 'knotting' of muscle tissue, or narrowing of, for example, a blood vessel.

sprain: wrenching or twisting of joint, damaging ligaments and perhaps adjacent soft tissues such as tendons, muscles, nerves and blood vessels.

stereotypie: non-productive behaviour resulting from psychological distress; 'stable vice'.

stimulant: energy-producing.

strain: to over-pressurise mentally or physically; to over-exercise, over-extend, over-exert.

stress: a forcibly exerted influence on the body such as compression or tension; adverse physical or psychological factor which over-taxes the organism and may adversely affect health, wellbeing and functioning.

sub-clinical: disease not showing symptoms obvious enough to be observed.

subcutaneous: under the skin.

succussion: homoeopathic process of violently shaking a solution of a substance, to increase the potency of a remedy by magnetically changing its molecular structure.

suspension: liquid preparation in which fine particles of a solid substance are evenly distributed without sinking to form a sediment.

sycosis: in homoeopathy, the excessive reaction of the body to disease.

symbiosis: close relationship of two organisms, from which both benefit.

symmetry: balance or evenness.

synergy: in herbalism, homoeopathy and nutritional therapy, the greater effect produced by two substances working together than when each is given separately. You could say '2+2=6'!

systemic: throughout the body systems; affecting the whole body.

tarsal: relating to the hock in the horse, and the ankle in the human.

therapeutic: having healing qualities; relating to healing.

thermography/thermal imaging: a standard veterinary diagnostic technique (often used in acupuncture practice) using a thermal imaging camera to produce a 'temperature picture' showing areas of unusual warmth or coolness.

thorax, thoracic: relating to the chest/ribcage area.

tincture: herbal liquid remedy prepared usually with alcohol as a preservative. Soaking plant material in alcohol to extract the active ingredients.

tissue: a layer or group of specialised cells, eg muscle tissue, lung tissue, connective tissue.

tonification: in Chinese medicine, strengthening and supporting Chi or energy.

topical: relating to a localised area, such as a wound on skin.

trauma: a wound, injury or severe psychological stress.

trigger point: colloquial term for a reflex point; sensitive point, stimulation of which sets off a reflex action.

tympany: accumulation of gas in, usually, digestive tract causing stretched intestinal walls, pain and, in extreme cases, rupture of tissues.

vaccinosis: disease occurring as a result of vaccination.

vascular: relating to the blood system.

venous: relating to veins.

ventral: relating to abdomen or belly/breast surface; opposite to dorsal.

vermifuge: complementary medical term for substance which expels worms from intestines.

vibrational medicine: another term for energy medicine, in which the body's energy (which 'vibrates') is used to bring about healing.

volatile: the quality of evaporating at room temperature, about 20°C.

voluntary: within the control of the conscious will.

vulnerary: in herbalism, substance which promotes wound healing.

wort: Anglo-Saxon word for plant, from which the word 'weed' developed. Restorative traditional drink for debilitated or convalescent horses made from hops or barley grains.

Yang: the positive aspect of Yin and Yang, the polar opposite aspects of Chinese medicine.

Yin: the negative aspect of Yin and Yang, the polar opposite aspects of Chinese medicine.

Useful Addresses

The following list is as up to date as we can reasonably make it. For the sake of economy of space, we have normally given only one main address for each therapy as an initial contact point. Where we feature a therapy but have been unable to find a main, national contact for it, readers who wish for further information are advised to contact one of the 'umbrella' organisations which deal with complementary therapies in general. A stamped, addressed envelope would always be appreciated, large enough to take brochures. Also, asking at your local reference library and looking in local directories will produce a contact.

UK (GENERAL)

ADAS (Food, Farming, Land and Leisure, Equine Services Dept) (see local directories)

Association for the Promotion of Animal Complementary Health Education (UK) (APACHE)
Archers Wood Farm, Coppingford Road, Sawtry, Huntingdon, Cambridgeshire, PE17 5XT
Helps you find a complementary therapist/practitioner in your area. Seminars and newsletters for practitioners and lay members alike.
Tel: (070) 5024 4196

British Association of Holistic Nutrition and Medicine (BAHNM)
Borough Court, Hartley Witney, Basingstoke, Hants, RG27 8JA
Tel: (01252) 843282
Fax: (01252) 845750

British Complementary Medicine Association
39 Prestbury Road, Cheltenham, Glos, GL52 2PT
Tel: (01242) 519911 and
9 Soar Lane, Leicester, LE3 5DE

British Equine Veterinary Association
5 Finlay Street, London, SW6 6HE
Helps find an equine vet in your area.
Tel: (0207) 610 6080
Fax: (0207) 610 6823

Council for Complementary and Alternative Medicine
206–8 Latimer Road, London, W10 6RE
Tel: (0208) 735 0632

Enlightened Equitation
East Leigh Farm, Harberton, Totnes, Devon, TQ9 7SS
'A Kinder Way To Ride': courses and lessons from Heather Moffett, teacher, lecturer and author of Enlightened Equitation (David & Charles). Remedial students and horses a speciality. School horses for non-owners (home or away). Saddles, back-savers and seat-savers
Tel: (01803) 863676

Equine Behaviour Forum
Grove Cottage, Brinkley, Newmarket, Suffolk, CB8 0SF
Tel: (01638) 507502
Fax: (01772) 786037
International, voluntary, non-profit-making group which aims to advance the sympathetic management of horses by promoting a better understanding of the horse's mind. Visits, seminars, quarterly journal. UK enquirers, please send sae for details.

Institute for Complementary Medicine
Unit 15, Tavern Quay, Commercial Centre, Rope Street, London, SE16 1TX
Tel: (0207) 237 5165 and
PO Box 194, London, SE16 1QZ

Susan McBane HNC Equine Science and Management
63 Chaigley Road, Longridge, Preston, Lancashire, PR3 3TQ
Tel/fax: (01772) 786037
Freelance classical riding tuition and horse management advice. Shiatsu therapy for horses, dogs and riders. Classical Riding Club member listed in CRC Trainers Directory. Shiatsu for Horses level 2 practitioner.

Soil Association
Bristol House, 40-56 Victoria Street, Bristol, BS1 6BY
Tel: (01179) 290661
Tel: (01179) 252504
Organic land management and animal production

Tony Hall
5 Mill Street, Preesall, Poulton-le-Fylde, Lancs FY6 0NN
Tel: (01253) 812051
Freelance trainer specialising in traditional backing and riding away.

UK (BY THERAPY)

ACUPRESSURE AND ACUPUNCTURE
British Veterinary Acupuncture Association
East Park Cottage, Handcross, West Sussex, RH17 6BD
Tel: (01444) 400213

The British Acupuncture Council
Park House, 206–8 Latimer Road, London, W10 6RE
Tel: (0208) 964 0222

Jacqueline Cook, BHSAI, NCMH, ANCMH
Equine and Canine Acupressure
Tel/fax: (07721) 739973

ALEXANDER TECHNIQUE
Society of Teachers of the
Alexander Tecnique
10 London House, 266 Fulham Road,
London, SW10 9EL
Tel: (0207) 351 0828
Fax: (0207) 352 1556

ALOE VERA
Forever Living
53 Lower Road, Huxtable,
Kent, BR8 7RY
Tel/fax: (01322) 664973/409541

AROMATHERAPY
Aromatherapy Organisations
Council
201 Selhurst Road, London, SE25 6LB
Tel: (0208) 251 7912

Equine Aromatherapy Association
PO Box 19, Hay on Wye,
Hereford, HR3 5AE
Tel: (01455) 619608

BIOFEEDBACK
The Acumedic Centre
101–103 Camden High Street,
Camden, London, NW1 7JN
Tel: (0207) 388 6704

BOWEN TECHNIQUE
Equine Bowen
Beth Darrall, MBTER
De Mara, Douro Road,
Cheltenham, Glos, GL50 2PD
Tel: (01242) 251465

European College of Bowen Studies
38 Portway, Frome, BA11 1QU
Tel: (01373) 461873

CELL INJECTION THERAPY
British College of Naturopathy and
Osteopathy

6 Netherhall Gardens,
120–122 Finchley Road,
London, NW3 5HR
Tel: (0207) 435 7830

CENTRED RIDING
Jo Brown, MCSP
(01890) 761752

CHI KUNG/QI GONG
British Council for Chinese
Martial Arts
110 Frenhsam Drive, Nuneaton,
Warks, CV10 9QL
Tel: (02476) 394642

CHIROPRACTIC
McTimoney Chiropractic Association
21 High Street, Eynsham,
Oxford, OX8 1HE
Tel: (01865) 880974
Fax: (01865) 880975

CHROMOTHERAPY
Rupinder Mangat, DCT, BRCP, DM,
SNAMAP, GNOMA
Tel: (020) 8571 9294

The Hygeia College of Colour
Therapy
Brook House, Avening, Tetbury,
Glos, GL8 8NS
Tel: (01453) 832150

CLASSICAL RIDING
Classical Riding Club
Eden Hall, Kelso, Roxburghshire,
Scotland, TD5 7QD
Fax: (01890) 830667

COPPER THERAPY
Forbes Copper
The Old Rectory, Farnham,
Dorset, DT11 8DE
Tel: (01725) 516474
Fax: (01725) 516484

CRANIO-SACRAL THERAPY
The Cranio-Sacral Therapy
Association

Monomark House,
27 Old Gloucester Street,
London, WC1N 3XX
Tel: (07000) 784735

CRYSTAL AND GEM THERAPY
The Institute of Crystal and Gem
Therapists
PO Box 6, Exminster,
Exeter, Devon, EX6 8AY
Tel: (01392) 832005

**DANCE AND MOVEMENT
THERAPY**
Shamanic Workshops in Britain
(London and Manchester)
Eve Cunningham
61 Eldon Road, Wood Green,
London, N22 5ED
Tel: (0208) 888 8178

ELECTRO-CRYSTAL THERAPY
The School of Electrocrystal
Therapy
117 Long Drive, South Ruislip,
Middlesex, HA4 0HL
Tel: (0208) 841 1716

EQUINE DENTISTRY
British Veterinary Dental
Association
British Equine Veterinary Association
5 Finlay Street, London, SW6 6HE
Tel: (0207) 222 2001

FAITH HEALING
National Federation of Spiritual
Healers
Old Manor Farm Studio, Church
Street, Sunbury-on-Thames,
Middlesex, TW16 6RG
Tel: (01932) 783164

FARRIERY
Farriers Registration Council
Sefton House, Adam Court,
Newark Road, Peterborough,
Cambs, PE1 5PP
Tel: (01733) 319911
Fax: (01733) 319910

FELDENKRAIS
Balance (Feldenkrais for Riders)
Westcott Venture Park, Westcott,
Aylesbury, Bucks, HP18 0XB
Tel: (01296) 658333

The Feldenkrais (UK) Guild
East Holcombe, Shillingford,
Devon, EX16 9BR
Tel: (07000) 785506

FENG SHUI
The Feng Shui Company
15 The Regency, Esterbrooke Street,
London, SW1P 4NL
Tel: (07000) 781901

Feng Shui Network
UK representative: Liza Evans
Tel: (0208) 547 2797

FLOWER REMEDIES
The Dr Edward Bach Centre
Mount Vernon, Sotwell, Wallingford,
Oxon, OX10 0PX
Tel: (01491) 834678
Fax: (01491) 825022

HERBALISM
The British Herbal Medicine Association
1 Wickham Road, Bournemouth,
Dorset, BH7 6JX
(01202) 433691

Ellen Collinson
Nuppend Farm, Clanna Lane,
Alvington, Gloucester, GL15 6BD

The Herb Society
Deddington Hill Farm, Warrington,
Banbury, Oxon, OX17 1DF
Tel: (01295) 692000

Hilton Herbs Ltd
Downclose Farm, Downclose Lane,
North Perrott, Crewkerne,
Somerset, TA18 7SH
Tel: (01460) 78300
Fax: (01460) 78302

Register of Chinese Herbal Medicine
Office 4, Garden Studios,
11 Betterton Street,
London, WC2H 9BP
Tel: (0207) 470 8740

HOMOEOPATHY
British Association of Homoeopathic Veterinary Surgeons
Alternative Medicine Centre,
Chinham House, Stanford in the
Vale, Faringdon, Oxon, SN7 8NQ
Tel: (01367) 710324

Society of Homoeopaths
4a Artizan Road,
Northampton, NN1 4HU
Tel: (01604) 621400

HORSE WHISPERING
Gaynor Davenport
11A Old Bakery Cottage, Tetbury
Street, Minchinhampton,
Glos, GL6 2JG

Think Equus
Michael Peace: Ambergate Barn,
PO Box 230, Kidlington,
Oxford, OX5 2TU
Tel/fax: (01865) 842806

HYPNOTHERAPY
Central Register of Advanced Hypnotherapists
PO Box 14526, London, N4 2WG
Tel: (0207) 354 9938

Hypnotherapy Register
Tel: (01590) 645570

INTEGRATION THERAPY
Caroline Dow Thomas, BHSII, ITEC, TMAP
Email:
carolinedowthomas@hotmail.com

IRIDOLOGY
British Society of Iridologists
998 Wimborne Road,

Bournemouth, BH9 2DE
Tel: (01202) 518078

Ellen Collinson (Equine iridologist)
see entry above in HERBALISM

JIN SHIN JYUTSU
Rae Wilder-Smith (Equine Specialist)
Tel: (01929) 424558

KINETIC EQUESTRIAN TRAINING
Artaine Jewell
Tel: (01285) 655886 and 659190

KINESIOLOGY
Kinesiology Federation
PO Box 83, Sheffield, S7 2YN
Tel: (0114) 281 4064

Pat Ki
115 Swarcliffe Road, Harrogate,
N. Yorks, HG1 4QY
Tel: (01423) 888528

MAGNETIC THERAPY
Adrenaline Sports Ltd
21 Scotlands Close, Haslemere,
Surrey, GU27 3AE
Tel: (01306) 885511
Tel: (01306) 882211

Equine Athletic Performance Unit
Shuttleworth College, Old Warden
Park, Biggleswade, Beds, GS18 9EA
Tel: (01767) 626200

Jo Hodges, practitioner
Maple Pound, Church Farm Barn,
Rushden Road, Newton Bromswold,
Rushden, Northants, NN10 0SP
Tel: (01767) 626218

Magno-Pulse Ltd
Cromhall Farm, Easton Piercy,
Chippenham, Wiltshire, SN14 6JU
Tel: (01179) 710710

MASSAGE
Equine Sports Massage Association
17 Gloucester Road, Stratton,

Cirencester, Glos, GL7 2LB
Tel: (01285) 650275

Horse & Rider Consultancy
Jo Hodges: Maple Pound, Church
Farm Barn, Rushden,
Northants, NN10 0SP
Tel: (01767) 626218

METAPHYSICS
One Way to Oneness
Wendy Price: 11 Churchill Drive,
Upper Bruntingthorpe, Lutterworth,
Leicestershire, LE17 5QX
Tel: (0800) 783 0292

NATUROPATHY
**British College of Naturopathy &
Osteopathy**
6 Netherhall Gardens,
120–122 Finchley Road,
London, NW3 5HR
Tel: (0207) 435 7830

School of Natural Health Sciences
Dept 10, 2 Lansdowne Row,
Berkeley Square, London, W1X 8HL
Tel: (0207) 413 9577
Fax: (0207) 493 4935

NEURO–LINGUISTIC
PROGRAMMING
Malcolm Bray/Heather Smiles
Tel: (01756) 791110

Liz Morrison
Tel: (01403) 752845

NUTRITIONAL THERAPY
**British Association of Holistic
Nutrition & Medicine**
Borough Court, Hartley Wintney,
Basingstoke, Hants, RG27 8JA
Tel: (01252) 843282

OSTEOPATHY
British Osteopathic Association
Langham House, Mill Street,
Luton, Beds, LU1 2NA
Tel: (01582) 488455

David Gutteridge
Spring Bank, 202 Preston New Road,
Blackburn, Lancs, BB2 6PN
Tel: (01254) 52143

Gavin Schofield
Tel: (01233) 750228

PHYSIOTHERAPY
**Association of Chartered
Physiotherapists in Animal Therapy**
Morland House, Salters Lane,
Winchester, Hants, SO22 5JP
Tel/fax: (01962) 863801

**National Association of Animal
Therapists**
Tyringham Hall, Cuddington,
Bucks, HP18 0AP
Tel: (01844) 291526

PROPOLIS
Bee Health Ltd
The Honey Farm, Racecourse Road,
East Ayton, Scarborough,
N. Yorks, YO13 9HT
Tel: (01723) 864001

Flynn's Bee Farms Ltd
Double J Farm, Elmley Road,
Minster, Sheppey, Kent, ME12 3SS
Tel: (01795) 874935

RADIONICS
The Radionic Association
Berlein House, Goose Green,
Deddington, Banbury, Oxon, OX15 0SZ
Tel/fax: (01869) 338852

The Radionic & Radiesthesia Trust
Home Farm, Maperton, Wincanton,
Somerset, BA9 3EH
Tel: (01963) 32651
Fax: (01963) 32626

REFLEXOLOGY
The British Reflexology Association
Monk's Orchard, Whitbourne,
Worcestershire, WR6 5RB
Tel: (01886) 821 1207

REIKI
**Equine Reiki:
Jodi Canti**
(01460) 281793

The Reiki Association
Cornbrook Bridge House, Clee Hill,
Ludlow, Shropshire, SY8 3QQ

SADDLING
Balance
Westcott Venture Park, Westcott,
Aylesbury, Bucks, HP18 0XB
tel: (01296) 658333

**British Association of Holistic
Nutrition and Medicine**
Borough Court, Hartley Wintney,
Basingstoke, Hants, RG27 8JA
Tel: (01252) 843282
Fax: (01252) 845750

Society of Master Saddlers (UK) Ltd
Kettles Farm, Mickfield, Stowmarket,
Suffolk, IP14 6BY
Tel: (01449) 711642

SHIATSU
The Shiatsu Society
Eastlands Court, St Peters Road,
Rugby, CV21 3QP
Tel: (01788) 555051
Fax: (01788) 555052

**Jacqueline Cook BHSAI, NCMH,
ANCMH
Shiatsu Practitioner/teacher**
Level III Certified for the Horse,
Rider & Dog
Tel: (07721) 739973

Rosewell Shiatsu Centre
Tel: (01780) 410072

TAI CHI (TAI JI)
**British Council for Chinese Martial
Arts**
31 Neale Drive, Greasby,
Wirral, L49 1SE
Tel: (0151) 6767 4471

Tai Chi Union for Great Britain
1 Littlemill Drive, Balmoral Gardens,
Crookston, Glasgow, G53 7GE
Tel: (0141) 810 3482
Fax: (0141) 810 3741

**TELLINGTON-TOUCH EQUINE
AWARENESS METHOD (TTeam)**
Sarah Fisher: South Hill House,
Radford Hill, Timsbury,
Bath, BA3 1QQ
Tel: (01761) 471182

**YOGA
The British Wheel of Yoga**
1 Hamilton Place, Boston Road,
Sleaford, Lincs, NG34 7ES
Tel: (01529) 306851

USA AND CANADA

**American Association of Oriental
Medicine (AAOM)**
433 Front Street,
Catasauqua, PA 18032
Tel: (610) 266–1433

American Herb Association
Box 1673, Nevada City, CA 95949
Tel: (530) 265–9552

American Herbalists Guild
1931 Gaddis Rd., Canton, GA 30115
Tel: (770) 751-6021

**American Holistic Veterinary
Association**
2218 Old Emmorton Road, Bel Air,
MD 21015
Tel: (410) 569–0795

**American Organization for
Bodywork Therapies of Asia
(AOBTA)**
1010 Haddonfield–Berlin Rd., Suite
408, Voorhees, NJ 08043
Tel: (856) 782–1616

Botanical Society of America
1735 Neil Ave., Columbus, OH 43210
Tel: (614) 292–3519

The Chi Kung School
2730 29th Street, Boulder, CO 80301
Tel: (303) 447–0484

Dances With Horses
Frank Bell: PO Box 1030, Castlerock,
CO 80104
Tel: (303) 681–3723

Herb Research Foundation
1007 Pearl Street, Suite 200,
Boulder, CO 80302
Tel: (303) 447–2265

**International Chi Kung/Qi Gong
Directory**
PO Box 19708, Boulder, CO 80308

**International Veterinary
Acupuncture Society**
PO Box 271395, FT. Collins,
CO 80527–1395
Tel: (970) 266–0666

**National Accreditation Commission
for Schools and Colleges of
Acupuncture and Oriental
Medicine (NACSCAOM)**
1010 Wayne Avenue, Suite 1270,
Silver Springs, MD 20910
Tel: (301) 608–9680

**National Acupuncture and Oriental
Medicine Alliance (National Alliance)**
14637 Starr Road, SE,
Olalla, WA 98359
Tel: (253) 851–6896

**National Commission for the
Certification of Acupuncturists
(NCCA)**
PO Box 97075,
Washington DC 20090-7075
Tel: (202) 232–1404

Ontario Herbalists Association
R.R.#1, Port Burwell, Ontario, OJ1T0,
Canada
Tel: (416) 536–1509

Qigong Academy
8103 Marlborough Avenue,
Cleveland, OH 44129
Tel: (440) 536–1509

Shiatsu With Horses
Pamela Hannay
31 Park Place, Flanders, NJ 07836

AUSTRALASIA
**Australian Natural Therapists
Association**
PO Box 308, Melrose Park 5039,
South Australia

**Australian Traditional Medicine
Society Ltd**
PO Box 1027,
Meadowbank, NSW 2114

College of Naturopathic Medicine
Box 4529, Christchurch, NZ

**National Herbalist Association of
Australia**
27 Leith Street, Coorparoo,
Queensland, 4151
also
Box 65, Kingsgrove, NSW 2208

**New Zealand Register of
Acupuncturists Inc**
PO Box 9950, Wellington 1, NZ

Qi Gong Association of Australia
458 White Horse Road, Surrey Hills,
Victoria, 3127

Index